Living in a World of Neighbours

CHURCH OF SWEDEN RESEARCH SERIES

۶

The Church of Sweden Research Series promotes research investigating the intersections of church, academy, and society. Its focus is on theology that is in lively conversation with the pressing issues of the world today, both from an academic and from an ecclesial perspective. What is the role of the churches in ever changing ecological, political, cultural, social and religious contexts? How is Christian teaching and practice affected by these changing currents? And how is the Lutheran tradition evolving amid such challenges? Through monographs and anthologies, the series makes available Swedish and Scandinavian scholarship in the English-speaking world, but also mirrors the worldwide connections of the Church of Sweden as part of its own identity.

General editor of CSRS (since 2020): Michael Nausner

VOLUMES PUBLISHED

1. Göran Gunner, editor, *Vulnerability, Churches and HIV* (2009)
2. Kajsa Ahlstrand and Göran Gunner, editors, *Non-Muslims in Muslim Majority Societies with Focus on the Middle East and Pakistan* (2009)
3. Jonas Ideström, editor, *For the Sake of the World: Swedish Ecclesiology in Dialogue with William T. Cavanaugh* (2010)
4. Göran Gunner and Kjell-Åke Nordquist, *An Unlikely Dilemma: Constructing a Partnership Between Human Rights and Peace-Building* (2011)
5. Anne-Louise Eriksson, Göran Gunner, and Niclas Blåder, editors, *Exploring a Heritage: Evangelical Lutheran Churches in the North* (2012)
6. Kjell-Åke Nordquist, editor, *Gods and Arms: On Religion and Armed Conflict* (2012)
7. Harald Hegstad, *The Real Church: An Ecclesiology of the Visible* (2013)
8. Carl-Henric Grenholm and Göran Gunner, editors, *Justification in a Post-Christian Society* (2014)
9. Carl-Henric Grenholm and Göran Gunner, editors, *Lutheran Identity and Political Theology* (2014)
10. Sune Fahlgren and Jonas Ideström, editors, *Ecclesiology in the Trenches: Theory and Method Under Construction* (2015)

11. Niclas Blåder, *Lutheran Tradition as Heritage and Tool: An Empirical Study of Reflections on Confessional Identity in Five Lutheran Churches in Different Contexts* (2015)

12. Ulla Schmidt and Harald Askeland, editors, *Church Reform and Leadership of Change* (2016)

13. Kjell-Åke Nordquist, *Reconciliation as Politics: A Concept and its Practice* (2016)

14. Niclas Blåder and Kristina Helgesson Kjellin, editors, *Mending the World? Possibilities and Obstacles for Religion, Church and Theology* (2017)

15. Tone Stangeland Kaufman, *A New Old Spirituality? A Qualitative Study of Clergy Spirituality in the Nordic Context* (2017)

16. Carl Reinhold Bråkenhielm, *The Study of Science and Religion: Sociological, Theological, and Philosophical Perspectives* (2017)

17. Jonas Ideström and Tone Stangeland Kaufman, editors, *What Really Matters: Scandinavian Perspectives on Ecclesiology and Ethnography* (2018)

18. Dion Forster, Elisabeth Gerle, and Göran Gunner, editors, *Freedom of Religion at Stake: Competing Claims Among Faith Traditions, States, and Persons* (2019)

19. Marianne Gaarden, *The Third Room of Preaching: A New Empirical Approach* (2021)

20. André S. Musskopf, Edith González Bernal and Maurício Rincón Andrade, editors, *Theology and Sexuality, Reproductive Health, and Rights: Latin American Experiences in Participatory Action Research* (2022)

21. Karin Johannesson, *Thérèse and Martin: Carmel and the Reformation in a New Light* (2023)

22. Harald Hegstad with Steinunn Arnþrúður Björnsdóttir, Magnus Evertsson, Jonas Adelin Jørgensen, and Jyri Komulainen, editors, *Baptism in Times of Change: Exploring New Patterns of Baptismal Theologies and Practices in Nordic Lutheran Churches* (2025)

23. Ryszard Bobrowicz, Anna Hjälm, Ulrich Schmiedel, editors, *Living in A World of Neighbours: Activists and Academics in Conversation about Multi-Faith Refugee Relief* (2025)

Living in A World of Neighbours

*Activists and Academics in Conversation
about Multi-Faith Refugee Relief*

Edited by
RYSZARD BOBROWICZ, ANNA HJÄLM,
& ULRICH SCHMIEDEL

PICKWICK *Publications* · Eugene, Oregon

LIVING IN A WORLD OF NEIGHBOURS

Activists and Academics in Conversation about Multi-Faith Refugee Relief

Church of Sweden Research Series 23

Copyright © 2025 Wipf and Stock Publishers. All rights reserved. Except for brief quotations in critical publications or reviews, no part of this book may be reproduced in any manner without prior written permission from the publisher. Write: Permissions, Wipf and Stock Publishers, 199 W. 8th Ave., Suite 3, Eugene, OR 97401.

Pickwick Publications
An Imprint of Wipf and Stock Publishers
199 W. 8th Ave., Suite 3
Eugene, OR 97401

www.wipfandstock.com

PAPERBACK ISBN: 979-8-3852-3587-2
HARDCOVER ISBN: 979-8-3852-3588-9
EBOOK ISBN: 979-8-3852-3589-6

Cataloguing-in-Publication data:

Names: Bobrowicz, Ryszard, editor. | Hjälm, Anna, editor. | Schmiedel, Ulrich, editor.

Title: Living in a world of neighbours : activists and academics in conversation about multi-faith refugee relief / edited by Ryszard Bobrowicz, Anna Hjälm, and Ulrich Schmiedel.

Description: Eugene, OR: Pickwick Publications, 2025. | Church of Sweden Research Series 23. | Includes bibliographical references and index.

Identifiers: ISBN 979-8-3852-3587-2 (paperback). | ISBN 979-8-3852-3588-9 (hardcover). | ISBN 979-8-3852-3589-6 (ebook).

Subjects: LCSH: Emigration and immigration—Social aspects. | Religion and social problems. | Refugees—Government policy.

Classification: BV2695.E4 L45 2023 (print). | BV2695.E4 (ebook).

VERSION NUMBER 08/19/25

Unless otherwise noted, quotations from the New Revised Standard Version of the Bible, copyrighted © 1989 by the Division of Christian Education of the National Council of Churches of Christ in the United States of America and are used by permission

Scripture quotations marked (NKJV) are taken from the New King James Version. Copyright © 1982 by Thomas Nelson, Inc. Used by permission. All rights reserved.

Scripture quotations marked (ASV) are taken from the American Standard Version is in the public domain.

Contents

Acknowledgments | *xi*

Contributors | *xiii*

Introduction: Why We Need a World of Neighbours | 1
  RYSZARD BOBROWICZ AND ULRICH SCHMIEDEL

PART I   THE CHALLENGE

1   Embroidering Theology, or How to Make the Theology Behind the Practice Visible | 21
    MARIA KJELLSDOTTER RYDINGER

2   Crimes Against the Soul and Potential for Repair | 32
    VANESSA BARKER

3   All You P*k*s F**k Off Home | 45
    AMJID KHAZIR

4   Race, Religion, and Refugees in Europe: Past and Present | 56
    ANYA TOPOLSKI

5   Reality Checking the Economics of Migration: Why Refugees Aren't Fiscal Burdens | 72
    PEO HANSEN

6   "Sabina, You Must Promise Me You Won't Tell My Father":
    Stories of Social Work | 84
    SABINA ESP

7   The Vigil: On Silence, Grief, Sight, and the Power of Belief:
    A Conversation with Anna Hjälm | 94
    AUDE SATHOUD

PART II   THE CALL

8   Arriving with Empty Hands: A Theological Case
    for a Post-Help Praxis | 107
    RIKKO VOORBERG

9   Finding One's Place at a Busy Intersection: The Methodology of
    the A World of Neighbours Practitioners' Network | 116
    RYSZARD BOBROWICZ

10 Responsible Research Projects within A World of Neighbours:
    Decolonizing Research Ethics | 128
    MAJBRITT LYCK-BOWEN

11 At Calais: A Refugee with a Red Passport | 139
    AMLOUD ALAMIR

12 Athliens: À nos corps étrangers | 145
    AUDE SATHOUD

13 Social Media and Migration: The Polish Case | 155
    KAROL WILCZYŃSKI

14 From Narrative to Policy and Back: A Glimpse
    into the Potential of Practitioners | 166
    ALESSIA PASSARELLI

PART III THE CHANGE

15 The Evolving Torah of Human Migration: Notes on a Jewish Theology of Migration | 181
    REBECCA LILLIAN

16 At the Table of Jesus: The Theology of the Open Supper | 189
    MÁRTHA BOLBA

17 The Significance of Ethnic and Religious Identity for Refugee Support: The Case of Muslim Communities | 197
    ATALLAH FITZGIBBON

18 Making Space for the Other | 203
    JAKOB WIRÉN

19 Collaboration Beyond Borders: When Felix Unogwu and Anne Kjaer Bathel Met | 215
    CECILIA SAHLSTRÖM

20 Fighting Now, Dreaming Ahead: A Conversation with Anna Stamou | 223
    AUDE SATHOUD

21 Just Care: Ethics in A World of Neighbours | 229
    ULRICH SCHMIEDEL

Conclusion: "You Have A World of Neighbours" | 244
    ANTJE JACKELÉN

A World of Neighbours: What Guides Us | 262

Index | 265

Acknowledgments

MIGRATION IS STIRRING UP controversy across Europe. In many countries, politicians and pundits point to conflicts and clashes that—or so the story goes—flare up when people of different religious and non-religious ways of life come together. This book brings together the voices of activists and academics who are affiliated with A World of Neighbours, a multi-faith network working with people on the move in every corner of Europe. These voices share their experiences and their expertise in the practice of multi-faith refugee relief to tell a different story for Europe, a story which revolves around "neighbourliness"—rather than clash or conflict—as its key concept. Taken together, the voices in this book present a comprehensive and constructive interpretation of A World of Neighbours to make a case for the significance of multi-faith refugee relief in contemporary Europe.

Given how fast and furious events are unfolding, many of the facts and figures collected in this book might be outdated by the time it is published. Yet the story that it tells might still—or so we hope—be important, instructive, and inspiring.

As co-editors, we are grateful for the support we received from a variety of institutions and individuals. This book is one of the results of the research for "Welcoming the Stranger: Resources for a European Multi-Faith Ethics of Migration," funded by a Saltire International Collaboration Award from the Royal Society of Edinburgh and the Birgit och Sven Håkan Ohlssons Fond. In addition, we gratefully acknowledge the support we received from Lunds Missionssällskap, which has shaped the conversations behind this book in many ways. We are grateful for the insights of İdil Akıncı-Pérez, Rana Alsoufi, Johanna Gustafsson Lundberg, Majbritt Lyck-Bowen, and Anya Topolski who all contributed to the research that has formed and informed this compilation in many ways. Funding from the Church of Sweden allowed us to cover the production and printing costs. Thanks are due to Sigrid Elise Strømmen, whose eagle-eyed work on the manuscript has helped us to improve the structure, the style, and the substance of the contributions. Of course, there will still be mistakes here and there—these are entirely our own. We are also grateful to the editors of the Church of Sweden Research Series, particularly Kristina Helgesson Kjellin and Michael Nausner, for taking the risk to include a book that aims to be more than "just" academic into their programme. Last but not least, we would like to thank all the contributors to this book.

We dedicate this book to Dirk Ficca, whose energy and enthusiasm continues to shape the A World of Neighbours Practitioners Network. Thank you, Dirk!

Leuven, Jerusalem, and Lund
Ryszard Bobrowicz, Anna Hjälm, and Ulrich Schmiedel

Contributors

Amloud AlAmir is a Syrian-German journalist. She has been living in Berlin since 2014. She works at Amal Berlin, a news portal that covers current events in several languages. She also serves on the Advisory Board on Migration and Integration in the Protestant Church in Berlin. She is a board member of A World of Neighbours.

Vanessa Barker is Professor of Sociology at Stockholm University in Sweden. She is the author of *Nordic Nationalism and Penal Order* (2017) and *The Politics of Imprisonment* (2009). She researches questions of democracy, immigration, punishment, borders, and civil society.

Ryszard Bobrowicz is a Visiting Professor of Comparative Law and Religion at Bonn University in Germany and a Researcher in Systematic Theology at the Catholic University of Leuven in Belgium. His recent books include *The Politics of Multifaith* (2024) and *Dissenting Church* (2024), coedited with Judith Gruber and Michael Schuessler.

Marta Bolba is a Lutheran Pastor based in Budapest, Hungary. She is leading two community centres. The Mandák House is active in community organizing, cooperating with a variety of NGOs. The Dévai Inn focuses on supporting refugees.

Sabina Esp is a social worker from Sweden who has been engaging with people on the move since 2008. She works primarily with young refugees, including unaccompanied minors. She specializes in accompaniment, concentrating in particular on the roles of receiving communities. She has been a practitioner in A World of Neighbours since 2019.

Atallah FitzGibbon has worked in economic and social development both inside and outside the UK. Over the last twenty years, he has served at Islamic Relief Worldwide as International Programmes Director, Head of Policy and Strategy, and Head of Global Advocacy. Currently, he leads Islamic Relief Worldwide's engagement with faith-based approaches to tackling the major challenges of our time, including the support for social justice, dialogue, and integration of migrants in Europe.

Peo Hansen is Professor of Political Science at the Institute for Research on Migration, Ethnicity and Society (REMESO) at Linköping University in Sweden. His books include *A Modern Migration Theory: An Alternative Economic Approach to Failed EU Policy* (2021) and *Eurafrica: The Untold History of European Integration and Colonialism* (2014), co-authored with Stefan Jonsson.

Anna Hjälm is currently the Director of the Swedish Theological Institute in Jerusalem, a centre for theological, interreligious, and contextual research, as well as education and dialogue. From 2018 to 2022 she served as the Church of Sweden's Programme Director for A World of Neighbours. Together with Dirk Ficca, she was responsible for setting up the programme. She gained her doctorate in Human Geography from the University of Umeå. She has served as Ecumenical Officer for the World Council of Churches' Jerusalem Office.

Antje Jackelén, Archbishop emerita, was the Primate of the Church of Sweden between 2014 and 2022 and Bishop of the Diocese of Lund between 2007 and 2014. She worked as a Professor of Systematic Theology/Science and Religion at the Lutheran School of Theology at Chicago, USA, where she directed the Zygon Center for Religion and Science. She was also the President of the European Society for the Study of Science and Theology. In addition to a PhD in theology, she holds three honorary degrees. Currently, she serves as senior advisor at Lund University in Sweden.

Amjid Khazir is the Director of Media Cultured, a UK-based education and training provider. He has over two decades of experience in anti-racism work and social cohesion initiatives. He is widely acclaimed for his pioneering work to tackle racism, Islamophobia, antisemitism, and extremism. The use of film, sport and art to deliver key messages of unity has been particularly lauded.

Anne Kjaer Bathel is the Co-Founder of ReDI School of Digital Integration, a vocational training programme teaching programming and tech skills to refugees, migrants and marginalised locals. As the CEO of ReDI, Anne is convinced that technology can break down barriers and bring people together to build new solutions to old problems. The idea of ReDI was sparked by the insight that amongst the refugee population there are incredible talents eager to contribute, who could help fill the hundreds of thousands of open IT jobs in Europe.

Maria Kjellsdotter Rydinger is a Minister in the Lutheran Church of Sweden, where she currently serves as an advisor and coordinator for interreligious practice at the central church office. She served as one of the project leaders who initiated the programme A World of Neighbours and has been one of the directors who led the programme in the transition to become an independent organization for practitioners in Europe. In Sweden, she coordinates the regional AWoN-network of interreligious practitioners working for people on the move.

Rebecca Lillian serves as Rabbi of two progressive Jewish congregations in Scandinavia, Sukkat Shalom in Stockholm and Shir Hatzafon in Copenhagen. She has been an activist for welcoming refugees since 2015. She is currently chair of the board of A World of Neighbours.

Majbritt Lyck-Bowen is a Senior Lecturer in the Department of Social Sciences and a Research Fellow at the Centre for Religion, Reconciliation and Peace at the University of Winchester in the UK. She is the programme leader of an online MA in Reconciliation and Peacebuilding, and she has extensive experience in carrying out research on sensitive issues in complex contexts.

Alessia Passarelli is a Researcher in Social Anthropology affiliated with the Fondazione per gli Studi Religiosi in Bologna, Italy. The co-author of *Mapping Migration: Mapping Churches' Responses in Europe* (2021), her research focuses on the intertwining of religion, migration, and integration studies. She has worked for the Churches' Commission for Migrants in Europe from 2005 to 2008, where she continues to contribute to the mapping migration project. Since 2022, she has been the Principal of the Liceo Valdese in Torre Pellice.

Cecilia Sahlström is a full-time author with a background in cultural studies. She worked for almost twenty years in the Swedish police force. After she left the police, she worked as a leadership consultant and in the social service of a Swedish municipality. She has written eleven books, mainly crime novels, since 2016. Her driving force is to write about current social issues, presenting vulnerability in today's society.

Aude Sathoud, wa/ondering between space and time, Athens, Paris, and Brazzaville, attempts at making sense of our chaotic worlds and opening possibles through advocacy, theory, performance, and poetry.

Ulrich Schmiedel is Professor of Global Christianities at Lund University in Sweden, where he runs a research project on "Faith-Based Refugee Relief in Europe," funded by the European Research Council. He also leads the Research Team of the A World of Neighbours Practitioners Network. His books include *The Claim to Christianity: Responding to the Far Right* (2020), co-authored with Hannah Strømmen, and *Religion in the European Refugee Crisis* (2018), co-edited with Graeme Smith.

Anya Topolski is an Associate Professor in Ethics and Political Philosophy at Radboud University Nijmegen in the Netherlands. Her PhD in Philosophy on Hannah Arendt, Emmanuel Levinas, Judaism, and Relationality was awarded the Auschwitz Foundation Stichting Prize. In 2009, she engaged in post-Srebrenica research on genocide, dehumanization, and responsibility as an NWO-Dutch post-doctoral researcher. In 2012, she was awarded a post-doctoral grant to investigate European Identity and Exclusion, antisemitism, and Islamophobia. Her current research is in the field of critical philosophy of race and focuses on the race-religion intersection in Europe.

Felix Unogwu is the Local Head of ReDI School of Digital Integration in Malmö, Sweden. He served as a political scientist and conflict resolution specialist, amassing eighteen years of experience across twenty-six different countries. His expertise encompasses addressing youth armed conflicts, child soldier rehabilitation, radicalization, and de-radicalization. Felix has actively participated in initiatives aimed at helping young individuals disengage from violent extremist groups in conflict zones worldwide. Over the years, Felix has dedicated himself to developing preventive strategies and methodologies that provide concrete alternatives to fragile target groups.

Rikko Voorberg is a Dutch theologian and organizer of artistic and activist interventions. He is known for his work on constructive anger and creative resistance. As an activist, he initiated several Dutch and European movements to draw attention to the situation of marginalized people. He has written several books on theology and activism, runs a daily podcast, and serves as the Director of the A World of Neighbours Practitioners Network.

Karol Wilczyński is a community organizer and communication strategist who provides leadership, media, and migration training. He supports victims of Islamophobia, works on combating Islamophobia in social and media spaces, and lectures on migration, Islamophobia, and the politics of fear at Jagiellonian University in Poland. For the past eight years he has been involved in work with people on the move and forced migration. As a journalist he visited various places experiencing forced migration, including Syria, Lebanon, Egypt, Morocco, Turkey, Belarus, and camps in the EU.

Jakob Wirén is Adjunct Associate Professor of Theology of Religions at Lund University in Sweden. He is theological advisor to the Archbishop of the Church of Sweden. Among his recent books are *Att ge plats för den andre?* (2021) and *Hope and Otherness* (2018).

It's the Movement that Endures

Various institutional actors will come and go. Policy and funding will change according to ever-fluid circumstances, the good will and whims of politics, the varying dictates of bureaucracy. People will always be on the move, seeking welcome. That will never change. Receiving communities and practitioners will always accompany them on their journey, and work in the broader society to encourage their welcome. The fragile yet persistent grassroots infrastructure to do that, the dynamism of this human-and-community-centered network, will always need to be nurtured. A World of Neighbours is one such effort to do just that.

DIRK FICCA (1955–2021)

Introduction

Why We Need a World of Neighbours

Ryszard Bobrowicz and Ulrich Schmiedel

Migration is stirring up controversy across Europe. In many countries, politicians and pundits point to clashes that—or so the story goes—flare up when people of different religious and non-religious ways of life come together. This book challenges that story. Setting an experimental and explorative agenda, it brings together the voices of activists and academics who are affiliated with A World of Neighbours (AWoN), a multi-faith network that has been engaging with people on the move across Europe. Coming from a wide variety of contexts and countries, these voices share their experiences and their expertise in the practice of multi-faith refugee relief to tell a different story. We are already living in a world of neighbours, whether we like or dislike it. The question, then, is not *whether* we want to live in a world of neighbours but *which* world of neighbours we want to live in. The wager of this book is that AWoN can help us to find answers to this very question. The book presents a comprehensive and constructive interpretation of the practices and principles of AWoN to make a case for the significance of multi-faith refugee relief in contemporary Europe.

In this introduction,[1] we contextualize and characterize the chapters of this book. We contend that AWoN counters the standard story of migration *by example*. Since the example set by AWoN cannot be captured by research on migration that draws a strong and stable distinction between "migrants" and "non-migrants," we convene a conversation between people who have and people who have not been on the move. They come from different non-religious and different religious backgrounds, including Judaism, Christianity, and Islam. Their conversation features more than twenty voices from more than ten countries. It is not "about" migration. It is about people who are trying to make our neighbourhoods more welcoming. The conversation in this book clarifies that a world of neighbours is both something that we have and something that we have to work for. The example of AWoN tells the story of a world of neighbours worth living in—now.

THE WORLD OF NEIGHBOURS WE HAVE

While migration has been a constant throughout history, the twenty-first century has been called "the age of migration."[2] Across the globe, more and more people are on the move. Sometimes they are free to move, sometimes they are forced to move, and sometimes it is difficult to tell the difference between "free" and "forced."[3]

According to the United Nations High Commissioner for Refugees (UNHCR), the rift between displaced people and provisions for displaced people has been widening since 2010.[4] In Europe, the narrative of a crisis has haunted public squares and political spheres since 2015, when millions of people on the move—mainly from Syria—made it over the borders and onto the beaches of the continent. Europe has been in thrall of what came to be called the current "migration crisis." Yet the fact that, of the global displaced population, about 90 percent are accommodated in developing countries, while about 10 percent are accommodated in developed countries,[5] casts doubt on the conceptualization of a cur-

---

1. Throughout this introduction, we build on the analysis and argument in Schmiedel, "Om gåshud."

2. See Haas et al., *Age of Migration*. For a theological take, see the contributions in Phan, *Christian Theology in the Age of Migration*.

3. Alexander Betts has suggested to refer to "survival migration." See Betts, *Survival Migration*.

4. UNHCR, *Global Trends Report*, 8.

5. UNHCR, *Global Trends Report*, 2–3. Recently, the UNHCR has changed the way

rent migration crisis in Europe.[6] If there is a migration crisis, it is not in Europe. And if there is a crisis in Europe, it is not a migration crisis.[7] On the contrary, the narrative of crisis covers up the "breakdown of modern European humanism."[8] The fallout is a death toll that makes the border around Europe "the world's deadliest border,"[9] while the number of people who have been forced to flee continues to rise rapidly.[10]

Crucially, Europe's response to the Russian invasion of Ukraine has not countered but contributed to the breakdown of European humanism. As we write, statistics of the UNHCR show that more than six million people are displaced outside, and more than three million people are displaced inside Ukraine.[11] More than fourteen million people living in Ukraine are in need of urgent humanitarian assistance. Several countries which had slammed their doors shut to people on the move have now opened them to Ukrainians. Yet these open doors must not camouflage how racist discourse and religious discrimination continue to run through both migration politics and migration policy. Many refugee relief organizations such as AWoN point out that a dubious and dangerous differentiation between people on the move has been set up. On the one hand, Ukrainian people, considered fellow Europeans and therefore "deserving" of "our" hospitality and, on the other hand, non-Ukrainian people, not considered Europeans and therefore "undeserving" of "our" hospitality. As Moustafa Bayoumi argued in *The Guardian* immediately after the invasion of Ukraine:

> If we decide to help Ukrainians in their desperate time of need because they happen to look like "us" or dress like "us" or pray like "us" . . . then we have not only chosen the wrong reasons to support another human being. We have also, and I'm

---

it categorizes countries. The new categorization shows that only about 20 percent of the displaced population are hosted in high income countries. Germany is still the only European country that is listed among the top five hosting countries. For current statistics, see UNHCR, "Figures at a Glance."

6. See Bauman, *Strangers at Our Door*. For theological and sociological analyses, see the contributions to Schmiedel and Smith, *Religion in the European Refugee Crisis*.

7. Dirk Ficca, the former co-director of AWoN, stressed the incongruency of these crises.

8. Squire, *Europe's Migration Crisis*, 12. Squire points to the role that colonialism has played in this European humanism. See also Hansen and Jonsson, *Eurafrica*.

9. Jones, *Violent Borders*, 12.

10. For current statistics, see UNHCR, "Figures at a Glance."

11. See UNHCR, "Emergency Appeal."

choosing these words carefully, shown ourselves as giving up on civilization.[12]

Encounters across racist and religious boundaries, then, are as crucial as—perhaps more crucial than—ever before to counter the breakdown of European humanism in our world of neighbours.

Of course, Bayoumi alludes to Samuel Huntington's construct of the clash of civilizations, the conjecture that there is a combat for cultural dominance in which Christians clash with Muslims as much as Muslims clash with Christians.[13] This construct has been persistent in the public perception of religion, fuelling the Islamophobia that distinguishes "deserving" from "undeserving" people. As a racism that targets "Muslimness" or perceived "Muslimness," Islamophobia thus ties together racist discourse and religious discrimination.[14] Islamophobic agendas have made it into the parliaments and the public spheres of many European countries. Across Europe, there are many who simultaneously construct and cash in on the clash of civilizations.

AWoN emerged as a response to the conditions under which people on the move continue to find themselves when attempting to enter Europe. In 2015, the network was set up at the initiative of then Archbishop of Uppsala, Antje Jackelén. AWoN has been one intervention in a variety of national and international activities spearheaded by the Church of Sweden.[15] While kickstarted by this Church, AWoN has been a multi-faith network—featuring *both* different religious *and* different non-religious people—from the very beginning. In a statement that addressed the members of AWoN, Jackelén stressed: "We want to reach out across social, cultural, and religious borders to create bonds of solidarity, bonds between people—a world of neighbours." Under Jackelén's leadership, the Church of Sweden has been vital for the reception of people on the move, offering a variety of services to the newcomers.[16]

Acknowledging both the scale and the significance of the challenge of migration for Europe, Jackelén started to ask what role communities of faith could and should play in addressing it. Together with a variety

---

12. Bayoumi, "They Are 'Civilised.'"
13. Huntington, "Clash of Civilizations?"; *Clash of Civilizations*.
14. See Strømmen and Schmiedel, *Claim to Christianity*.
15. Ryszard Bobrowicz's chapter in this book offers a short overview of these activities, contextualizing the AWoN network in the ecology of migration of 2015.
16. Hellqvist and Sandberg, *Time of Encounters*.

of national and international activities, she initiated AWoN as a European project, entrusting it to Dirk Ficca and Anna Hjälm. After careful planning, the directors met with more than one hundred actors in more than ten countries to evaluate the ecology of migration across the continent. This evaluation culminated in a meeting in Malmö, Sweden, in 2020, a few weeks before the pandemic would make collaborations much more challenging. Among the gaps in the ecology of migration that were identified at the meeting was the lack of cross-country support for practitioners who work with people on the move.[17] In response to this gap, the practitioners' network of AWoN was built to connect religious and non-religious practitioners in all corners of Europe. These practitioners—many with a history of migration themselves—have been engaged in acceptance, accompaniment, and advocacy for people on the move. They work in all sorts of organizations, sometimes faith-based and sometimes not faith-based.

While the pandemic challenged all of the projects that followed from the meeting in Malmö, the network of practitioners took shape in the "zoom revolution." The practitioners were recruited in cohorts of ten. These cohorts were familiarized with the network through a mix of materials to read, meetings to run, and one-to-one conversations—everything online. When the pandemic loosened its grip on the continent, the network was ready for a face-to-face meeting. In 2022, the practitioners met in Brussels. What had been an initiative started and sustained by the Church of Sweden was transformed into a standalone organization led by the practitioners themselves. One of them, Rikko Voorberg, stepped up to take the new role of network director. Guided by a Board with people from different religious and non-religious backgrounds, many of whom had fled their homes before arriving in Europe, he established a foundation with its seat in Amsterdam. In 2023, the practitioners met in Budapest to set a new agenda for the newly founded network, taking the vision of its initiators forward.

Until his untimely death, Ficca insisted that AWoN cannot be "centrally controlled."[18] It had to be on the ground, at the grassroots, and "hands-on."[19] Ficca's insistence still influences the network. The practitio-

---

17. For overviews of all the challenges that were identified at the meeting in Malmö, see Bobrowicz, "Working Group on Policy Making"; "Working Group on Social Cohesion"; "Working Group on Media and Narratives."

18. Ficca, "Power of Accumulated Smallness."

19. Ficca, "Power of Accumulated Smallness."

ners are doing what it takes to work for a world of neighbours predicated on the "transformative power of connection."[20] Through AWoN, "these committed and courageous individuals find mutual support in a community of practice."[21]

> We believe that global coexistence starts on a small scale: the practice of living together with those nearby. That's why we are building a network from the bottom up, where people of different faiths . . . [can] learn from one another, in their encounter with refugees . . . because we're all neighbours.[22]

The practitioners bring people together, attempting to prove through their day-to-day practice that there is no clash of civilizations in which Islam(ization) can be conjured up as a threat to the racist and religious purity of our neighbourhoods. Of course, there are conflicts and controversies, probably inside the network as much as outside the network. Yet by living in a world of neighbours, AWoN seeks to shape a world of neighbours in which all are welcome.

THE WORLD OF NEIGHBOURS WE HAVE TO WORK FOR

Encounters across borders are at the core of AWoN's work for a world of neighbours. As one of the practitioners argues:

> I don't think there's any way we can exist together without . . . considering the fact that we are a multi-faith world. . . . It doesn't mean that we have to come to some sort of agreement. . . . Just working with the fact that we—some are believers, some aren't—we might believe different things. We might even believe, you know, contradictory things, but we can still work together or we have to work together. . . . It makes a difference because it's something that has to be done by example.[23]

Crucially, the example set by AWoN revolves around the principle that "another world is possible."[24] As anarchist anthropologist David Graeber argues: "To commit oneself to such a principle is almost an act of

---

20. AWoN, *Keeping Our Humanity*, 4.
21. AWoN, *Keeping Our Humanity*, 4.
22. AWoN, *Keeping Our Humanity*, 31.
23. Interview with AWoN practitioner, 2020.
24. Graeber, *Fragments of an Anarchist Anthropology*, 10.

faith, since how can one have . . . knowledge of such matters?"[25] While agreements between anarchists and archbishops might be somewhat surprising, Jackelén also argues that "hope is nourished by our . . . experience of faith."[26]

Graeber examines the faith—in his case, it is likely a non-religious rather than a religious faith—that he experienced in the events of Occupy Wall Street, the 2011 protests against inequality and the influence of "big money" on politics in New York City that gave rise to the wider Occupy Movement. "Much of our political culture . . . makes us feel that such events are simply impossible (indeed, there is reason to believe that our political culture is designed to make us feel that way)."[27] Yet once you experience that they are not impossible but possible, the feeling changes: "The experience of those who live through such events is to find our horizons thrown open; to find ourselves wondering what else we assume cannot really happen actually can. Such events cause us to reconsider everything we thought we knew."[28]

Graeber captures the change with the concept of "contaminationism": the activities of networks such as AWoN are "premised on the assumption that the experience . . . is infectious, that anyone who takes part . . . is likely to be permanently transformed by the experience, and want more."[29] Participation is the key to contaminationism: through participation, the spark of hope jumps from participant to participant, thus nourishing the network.[30] Participation in AWoN is about doing rather than describing—Ficca's "accumulation of smallness," changing Europe step-by-step, one encounter at a time.

The practitioners of AWoN describe experiences of faith, both religious and non-religious. Of course, the figure of the neighbour is central to all Abrahamic faiths.[31] We are called to love our neighbours, no matter who they are.[32] As one of the practitioners puts it: "I'm realising that I

25. Graeber, *Fragments of an Anarchist Anthropology*, 10.
26. Jackelén, "What May We Hope?," 18.
27. Graeber, *Democracy Project*, 4.
28. Graeber, *Democracy Project*, 5.
29. Graeber, *Direct Action*, 211.
30. See Nausner, *Theologie der Teilhabe*, particularly the chapter on the significance of experience, 145–68.
31. We use "Abrahamic" as a shorthand here, although we are aware that it is a tricky term. See Hughes, *Abrahamic Religions*.
32. See Kartzow, *Ambiguous Figure of the Neighbour*, 1–22.

have lost faith in our system and our justice system. But I have found faith in God—and that's bigger."³³ She points to a shift in her view of the world: "I'm not helping you because you're Christian. . . . I'm helping you because *I'm Christian*." The shift allows for her faith to transgress borders: "My motivation now is that I've come to realise that it's all about one humanity, and if there is one undocumented person, then the whole of humanity is undocumented."

Drawing on these experiences of faith, the practitioners imagine what a more welcoming Europe could and should look like. Graeber calls it "outbreaks of imagination."³⁴ During one of the summits that brought all practitioners together, the outbreak of imagination was captured in a communal dream for a Europe "without borders in our faith communities," where "faith is a home away from home," so that one feels "safe" in a new community, no matter where one comes from.³⁵ Christians celebrating services with Muslims, Muslims celebrating services with Christians, for instance. In the Europe of their dream, the network of faith communities exemplified what it means to respond to people on the move in human and humane ways. The example would be too provocative and too powerful to be ignored by politicians and policymakers, so it caused "political change." The communal dream went on.

Given the migration regimes in Europe, the dream sounds like a dream indeed. As we write, the European Union is debating new regulations which include a more restrictive and rigid approach to people on the move who come to Europe to claim asylum. There is evidence of pushbacks by the European Union's border forces, FRONTEX, breaking national and international laws.³⁶ The conditions for the people who end up in camps on the continent are catastrophic, both inside and outside the EU.³⁷ The death toll is rising.³⁸ The practitioners, however, dream on. For them, their dream is more than a dream, because they have experienced how their collaboration has transformed them—one multi-faith encounter at a time. They have found their horizons thrown open. "Yes, I think you need a hope," one of the practitioners insists:

33. Interview with AWoN practitioner, 2020.
34. Graeber, *Democracy Project*, 5.
35. Authors' field notes from AWoN summit, 2022.
36. See Squire, *Europe's Migration Crisis*, 201. See also Fallon, "Revealed."
37. See Grillmeier, *Insel*.
38. See the data collected by the research project on the "Human Cost of Border Control" at the Free University of Amsterdam (http://www.borderdeaths.org).

> Hope which is not optimism or hope which is not pessimism, but hope which is, uh, realism. So you really stick to the ground to see what you are doing right now will have fruits. . . . So when I say "hope" it's not, like, mystical, a belief that there is a god who will do everything good. When I say "hope," it's a very realistic position towards the world. . . . Hope is always concrete.[39]

The practitioners, then, have a contagious hope which is neither esoteric nor escapist—even if their dream for Europe might sound a bit like it—but a hope that leads those who have caught it to transform hope into action, just like the anarchist and the archbishop argue. According to Jackelén, "hope is a gift," but the "possession of this gift may imply struggle" because it calls for change.[40] "Change is possible."[41]

A BOOK FOR A WORLD OF NEIGHBOURS

This book brings together activists and academics in conversation about the contagious hope that calls for change, provoking us to move from the world of neighbours we have to the world of neighbours we have to work for. Methodologically, we aim to stage this conversation in a way that allows the experiences of activists to inform academics and the expertise of academics to inform activists. Of course, such a conversation comes with challenges.

In the academy, neutrality has been the criterion for deciding between "scientific" and "unscientific" knowledge. Normativity—the idea that scholars could *both* study *and* shape the world—has been sniffed at. Scholars of religion, particularly theologians, have been uneasy with this ban on normativity from the very beginning, spearheading a debate that has spawned into fields such as philosophy, sociology, anthropology, and ethnography.[42] Lori Beaman, a scholar known for her work on religious and non-religious diversity, has assessed the relation between academic and activist work as "complementary."[43] Reflecting on her own career as a scholar, she looks back at how her sociological study has informed her advocacy work and how her advocacy work has informed her sociological

---

39. Interview with AWoN practitioner, 2020.
40. Jackelén, "What May We Hope?," 18.
41. Jackelén, "Need for a Theology of Resilience," 20.
42. For a short summary, see Lewis, "On the Role of Normativity."
43. Beaman, "Woven Together."

study, so that the two are "inextricably bound together."[44] Building on Beaman, it makes sense to interpret the relation between academic and activist work as running both ways: research can benefit from a bit of commitment and commitment can benefit from a bit of research.

As it turns out, many of the activists whose voices are gathered in this book also have academic expertise and many of the academics whose voices are gathered in this book also have activist experiences. It is not always easy to distinguish between "activist" and "academic" chapters. All of the contributors have engaged with AWoN, sometimes more directly and sometimes more indirectly. As a consequence, readers who are looking for abrasive or acerbic critiques of what is going on in AWoN will be disappointed. The contributors who write in this book want to make a case for the significance of the practices and the principles of multi-faith refugee relief that brings together religious and non-religious people with and without "migration background." Of course, the contributors at times agree and at times disagree with what is going on in the network, but they all argue that networks like AWoN are important, instructive, and inspiring for contemporary Europe. If what they have written leaves readers with the impression of a manifesto for multi-faith refugee relief, then that is not an impression that the contributors would want to correct—at least not in this book.[45]

However, the conversation between them is *not* intended as a self-promoting presentation of AWoN. Given the permeability and plasticity of networks such as AWoN, the contributors are neither only "insiders" nor only "outsiders," but often blur the boundary between insider and outsider positions. Hence, they offer critical and constructive accounts of the challenges and the chances sparked by AWoN's work. Taken together, these accounts counter a type of academic endeavour that is un-critical with activists and a type of activist endeavour that is un-critical with academics. We need a bridge between the activists and academics so that they can listen and learn from each other. This book would like to build such a bridge, allowing for the co-creation of knowledge by activists and academics. While the connections between the chapters are sometimes more implicit and sometimes more explicit, the book can be characterized as a conversation if it is read as a whole. This conversation is structured in three sections: "The Challenge," "The Call," and "The Change."

---

44. Beaman, "Woven Together," 279.

45. For a compelling and crucial critique of the harmony business that can come out of multi-faith initiatives, see Omer, *Decolonizing Religion and Peacebuilding*.

The Challenge

This section charts the situation in Europe on both national and supranational levels, challenging the legal, social, cultural, political, and economic status quo.

Maria Kjellsdotter Rydinger's chapter, "Embroidering Theology," sets the scene by challenging the idea that theology is only an academic endeavour. Through the example of an embroidery competition, in which the members of the Church of Sweden were invited to embroider sentences and slogans sustaining practitioners such as the people working with AWoN, Kjellsdotter Rydinger shows how theology inhabits their praxis. Practitioners are not passive receivers of a theology that trickles down from experts. On the contrary, they make theology through their day-to-day practice. It is this theology that can take the challenges confronting people who are and people who are not on the move seriously.

Vanessa Barker discusses the legal, ethical, and political fallout of what she calls "crimes against the soul," violations of our shared humanity. She suggests that such crimes catapult Europe into a "doom loop" that destroys what it claims to defend. Of course, racism is central to this doom loop.

The following two chapters characterize the intersection of racist and religious discrimination in debates about migration, one from a more practical angle and one from a more theoretical angle. In "All You P*k*s F**K Off Home," **Amjid Khazir** reports about this encounter with racism. His reflection shows how racist and religious discrimination come together to create a cycle of violence that has to be broken. **Anya Topolski** contextualizes stories such as Khazir's by criticizing the very constitution of the nation state as we know it, a nation state that requires differentiation between insiders and outsiders. Topolski's takedown of the simplistic binary between "inflexible" nature and "flexible" culture demonstrates that the categories of race and religion have been tied together for a long time. It makes no sense, then, to speak of Islamophobia as a form of religious rather than racist discrimination. On the contrary, it is a racism with a very long history.

Peo Hansen moves us to economics. He offers a "reality check" of the assumption that migrants are a burden rather than a benefit to economies across Europe. He counters the "toxic debate" over the costs that people on the move create by drawing on modern monetary theory. The example of Sweden shows that investing in people on the move who have arrived in the country pays off—for people with and for people without a history of migration. **Sabina Esp**'s chapter follows on from Hansen's "reality check," presenting the day-to-day struggles that social workers are confronted with, not only because of flawed cost calculations. Telling five stories from her own experience, she tackles the consequences of policies against people on the move—in her case, unaccompanied minors—as they play out on the ground.

The section concludes with a conversation between **Aude Sathoud** and **Anna Hjälm** that showcases the thinking-on-the-move that has shaped AWoN since its inception.

Taken together, the chapters in this section suggest that the challenge of migration can be addressed from the bottom up, with actions and activities that draw in more and more people. Migration cannot be isolated as if it were only about "the migrants" as opposed to "the non-migrants." The challenge concerns everybody. Everybody is called to change the status quo.

The Call

This section concentrates on how the activists affiliated with A World of Neighbours have responded to the call to change the status quo.

In his chapter on "empty hands," **Rikko Voorberg** makes the case for a "post-helping praxis" that revolves around a simple but striking suggestion: encounters that lead to spending time together need to replace the structural inequality that the very idea of "help" implies. This suggestion is grounded in a radical theology that has consequences for how to be on the quest for truth in which activists and academics might share.

Ryszard Bobrowicz's "Finding One's Place at a Busy Intersection" offers an overview of the ways in which the activists in AWoN work together, showing how difficult and demanding it can be to work together with "empty hands." Tackling the significance of mutual transformation that is triggered by encounters, he tells the story of the origins and the organization of AWoN.

Majbritt Lyck-Bowen reflects on the work of the research team that has been affiliated with AWoN from the get-go, shedding some light on the research ethics that ought to guide collaborations between activists and academics. This ethics is driven by the hope that the activists find themselves to be subjects rather than objects of the research—practitioners as partners in the co-creation of knowledge.

The following two chapters show the connections and disconnections between ethical and existential issues that the activists affiliated with AWoN are confronted with. **Amloud AlAmir**'s personal piece, "At Calais," captures a situation of being in-between. Seeing herself as being a refugee and not being a refugee at the same time, she draws attention to the search for a sense of security and stability amid the aggressions that target her. **Aude Sathoud**'s poetic piece "Athliens" also captures a situation of being in-between. They had relocated to Athens, Greece, to work with people on the move, a move which triggered personal and political struggles with constructions of identity. Situating this struggle in the context of a humanitarianism that is driven by the demands of capitalism, they show the pressures and counter-pressures that confront people who want to change lives.

Combining academic and activist backgrounds, **Karol Wilczyński** presents social media as a challenge and a chance for the work with people on the move. While he details the polarizing effect that social media has on societies through the example of Poland, he offers concrete and clear recommendations for how to change the situation for the better.

Alessia Passarelli's chapter concludes this section by clarifying how activist and academic concerns can come together in AWoN. Offering an overview of some of the quantitative-empirical and qualitative-empirical explorations conducted about the network in a pilot research project, she shows that the mismatch of the perception of people on the move, on the one hand, and the position of people on the move, on the other hand, is a pressing issue for everybody who is working with people on the move. The practitioners of AWoN, she proposes, are in a promising position to address this very mismatch. Of course, the activities of the network could and should be criticized, but her point is that any criticism needs to take the practitioners' position seriously.

The call that is characterized by the chapters in this section, then, rests on concrete materialities, controversial meanings, and clear motivations. This complexity is at the core of the change that AWoN is working towards.

The Change

This section captures the change that the activists of AWoN have instigated across the continent, clarifying the significance of faith and multi-faith engagements for their continuing commitment. It takes stock of the activities of AWoN, pointing to future possibilities for multi-faith refugee relief.

The section is opened by three chapters that tackle both migration and the consequences of migration from the perspectives of the three Abrahamic—perhaps it would be better to point to Hagaramic[46]—faiths. Drawing on her experiences as a Rabbi, **Rebecca Lillian**'s "The Evolving Torah of Human Migration" offers a reading of Jewish traditions and Jewish theologies to suggest that it is not sufficient to say that Judaism has a theology of migration. On the contrary, Judaism *is* a theology of migration, which plays out theoretically and practically.

Mártha Bolba explores the inspiration that she has taken from the table fellowship of Jesus of Nazareth for the "theology of the open supper" that is at the core of her congregation's work with people on the move in Budapest, Hungary. Like the Rabbi, she suggests that theology is more in the doing rather than the describing of relations. Her exploration points to the ripples of change that can run through a city when one congregation is courageous enough to open its table to others.

Atallah FitzGibbon details the role that Muslim communities play in welcoming people on the move in Europe. Drawing on his experiences as Advisor for Islamic Relief Europe, he discusses the complex interplay of ethnicity and religiosity in these communities, pointing to the emergence of a European Muslim community which slowly but surely transcends the divides that these concepts signal.

Tying together these three chapters, **Jakob Wirén** reflects on the practices and the potential of making space from the perspective of a theology of religions. He suggests that making space is marked by mutuality: it has to do with giving space and with being given space, thus cutting to the core of one's own theological tradition.

Exemplifying how people give space to each other, **Cecilia Sahlström** tells the story of the encounter between **Felix Unogwu** and **Anne Kjaer Bathel** through AWoN that sparked the spread of a school providing access to free digital education across several countries in Europe. It is followed by **Aude Sathoud**'s interview with **Anna Stamou**, which presents the struggle of the spokesperson of the Muslim Association of Greece. Given the rise of the far right inside and outside the country, her work with people on the move requires both inward-facing and outward-facing

---

46. For the concept of the Hagaramic, see Sherwood, "Migration as Foundation."

activities which are connected in a holistic action plan that connects the Muslim Association to a wide variety of actors.

The section closes with **Ulrich Schmiedel**'s chapter "Just Care," which presents the ethics of AWoN as a postmigrant care ethics. Such an ethics counters the binary between "migrant" and "non-migrant" that has dominated the conversation about migration ethics in theology and philosophy. AWoN's prefiguration of a world of neighbours worth living in, then, could have crucial consequences for how migration into Europe is understood.

Taken together, the chapters in this section point to both the problematic and the promising circumstances that activists encounter in their day-to-day work, presenting a nuanced account of what AWoN has done so far. These presentations are taken as a point of departure to reflect on what still needs doing to move us from the world of neighbours we have to the world of neighbours we have to work for. **Antje Jackelén**'s conclusion draws on her own experiences as a migrant in order to pinpoint the work that still needs to be done in our neighbourhoods. AWoN, then, is not a point of destination but a point of departure for a world of neighbours.

NEW NEIGHBOURHOODS

Why, then, do we need a world of neighbours? Of course, the title of this book is equivocal: *Living in a World of Neighbours* could mean either living in the world of neighbours we have or living in the world of neighbours we have to work for—the normal world or the network's world, so to speak. But both have to do with neighbourhoods. As mentioned at the outset, the neighbour is crucial to all three Abrahamic faiths. The neighbour also features in non-religious and religious visions for how we want to live together.[47] AWoN puts these visions into practice, countering the stories of clash and conflict that are told about a Europe challenged by migration. The chapters that oppose these stories come in different and diverse genres, reaching from interviews through poetry to interpretations that the activists offer of their own work. Of course, the contributors who wrote these chapters do not have all the answers to the challenge of the age of migration. But, taken together, they tell a new story for Europe—a world of neighbours is possible. Against all odds, we are already living in it. And this might be just the story we need.

47. See the contributions in Kartzow, *Ambiguous Figure of the Neighbour*.

BIBLIOGRAPHY

Bauman, Zygmunt. *Strangers at Our Door*. Cambridge: Polity, 2016.
Bayoumi, Moustafa. "They Are 'Civilised' and 'Look Like Us': The Racist Coverage of Ukraine." *Guardian*, March 2, 2022. https://www.theguardian.com/commentisfree/2022/mar/02/civilised-european-look-like-us-racist-coverage-ukraine.
Beaman, Lori G. "Woven Together: Advocacy and Research as Complementary." *Religion* 44.2 (2014) 276–88.
Bett, Alexander. *Survival Migration: Failed Governance and the Crisis of Displacement*. New York: Cornell University Press, 2013.
Bobrowicz, Ryszard. "Working Group on Media and Narratives." *World of Neighbours*, June 20, 2019. https://aworldofneighbours.org/wp-content/uploads/2025/02/AWON-Narrative-and-Media-WG.pdf.
———. "Working Group on Policy Making." *World of Neighbours*, March 20, 2019. https://aworldofneighbours.org/wp-content/uploads/2025/02/AWON-Policy-WG.pdf.
———. "Working Group on Social Cohesion." *World of Neighbours*, November 7, 2019. https://aworldofneighbours.org/wp-content/uploads/2025/02/AWON-Social-Cohesion-WG.pdf
Fallon, Katy. "Revealed: EU Border Agency Involved in Hundreds of Refugee Pushbacks." *Guardian*, April 22, 2022. https://www.theguardian.com/global-development/2022/apr/28/revealed-eu-border-agency-involved-in-hundreds-of-refugee-pushbacks.
Ficca, Dirk. "The Power of Accumulated Smallness." *World of Neighbours*, February 2, 2024. https://aworldofneighbours.org/the-power-of-accumulated-smallness.
Graeber, David. *The Democracy Project: A History, A Crisis, A Movement*. London: Penguin, 2013.
———. *Direct Action: An Ethnography*. Edinburgh: AK, 2009.
———. *Fragments of an Anarchist Anthropology*. Chicago: Prickly Paradigm, 2004.
Grillmeier, Franziska. *Die Insel: Ein Bericht vom Ausnahmezustand an den Rändern Europas*. Munich: CH Beck, 2023.
Haas, Hein de, et al. *The Age of Migration: International Population Movements in the Modern World*. 6th ed. New York: Palgrave Macmillan, 2020.
Hansen, Peo, and Stefan Jonsson. *Eurafrica: The Untold History of European Integration and Colonialism*. London: Bloomsbury, 2014.
Hellqvist, Kristina, and Andreas Sandberg. *A Time of Encounters. The Work with Asylum Seekers and New Arrivals in the Parishes of the Church of Sweden 2015–2016*. Uppsala: Svenska Kyrkan, 2018.
Hughes, Aaron W. *Abrahamic Religions: On the Uses and Abuses of History*. Oxford: Oxford University Press, 2012.
Huntington, Samuel P. "The Clash of Civilizations?" *Foreign Affairs* 2.3 (1993) 22–49.
———. *The Clash of Civilizations and the Remaking of World Order*. New York: Simon and Schuster, 1996.
Jackelén, Antje. "The Need for a Theology of Resilience, Coexistence, and Hope." *The Ecumenical Review* 1 (2019) 14–20.
———. "What May We Hope?" *Dialog: A Journal of Theology* 61.1 (2022) 13–19.
Jones, Reece. *Violent Borders: Refugees and the Right to Move*. London: Verso, 2016.

Kartzow, Marianne Bjelland, ed. *The Ambiguous Figure of the Neighbour in Jewish, Christian, and Islamic Texts and Receptions.* London: Routledge, 2021.

Lewis, Thomas A. "On the Role of Normativity in Religious Studies." In *The Cambridge Companion to Religious Studies*, edited by Robert A. Orsi, 168–85. Cambridge: Cambridge University Press, 2011.

Nausner, Michael. *Eine Theologie der Teilhabe.* Leipzig: EVA, 2020.

Omer, Atalia. *Decolonizing Religion and Peacebuilding.* Oxford: Oxford University Press, 2023.

Phan, Peter, ed. *Christian Theology in the Age of Migration: Implications for World Christianity.* London: Rowman & Littlefield, 2020.

Schmiedel, Ulrich. "Om gåshud: Hopp om en värld av grannar." In *För Världens skull: En festskrift till ärkebiskop Antje Jackelén*, edited by Christina Grenholm et al., 187–203. Stockholm: Verbum, 2022.

Schmiedel, Ulrich, and Graeme Smith, eds. *Religion in the European Refugee Crisis.* New York: Palgrave Macmillan, 2018.

Schmiedel, Ulrich, and Hannah Strømmen. *The Claim to Christianity: Responding to the Far Right.* London: SCM, 2020.

Sherwood, Yvonne. "Migration as Foundation: Hagar, the 'Resident Alien,' as Euro-America's Surrogate Self." *Biblical Interpretation* 26.4–5 (2018) 439–68.

Squire, Vicky. *Europe's Migration Crisis: Border Deaths and Human Dignity.* Cambridge: Cambridge University Press, 2020.

United Nations High Commissioner for Refugees (UNHCR). "Emergency Appeal: Ukraine Emergency." UNHCR, February 2025. https://www.unhcr.org/emergencies/ukraine-emergency.

———. "Figures at a Glance." UNHCR, n.d. https://www.unhcr.org/about-unhcr/who-we-are/figures-glance.

———. *Global Trends Report 2021.* New York: UNHCR, 2022.

A World of Neighbours (AWoN). *Keeping Our Humanity.* Uppsala: AWoN, 2020.

Part I

The Challenge

1

Embroidering Theology, or How to Make the Theology Behind the Practice Visible

Maria Kjellsdotter Rydinger

How are theology and practice connected? Working with A World of Neighbours (AWoN) within a Swedish context, I have been trying to understand how theology is expressed in practical work and what motivates and assists practitioners in encounters across religious boundaries.

To gain more insight into how practitioners[1] working for the Church of Sweden perceive their role and needs, AWoN interviewed around 30 persons receiving people on the move in 2019, often in cooperation with other local actors. These interviews revealed a gap between what practitioners *do* and what they *perceive* to be theology. Although practitioners create space for religious encounters through language cafés, help centres and other activities in which existential questions and negotiations about faith and religion are processed by diapraxis,[2] they do not consider this

---

1. In this chapter, I refer to the AWoN definition of a practitioner: currently working in the field as a practitioner of accompaniment or social cohesion; demonstrated ability and experience in the support of practitioners in the field; demonstrated ability and experience in networking; clear alignment of current work with the mission and work of AWoN.

2. Lissa Rassmussen defines "diapraxis" as "the practical cooperation between different groups. The cooperation is meant to tear down prejudices, fear and hostility between people. Diapraxis takes place in the border zone between religion and

to be theological engagement and do not describe their work as interreligious dialogue. Theology is primarily associated with expert knowledge, theoretical systems, and ideas held by academically trained theologians. This separation between theology and practice is devastating, as it deprives practitioners of important tools and legitimacy in their encounters with colleagues and church structures, and leaves them with a sense of solitude.

To bridge that gap, AWoN searched for ways to aid the theological articulation of what practitioners do. The question was: How can their knowledge be made visible and, in turn, influence and challenge our understanding of issues around migration and religious encounters? This became one of the driving forces behind AWoN's approach, which step by step led us to publish a book about embroidery.

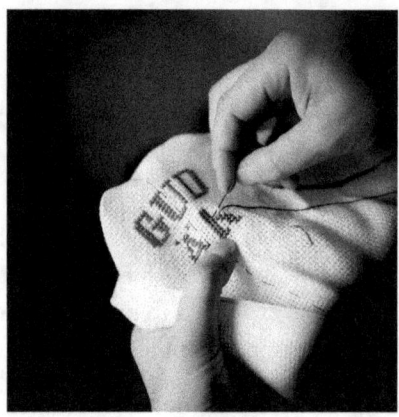

"God Is..."
Photo: Magnus Aronson.

Throughout this chapter, I will describe our approach and the process behind the embroidery project.

FROM HEROES TO ZEROES

In 2015, as Europe was accommodating an influx of people on the move, many of the practitioners we interviewed were among the first to offer help and volunteer with accompaniment. They described themselves as solution-oriented and quick to respond to what is happening in society.

---

culture." This definition is also used by the City Mission in their interreligious work in Sweden. See Gärde, "Diapraxis."

Initially their efforts were easy to justify, and many received grants from the state, municipalities, and religious communities to implement their work. However, gradually, interest waned. Negative narratives about migrants and refugees began to dominate, they were characterized as a problem, a threat, and as something we in Europe needed to protect ourselves against. Fears were fuelled by statistics and reports of "crises in the system." The belief in humanity, human rights, and inclusive societies was replaced by a general distrust that dehumanized and divided into "us" and "them." More and more people found "sensible" reasons to introduce stricter rules and more prudent migration policies. The previous open-minded approach was described as rose-tinted idealism that now needed to be replaced by a more mature realism.

In Sweden, the norm shifted. What was previously taken for granted as part of the foundation of our society, equal value and dignity of all, became a choice, a position that could be questioned and criticized. This affected the practitioners. They went from being celebrated heroes to being sees as naive, bleeding hearts, and even threats to society. Grants and operations were cancelled. When they pointed out problems in the system or defended the rights of migrants, they were often dismissed, met with silence, and sometimes accused of being troublemakers contributing to the undermining of the welfare system. Critical questions were asked. How do you know that these people you are helping are here legally? Do you think they should have the same rights as those of us who have lived here all our lives?

The tone also changed within faith-based communities and religious organizations. Practitioners had to answer questions such as: Why should we help people of other faiths in our community? How do you justify this in your religious tradition? The interreligious practice was increasingly described as something negative, a mixing of religions, where you had to compromise your own values and beliefs. The interreligious concept was politicized and categorized in the new landscape as part of a "left-wing project."

Within AWoN, we encountered more and more practitioners who felt inadequate, misunderstood, and isolated in their work. They were torn between, on the one hand, trying to take care of endless needs, while, on the other hand, receiving fewer and fewer resources, support, and encouragement. Ambition and empathy were pushed to one side and "compassion fatigue" became a term used to describe the situation that many found themselves in. Several practitioners quit their jobs and applied for other posts. Some did so because project grants ran out and operations were cancelled, and others because they simply could not cope with the situation.

Practitioners are people on the front line, those who first recognize major changes and challenges in society. The new worldview presented a more complex picture of migration, and the reaction of practitioners indicated that they were not equipped to respond to and manage it. Migration challenges Europe in many ways, but it is also a mirror that reflects who we are and the values around which we build our lives and society. It offers an opportunity to examine our identity, our fears and vulnerabilities. To question what we need to protect and secure—and what we fundamentally believe in and have to take a stand for. As new and old neighbours, we must embrace the challenge of how to live together in a diverse and complex world. We need to create conditions for a sustainable and resilient community.

In AWoN, we saw a need for an in-depth dialogue on what migration and encounters across religious boundaries meant. Several questions arose. What lessons can be learnt from the practitioners' experiences? How can we build resilience and hold on to important values when norms shift and we cannot live up to our ideals? Can practitioners' knowledge be both a resource for themselves, giving them confidence and courage in their work, and at the same time challenge the worldview which is under threat of becoming too narrow for us to live together as good neighbours?

THE CONTRIBUTION OF THEOLOGY

As a theologian, I believe that theology can offer a significant contribution to an understanding of our existence and living conditions. During times of societal upheaval, theology has been able to help people find a meaningful language that can accommodate contradictions and complexity, but also give them the tools to examine cultural norms and values.

In the current European climate of growing protectionism, where we are building walls and fences along our borders to protect ourselves from those fleeing and seeking shelter—but where many are also struggling not to dehumanize, shut down, and fall into compassion fatigue—theology can offer resources to go beyond a one-sided narrative of us versus them. In the formation of this theology, the experience of practitioners is an important resource in posing the right questions and understanding what we need, what is possible, and how we should act.

To facilitate conversations about interfaith practice, AWoN organized "fishbowl conversations"[3] in 2019, where practitioners and researchers could come together to listen and reflect upon one another's experience. In these conversations, practitioners described their work as a relationship-building approach that involves testing and changing strategies and solutions on an ongoing basis. They expressed confidence in their knowledge of how to create safe spaces where people with different needs, backgrounds, and religious identities can interact. But many also expressed concern that they did not have a theological basis for their praxis. They often had a narrow understanding of what theology is and can encompass, and hardly anyone saw their own activity as a form of theology. Some asked for more theological arguments, or a "new theology" of migration, something they could hold on to when they were criticized and questioned because they felt they were in an inferior position when they could not always explain their theology. Others tried as best as they could to legitimize their activities by referring to what they perceived to be an "approved theology," but by doing so they were at the same time undermining their own work and the theology expressed through it. As one deacon in the Church of Sweden put it: "We organize language cafés attended by many people from different backgrounds. People feel that they can be themselves there, practice the language but also talk about struggles, and what is happening in their lives—but yes, we talk about Jesus too. We actually do that!"

The researchers clarified that theology is not only expressed by the conceptualization of definitions and thoughts. Events such as language cafés or cooking groups can also be an expression of theology in many ways.[4] However, this understanding of their operational theology is of little benefit to practitioners if this knowledge is not validated or legitimized by themselves or those they work with. The interviews and conversations identified a gap that needed to be addressed—a lack of language that can help practitioners explain and legitimize their work in both a religious and secular context. Additionally, they showed that the radical theology expressed in practitioners' actions has no space to manifest itself in the broader conversations.

The identification of these gaps meant that we had to find a way to bridge them. If we want to live in an open society, side by side, we need

---

3. A form of dialogue where practitioners and researchers actively listen, comment, and discuss while receiving questions from an external audience.

4. See Nygaard, "Modes of Deacons Professional Knowledge."

training in how we can interact and benefit from our different experiences and religious backgrounds.[5] Interreligious encounters should be seen as something that is natural to society, and interreligious diapraxis should be able to develop curiosity and contribute to inherent processes of knowledge that are part of our culture.

FROM QUOTES TO EMBROIDERY

During the pandemic year of 2020, a lot of activities were put on hold, and people felt lonely and isolated. At the same time, interreligious cooperation was of great importance when reaching out to vulnerable groups and migrants with help and information. During this period, we regularly met with Archbishop Antje Jackelén to coordinate the work of AWoN. In one of the meetings, we talked about interreligious practice, the gap, and how practitioners were questioned even though it should be obvious that we should help fellow human beings regardless of their religious background. In response to this she said: "I think we need to help them to build some backbone."[6]

We liked her phrase "building backbone" but also wanted to emphasize that *we* should not be helping them by coming up with a new kind of "migration theology" imposed from above. Instead, we should ask *them* for help. Even though many practitioners did not consider themselves theologians, they certainly had sayings that have given them strength and inspiration in their work to face challenges—mottos and quotes that helped them to stand firm and believe in what they do. Therefore, we reached out to as many people as we could find in the interreligious network in Sweden and asked them to send in their favourite quotes and thoughts that, in various ways, give them courage. We quickly received many contributions.[7] From Amanda Gorman's quote, "There is always light, if only we are brave enough to see it. If only if we are brave enough to be it,"[8] to words from the Bible or the Qur'an such as "God is greater,"

---

5. Sturla Stålsett emphasizes the capacity for dialogue as one of three fundamental impacts that religious traditions have in a society in his *Det livssynsåpne samfunn*.

6. In Swedish there is a saying: to have "rye in the back" (råg i ryggen), which means that a person dares to speak up for themselves, taking a stand for something that matters to them.

7. Information about the process for "Råg i ryggen—en utställning" can be found online. See Church of Sweden, "Råg i ryggen."

8. From Amanda Gorman's poem "The Hill We Climb," performed at the inauguration of the US president in 2021. See Gorman "The Hill We Climb."

"Whatever you want others to do for you, do also the same for them," or from famous theologians, such as Hans Küng, "No peace among the nations without peace among the religions," and famous philosophers, such as Martin Buber, "All real living is meeting," but many also came up with their own thoughts and phrases. A former UN employee in Sudan wrote: "Isn't the meaning of life that we help others to live?" AWoN practitioners wrote: "What you see in others is in you," and, "You have a world of neighbours."

Several of the quotes were so powerful that we wondered how we could take care of these treasures. Could we make posters of them to display in appropriate public places, or as a reminder at practitioners' workplaces? Or could we make postcards and distribute them as widely as possible? In the end, we decided to honour an old tradition used to give status to words and ideas. Many of us had memories of cross-stitch samplers and intricately embroidered proverbs hanging on the wall at home or in church halls. Words that have become a reference point for an approach and have quietly influenced people for generations. What if the words shared about peaceful coexistence and the importance of encounters between people and religions, could be embroidered and become reference points that encourage reflection, signs that quietly speak in people's everyday lives?

In March 2021, we announced a competition in the press, inviting anyone who wanted to, to embroider one of the twelve quotes that we had selected. Entries of all sizes, shapes, and materials were received from all over Sweden. Some had embroidered tapestries to hang on the wall, others had embroidered on cushions, jackets, towels, tote bags, and recycled materials. Several also sent in their own thoughts that came to them while they were working. A woman who embroidered "You have a world of neighbours" wrote:

> Having neighbours from different parts of the world on my doorstep when I was growing up made this quote feel right. I wanted a globe to represent the world, and hands to represent the neighbours. With the hands, I also want to show that when you ask for help, there is always someone reaching out.

"You Have a World of Neighbours."
Embroidery: Petra Hall. Photo: Magnus Aronson.

Another who embroidered "God is greater" explained it more biblically:

> My inspiration for embroidery came from the creation story: In the beginning, God created the heavens and the earth. So it had to be the heavens. I tried to give the text a Star Wars feel, with the words rolling out into space. The star of Bethlehem was added to the embroidery and with a little imagination I can see that the star and the text formed a triangle Trinity.

"God Is Greater."
Embroidery: Gunilla Gustafsson. Photo: Magnus Aronson.

One parish submitted a joint piece with many different small embroideries and quotes illustrating how they live together with a diversity of opinions as neighbours. For them, the embroidery competition provided an opportunity to talk to many people about commitment and courage. They wrote another explanatory text: "In total, eighty-eight people participated in various ways, by embroidering or by sharing their opinion on what the quote means to them. Each image on the embroidery represents something that people have shared."

We chose handicrafts because they can have an impact on an individual level. They can constitute a personal time for thought and reflection. But they also open up the individual to a broader community, creating opportunities for social interaction and dialogue. Patterns, techniques, and materials have long travelled with people across territorial boundaries without the need to speak the same language or share a philosophy of life. Many thoughts and hours lie behind the entries submitted—sometimes days and weeks of personal commitment. This slow process of using one's hands, gives the mind a rest and offers new space for the change you want to see in yourself and in society. The theology emerges between the lines of the mosaic of different quotes and images that were collected. In this tapestry, there are common experiences that can be used to draw conclusions, but there are also contradictions and unique ideas. Some of them are linked to time and place. There is a richness that exposes the complexity of life. When it comes to action, there is no single manual, method, or theology that can be universally applied as the "correct" one.

Each embroidery was a gift which we then shared via social media and newsletters. They also became the basis for a traveling exhibition and a book which has been distributed in various contexts.[9] The Backbone project made interreligious practice visible. A year later, in the spring of 2023, AWoN, together with other organizations in Sweden, invited sixty new practitioners to an online gathering. During the meeting, there were several practitioners who, without knowing each other, used quotes from the *Book of Backbones*. For me, this proved not only that theology had become concrete, but also offered resilience to practitioners by creating meaning and hope.

---

9. See, again, Church of Sweden, "Råg i ryggen."

A BACKBONE FOR EUROPE

Throughout this chapter, I have focused on a concrete project rooted in a Swedish context. However, I believe that the "Backbone project" can provide insights for a broader European context. Thus, I would like to conclude with three constructive proposals.

"There Is Always Light, If Only We Are Brave Enough To See It.
If Only We Are Brave Enough To Be It."
Photo: Magnus Aronson.

First, a changing attitude to migration which begins to question core values like human dignity, requires development of a backbone of resilience. As frontline workers, migration practitioners have already developed sophisticated strategies to justify their work and sustain themselves throughout daily struggles. They also have experience in creating safe encounters across religious boundaries. Their actions and testimonies show that there are several ways of looking at migration and people on the move. They know that life is not about protecting our "external borders" and prosperity at all costs, but about protecting our empathy and our willingness to find common solutions so we can identify with one another. Their knowledge and voices must be valorised and made visible in different ways. Religious leaders, policymakers, and academics should acknowledge their experience and give them a seat at the table.

Second, there is a need to create space and time for reflection, both personal and communal. The Embroidery Project gave people space and time to recognize their sources of motivation, be constructive, and reflect, both by themselves and together with others. It countered a sense of isolation and solitude, showing that the practitioners were not as alone as they felt and that it is possible to draw strength from linking arms with others. Working with the embroideries embodied and made visible that "you have a world of neighbours." When stitches were added alongside stitches, a space for compassion was created. This sense of neighbourliness is necessary if we are to maintain our empathy and combat compassion fatigue.

Third, and finally, we need more of an embroidered theology approach. The Swedish practitioners were searching for theological guidance, a language that could give them courage and strengthen their backbone. The embroidery project showed that they do not necessarily need new theological handbooks, training programs, or policies. Instead, they needed support for a more comprehensive understanding of the fact that an intervention which starts with the hands rather than the brain, is a valid and valuable theological contribution.

This is especially important in the context of interfaith encounters. Numerous experts from different religious traditions have attempted to construct concrete rules for interreligious dialogue. However, these dialogues have rarely extended beyond academic circles or international conferences. To be relevant, interreligious encounters must be rooted in the local public sphere. This requires putting words to what occurs when people from different backgrounds come together in everyday settings, such as parishes, outreach camps, or language cafés. The embroidery project exemplified that through a conscious *diapraxis* a deeper theological reflection on religion can emerge. A backbone for Europe will require an embrace of these kinds of grassroot theological approaches.

BIBLIOGRAPHY

Church of Sweden. "Råg i ryggen—en utställning." *Svenska kyrkan*, December 18, 2024. https://www.svenskakyrkan.se/migration/envarldavgrannar/rag-i-ryggen.

Gärde, Johan. *Diapraxis: Interkulturell och—religiös samvaro/dialog som metod i social arbete*. Stockholm: Stockholms Stadsmission, 2013. https://www.stadsmissionen.se/sites/default/files/2019-12/Metodhandbok-Diapraxis.pdf.

Gorman, Amanda. *The Hill We Climb: An Inaugural Poem*. New York: Penguin, 2021.

Nygaard, Marianne Rodriguez. "Modes of Deacons Professional Knowledge: Facilitation of the 'Space of Possibilities.'" *Diaconia* 5.2 (2014) 178–200.

Stålsett, Sturla. *Det livssynsåpne samfunn*. Oslo: Cappelen Damm, 2021.

2

Crimes Against the Soul and Potential for Repair

Vanessa Barker

Blood, violence, and war have soaked the European continent for much of its history. Conflicts over territory, power, and population, rather than a relic of the past, continue to shape the life chances of anyone within Europe's borders and anyone who crosses them. This characterization of Europe as a site of struggle over territory and population, unrecognizable a mere ten years ago when the European Union won the Nobel Peace Prize for advancing peace, human rights, and democracy, has been made manifest through Russia's invasion of Ukraine. This war we can recognize and even understand in conventional terms as a fight for Europe and European values. At the same time, however, the European Union has been engaged in another fight for its values, its way of life, its territory and population. But this fight has been waged not against a hostile or rogue nation but against people on the move, those seeking safety, security, and refuge in Europe. This campaign is asymmetrical, dirty, and fought in border zones through passports, visas, and violence, and most recently in the dark forests of Belarus and Poland, in the Mediterranean and Aegean Seas, and along the Balkan borders.

Across Europe, Australia, the US, and the Global North more generally, unwanted mobility has been met with a series of restrictive migration policies and practices designed to keep migrants, particularly poor people, people of colour, and those from the global south, out of affluent societies.¹ These measures have escalated from administrative backlogs and bureaucratic nightmares² to the building of camps, detention centres, migration prisons, push-backs, and off-shore reception centres designed to house, contain, punish, and block onward mobility.³ The various forms and global scales of border violence⁴ have reached such a level of intensity and saturation they have become an assault on the lives of migrants.⁵ As I will suggest below, this is a self-destructive doom loop. When democratic societies rely so heavily on repression, such state coercion undermines the same values it seeks to preserve. This repression violates the social contract and social relations themselves. This is a historical and social process I call *crimes against the soul*.

Below I walk through one such example, although there are many more. I provide additional context for border closures, specifically around the criminalization of migration and increasingly the criminalization of humanitarian aid, and conclude with examples of resistance to Europe's hard borders. Here it is civil society, volunteers, social movements and activists, including networks such as A World of Neighbours (AWoN), who refuse to accept the inhumanity of contemporary border regimes. Instead, they challenge it as they provide aid, assistance, support, and mutual recognition. They stand up for our shared humanity and they remind us in no uncertain terms that "solidarity is not a crime," a transformative organizing principle for a social movement that supports the freedom and autonomy of migrants.⁶

NO WAY OUT

Through summer and autumn of 2021, Belarus provided travel visas to migrants and asylum seekers from Iraq, Afghanistan, and Syria promising them safe passage into Poland and the European Union. Belarus's apparent act of generosity was widely understood as a geopolitical stunt and payback for EU sanctions against the government for violently cracking down on peaceful protests and lack of free and fair elections. Belarus encouraged asylum seekers and other migrants to travel to Minsk

1. Walia, *Border & Rule*.
2. Billings, *Regulating Refugee Protection*; Canning, "Bureaucratised Banality."
3. Bosworth, *Inside Immigration Detention*, 199.
4. Jones, *Violent Borders*; FitzGerald, *Refuge Beyond Reach*.
5. Tazreiter et al., "Spectres of Subjugation"; Weber, "Welfare Policing."
6. See Tazzioli, "Crimes of Solidarity."

where they would be guided into Poland. Those who arrived from the Middle East quickly learned there was no safe passage. They were there as political pawns to antagonize Poland and the European Union. From Minsk, they were escorted to a remote border zone and told to cross into Poland through a razor wire fence, which had been cut open by Belarus border guards. On the other side, Polish border forces blocked their entry and pushed them back into Belarus. The Polish Parliament recently had passed the Act of Foreigners, enabling the border force to push anyone back for illegal entry and created a two-kilometre military zone along the Belarus border which prohibited any civil society organization, volunteer, lawyer, humanitarian worker, or journalist from accessing the zone or providing aid.[7] As reported to case workers for Human Rights Watch, several migrants were beaten, extorted, and subject to hardships and humiliations by border guards while others were warned: "Die here or go to Poland."[8] Blocked at the border by Polish border forces, who at one point used water cannons against them, and pushed back into Belarus, most were caught in a no man's land with no way out. For weeks, they were trapped in a remote forest without food, water, or shelter, unable to enter Poland and unable to return home. Several aid groups tried to provide relief by using GPS location data to drop caches of food, medicine, and water at great personal risk under the cover of night. As temperatures fell below zero, several people died in the woods from the cold and exposure. The West watched and did nothing. The European Union stood by Poland, and Belarus got away with it.

How are we to make sense of this border standoff and the total disregard for human life? How is it possible that the European Union, with its founding principles of human dignity, freedom of movement, equality, and human rights, did not intervene? No airlifts out of the forest? No sanctions against Poland, a fellow member? No humanitarian corridors to bring those asserting their rights or in need to safety? Are the founding principles empty words? Are they merely conditional? Are they fading in historical relevance or resonance? Is this level of hypocrisy simply accepted in democratic societies? Is Europe morally bankrupt? These may seem naïve questions, as scholars, activists, and commentators have all noted the return of hard borders across Europe and the Global North as democratic societies are inherently exclusionary and depend on the dirty

---

7. Boelpaep, "Migrants Freezing to Death."
8. HRW, *Die Here or Go to Poland.*

work of the state to preserve their way of life. Yet I do not think these are naïve questions but are essential to ask and get right.

As I will outline below, these kind of questions about life and death at the border and why and how they can take place within democratic societies should be placed front and centre, rather than dismissing them or even explaining them away as obvious in a world of global inequality or the prerogatives of nation-states. We need to ask these questions. They can help us pierce through all of the noise—what community organizer Maurice Mitchell calls the "the doom loop" of endless critique, or what sociologist Diana Mulinari calls the scholarship of despair and need for a scholarship of hope.[9] If we can get to the heart of the matter, we may be able to provide a way out, another way of thinking about old problems, and develop a new way of acting. As critical theorist Rahel Jaeggi explains, by examining the underlying structures of historical developments, critical scholars can identify the emancipatory possibilities from their internal tensions and contradictions.[10] To Jaeggi, critical scholarship can contribute in productive and emancipatory ways to a taken for granted structure of society by platforming and closely examining social and political crises. Asking questions about life and death, principles and ideals, can expose the false promises of security, border control, and repression. We know from the long history of the prison, taking away liberty never solved the crime problem or its underlying social causes. Closed borders, which make more people unfree and unsafe, will not stop migration or address the social fault lines around it. Violence usually does not solve social problems but makes them worse. Instead, we as scholars, activists, and community organizers should confront the normalization of violence within our societies that is carried out in our names and see it for what it is.

CRIMES AGAINST THE SOUL

Crimes against the soul are crimes against our shared human values, our shared humanity, our sense that we are part of something larger than ourselves but bound to each other as fellow humans. Crimes against the soul are violations of the bond that ties humans together. They are crimes against society itself; they are crimes against what Émile Durkheim would

---

9. See Mitchell, *Building Resilient Organisations*; Mulinari, "Postcolonial/Decolonial Traditions."

10. Jaeggi, "Crisis, Contradiction," 210.

have called the collective consciousness, our shared understandings of the social world that binds us together despite our differences.[11] Crimes against the soul include acts of violence, misrecognition, and indifference against individuals and groups. They entail violations of an individual's integrity, dignity, and sense of wholeness and as such they violate the social bond that ties that individual to society. As they crush individuals, they crush us all. Allowing people to die in the forest because they dared to cross a border to seek a better life, safety, and refuge is one such example. Slow death by bureaucracy, which fails to see and respond to the needs of human life, is another. Being beaten to death by the police as Tyre Nichols called out for his mother is one more. Tyre Nichols, a Black American, was pulled over by a special crime unit in the Memphis police department for an unclear traffic violation. When he left the scene, he was tasered, taunted, kicked, and pummelled by five Black police officers who failed to provide aid and have now been charged in his murder. Indifference towards others crushes the human spirit. It also evokes a deep social fear of abandonment as to be human is to be necessarily social, relational, and interconnected to others, to be recognized by others.[12] The quality and character of social ties are foundational to what makes or breaks a society. These interconnections, interdependencies, and the moral values that make them meaningful may change over time, but they are intrinsic to human society. Crimes against the soul destabilize these interconnections, social ties, and a shared sense of meaning about the world. When we normalize the infliction of violence against fellow humans and do so for our own benefit, we are breaking this shared social world.

A note for clarification. "Crimes against the soul" is a sociological concept that seeks to capture the specifically social aspects of the violations against individual dignity and humanity. It is a social offense that necessarily entails social effects. They cannot be separated. It is related to, but distinct from, crimes against humanity. Crimes against humanity as defined by Article 7 of the 1998 Rome Statute are specific acts committed against individuals or groups, including, but not limited to: extermination; forced displacement of a population; enslavement; sexual violence; torture. These are legal definitions with legal remedies such as the International Criminal Court established to prosecute them. Crimes against

---

11. On the collective consciousness, see Durkheim, *Division of Labor in Society*, 79–80.

12. Honneth, *Struggle for Recognition*; Lamont, "Addressing Recognition Gaps"; Hörnqvist, *Pleasure of Punishment*.

the soul is not a legal category but a social one that necessitates social remedies.

How has it come to this, where democratic societies routinely accept, if not demand, violence against others and outsiders? How has it become normalized? In the following section, I review key developments in European border practices that preceded the standoff between Poland and Belarus, practices which have been institutionalized across the region. It concludes on a more hopeful note with several examples of resistance and challenges to this paradigm, which might provide avenues, ideas, and practices to restore the soul.

CRIMINALIZATION OF MIGRATION

The EU has been restricting unwanted mobility since at least 2004 with an elaborate web of legal frameworks and anti-immigrant politics, which intensified after the 2015 refugee crisis. Political parties on the right and left have risen to power with various claims to limit migration and have done so in nearly all regions of the EU. Elections are often won or lost on the migration issue, which effectively ties together culture wars about values and identity with economic anxieties to bring together new electoral patterns and coalitions. Sweden, for example, recently elected a right-wing coalition government that includes a partnership with the explicitly anti-immigrant party, the Sweden Democrats, the second largest party in the country. Across the political spectrum, migrants, asylum seekers, refugees, especially those racialized from the global south, have been deemed a threat to the European way of life, its values, its identity, population, and resources. To respond to these perceived existential, social, and national security threats, member states have developed an array of security logics and criminalization practices to stop migration.

What this means is that migration has been deemed a crime and the migrant a criminal.[13] That it is to say, people who cross borders can be subject to criminal sanctions and put in prison-like facilities, even without committing a crime in the conventional sense of committing an offense such as robbery, assault, theft, or fraud, a violation of the criminal law. In Europe, migration is not a violation of the criminal law but is being treated as such by public authorities. Likewise, a person cannot be illegal. It is only through the law, through legal codes and legal frameworks, that certain actions can become a criminal offense. Border

---

13. Stumpf, "Crimmigration Crisis," 367–419; Franko, *Crimmigrant Other*.

activists have powerfully captured this sentiment in their organizing slogan: "no one is illegal." Legal scholars similarly have shown how the law is used and structured to create conditions of illegality[14]—the law makes people illegal, not the other way around.

The criminalization of migration also entails the use of criminal justice personnel to deal with migration. This means that the police are often called to handle migration issues even though domestic or local police forces are trained to deal with crime and disorder. What does it mean and what does it communicate to the public when we see the police escorting refugees, for example, to a reception centre? Many might say it simply means the police are there to provide some security or protection to the refugees, but we can also see how their presence may mean they are keeping us safe from the refugees. The policing of refugees is loaded with cultural significance as it reverses the nature of the threat: it portrays people who are fleeing violence, persecution, and forced displacement as a threat or security risk themselves.[15] Why not use the administrative authority responsible for migration such as the Migration Agency or work with civil society volunteers such as the Red Cross or Refugees Welcome? It is a lazy state that turns to the police over and over again to manage social issues that are outside their crime control jurisdiction and raison d'être.

The criminalization of migration can include changes to the substance or content of the criminal law. For example, legal scholars have identified the EU Returns Directive as the key legal framework that underpins the criminalization processes in Europe.[16] The directive indicates how immigration detention can be used and how the EU can remove or repatriate unwanted migrants.[17] Immigration detention centres are closed and locked facilities that restrict the freedom and movement of those inside; they are weigh stations for most who will be returned or repatriated to their country of origin. In Denmark, the government proposed the use of prison islands for refugees and asylum seekers to keep them locked up and locked out of Danish society.[18] As immigration detention necessitates the loss of liberty for noncriminal offenses, to legal scholars and

---

14. Dauvergne, "Making People Illegal."
15. Barker, *Nordic Nationalism and Penal Order*.
16. CEU, "Directive 2008/115/EC."
17. Mitsilegas, *Criminalisation of Migration in Europe*.
18. Barker and Smith, "This Is Denmark," 1540.

others, the use of immigration detention to house migrants in prison-like facilities violates the principle of proportionality and protection of human dignity in European law.[19] As much ethnographic research has found, they can also inflict harm on those on the inside by limiting their autonomy, increasing a sense of insecurity or uncertainty, and subjecting them to the stigma associated with imprisonment and wrongdoing.[20] As border criminologists have argued, the use of penal sanctions such as detention gives a false sense of legitimacy to the use of crime control measures to manage migration.

And perhaps one of the more insidious elements of the criminalization of migration involves shifts in the cultural frameworks for making sense of migration itself.[21] As migration becomes entangled or conflated with crime, disorder, and social threats, migrants become associated with wrongdoing. This way of making sense of migration not only legitimizes repressive responses, it disconnects or decouples migration from the political expression of rights. Migrants and migration become problems of order rather than a recognized part of a political order. This shift can minimize a state and society's responsibility towards noncitizens and outsiders. As the crime control paradigm becomes dominant, superseding but not yet replacing human rights and the freedom of movement embedded in international law, this paradigm reenforces national interests over international obligations. As philosopher Nancy Fraser[22] explains, the scales of justice have been domesticated within the nation-state frame and cut off from questions of global equality and global justice. In terms of border control, this historical process has been called penal nationalism, in which the hard and soft power of criminal justice is used to exclude and punish migrants, noncitizens, and other racialized groups to uphold and protect national interests, identities, and resources.[23] Penal nationalism is mobilized to protect the bubble of a certain way of life from the perceived existential threat of outsiders and others.

Penal nationalism, and its associated processes of criminalization of migration, exposes the underlying structure of human values embedded in law. It makes clear that even in the most equal and democratic

19. Cancellaro and Zirulia, "Controlling Migration Through De Facto Detention."
20. Canning, "Bureaucratised Banality," 210.
21. Franko, *Crimmigrant Other*; Woude et al., "Crimmigration in the Netherlands," 560–79.
22. Fraser, *Scales of Justice*.
23. Barker, "Penal Power at the Border," 441; Haney, "Prisons of the Past," 346–68.

societies, we tend to reproduce a violent and racialized hierarchy of human worth.

SOLIDARITY IS NOT A CRIME: MÖTE MELLAN MÄNNISKOR

The criminalization of migration follows an expansive logic. This means that rather than retract or narrow its aims, purposes and targets, or pull back when it is clear these practices do not work, it doubles down. It becomes a pervasive governing logic that seeks to solve problems of order through repression and reaches across policy domains.[24] As I have suggested above, this approach is self-destructive. Yet, it is not inevitable. Social movements from all directions and all walks of life have stood up for migrants and refused the legitimacy of violence. In the US and elsewhere, a newly invigorated abolition movement has emerged to protest policing and the prison, excessively deployed against people of colour and poor people. Across Europe and elsewhere, "no borders" movements have called for the abolition of state borders in recognition of a universal right to movement and human freedom. Migrant movements have provided aid, support, human contact, and political energy to those faced with coercion and the violation of rights and autonomy.

In 2015, in Sweden, for example, networks such as Refugees Welcome among many others, including the Red Cross, the Red Crescent, sports associations, and several parishes of the Swedish church, provided much needed human support to asylum seekers and refugees arriving in Northern Europe as they fled the civil war in Syria. AWoN was created in this very context. People met those entering Sweden at train stations and after a long journey, offered a warm cup of soup, a blanket, a glimpse of shared humanity.[25] In the Swedish language, these face-to-face encounters are called *möte mellan människor*, a meeting between people. But it carries a profound meaning of recognition—to see and be seen by another. This simple exchange has radical implications as it can connect humans outside their social parameters of citizenship, national origin, and territorial boundaries. It can threaten the authority of the state as civil society claims the ultimate responsibility to decide who belongs in

---

24. Simon, *Governing Through Crime*; Bosworth, "Border Control and the Limits of the Sovereign State."

25. Hellqvist and Sandberg, *En tid av möten*. Also available in English as Hellqvist and Sandberg, *Time of Encounters*.

the society, who to care for, who to connect with regardless of geographic boundaries and social borders. In its simplicity, it holds emancipatory potential.

So, it may not come as a surprise that this transformative moment was quickly met with closed borders, a backlash against migration, and a new level of criminalization. This time the criminalization process was aimed squarely at aid groups and volunteers themselves. The European Union has criminalized aspects of humanitarian aid in which anyone who helps a noncitizen cross a border or enter a territory where they are not a citizen or member, can be prosecuted. According to the EU Council Directive, these acts constitute a crime or breach of state law. The Crime of Facilitation of Entry and Transit, Article 1.1 (a) states: "Any person who intentionally assists a person who is not a national of a Member State to enter, or transit across, the territory of a Member State in breach of the laws of the State concerned on the entry or transit of aliens."[26]

The legal framework has been on the books since 2002, its application was expanded during the so-called refugee crisis of 2015–2016. In Sweden, for example, a Swedish television producer was arrested and prosecuted for transporting a young Syrian across the border. Volunteers in Malmö who tried to help those seeking asylum cross into Sweden and reach a Migration Reception centre feared reprisal for their help. Likewise, in France, particularly around the Italy-France border and in the Mediterranean Sea, as philosopher Martina Tazzioli[27] has shown, numerous NGOs and activists have been subject to criminalization and prosecution, including Doctors without Borders, Save the Children, SOS Méditerranée, Sea-Watch, and others. Their actions of support and aid have been twisted into the crime of human smuggling and trafficking for criminal gains. We might ask how is it possible that the duty of care has become a crime.

Returning to the Belarus-Polish border in 2021, we can see the entrenchment of the criminalization of humanitarian aid to such an extent that the Polish government created a two-kilometre militarized zone prohibiting the entry of civilians, including humanitarian workers, journalists, and volunteers. Those caught providing aid or support could be prosecuted. Given that both Polish and Belarus's border forces played human pin ball with migrants who were trapped, the threat of prosecution

---

26. CEU, "Directive 2002/90/EC."
27. Tazzioli, "Crimes of Solidarity."

or violence hindered much relief. And yet, people responded. Ordinary people, neighbours, volunteers, activists, and humanitarians with the aid of GPS tracking location technologies were able to reach those stuck in the forest to bring them food, water, medicine, legal aid if requested, and recognition of shared humanity. Members of AWoN were at this border too. These *möte mellan människor*, the meetings between people, may provide a way forward, a way out of the moral morass. Migrants and civil society actors who refuse to accept the violence of the state, to claim responsibility for another, to share humanity in a simple gesture of recognition hold an emancipatory potential to support human freedom and autonomy. These gestures of recognition are restorative for the soul and society. The question now is how to reproduce them on a grand scale?

BIBLIOGRAPHY

Barker, Vanessa. *Nordic Nationalism and Penal Order: Walling the Welfare State*. London: Routledge, 2018.

———. "Penal Power at the Border: Realigning State and Nation." *Theoretical Criminology* 21.4 (2017) 441–57.

Barker, Vanessa, and Peter Scharff Smith. "This Is Denmark: Prison Islands and the Detention of Immigrants." *British Journal of Criminology* 61.6 (2021) 1540–56.

Billings, Peter, ed. *Regulating Refugee Protection Through Social Welfare: Law, Policy and Praxis*. London: Routledge, 2022.

Boelpaep, Bruno. "Migrants Freezing to Death on Belarus-Poland Border." *BBC News*, September 23, 2021. https://www.bbc.com/news/av/world-europe-58671941.

Bosworth, Mary. "Border Control and the Limits of the Sovereign State." *Social Legal Studies* 17.2 (2008) 199–215.

———. *Inside Immigration Detention*. Oxford: Oxford University Press, 2014.

Cancellaro, Francesca, and Stefano Zirulia. "Controlling Migration Through De Facto Detention: The Case of the 'Diciotti' Italian Ship." *Border Criminologies* (blog), October 22, 2018. https://www.law.ox.ac.uk/research-subject-groups/centre-criminology/centreborder-criminologies/blog/2018/10/controlling.

Canning, Victoria. "Bureaucratised Banality: Asylum and Immobility in Britain, Denmark and Sweden." In *Refugees and the Violence of Welfare Bureaucracies in Northern Europe*, edited by Dalia Abdelhady et al., 210–26. Manchester: Manchester University Press, 2020.

Council of the European Union (CEU). "Directive 2002/90/EC." *Official Journal of the European Union* 328 (2002) 17–18. http://data.europa.eu/eli/dir/2002/90/oj.

———. "Directive 2008/115/EC." *Official Journal of the European Union* 348 (2008) 98–107. http://data.europa.eu/eli/dir/2008/115/oj.

Dauvergne, Catherine. *Making People Illegal: What Globalization Means for Migration and Law*. Cambridge: Cambridge University Press, 2008.

Durkheim, Émile. *The Division of Labor in Society*. Translated by George Simpson. New York: Macmillan, 1960.

FitzGerald, David. *Refuge Beyond Reach: How Rich Democracies Repel Asylum Seekers.* New York: Oxford University Press, 2019.

Franko, Katja. *The Crimmigrant Other: Migration and Penal Power.* London: Routledge, 2020.

Fraser, Nancy. *Scales of Justice: Reimagining Political Space in a Globalizing World.* Cambridge: Polity, 2008.

Haney, Lynne. "Prisons of the Past: Penal Nationalism and the Politics of Punishment in Central Europe." *Punishment & Society* 18.3 (2016) 346–68.

Hellqvist, Kristina, and Andreas Sandberg. *En tid av möten: Arbetet med asylsökande och nyanlända i Svenska kyrkans församlingar 2015–2016.* Uppsala: Svenska kyrkan, 2017.

———. *A Time of Encounters: The Work with Asylum Seekers and New Arrivals in the Parishes of the Church of Sweden 2015–2016.* Uppsala: Svenska Kyrkan, 2017.

Honneth, Axel. *Struggle for Recognition: The Moral Grammar of Social Conflicts.* Cambridge: Polity, 1995.

Hörnqvist, Magnus. *The Pleasure of Punishment.* London: Routledge, 2021.

Human Rights Watch (HRW). *"Die Here or Go to Poland": Belarus' and Poland's Shared Responsibility for Border Abuses.* New York: HRW, 2021. https://www.hrw.org/sites/default/files/media_2021/11/eca_migrant1121_web_0.pdf.

Jaeggi, Rahel. "Crisis, Contradiction, and the Task of a Critical Theory." In *Feminism, Capitalism, and Critique: Essays in Honor of Nancy Fraser*, edited by Banu Bargu and Chiara Bottici, 209–24. Cham: Springer International, 2017.

Jones, Reece. *Violent Borders: Refugees and the Right to Move.* London: Verso, 2017.

Kaufman, Emma. *Punish and Expel: Border Control, Nationalism, and the New Purpose of the Prison.* Oxford: Oxford University Press, 2015.

Lamont, Michèle. "Addressing Recognition Gaps: Destigmatization and the Reduction of Inequality." *American Sociology Review* 83.3 (2018) 419–44.

Mitchell, Michael. "Building Resilient Organizations: Toward Joy and Durable Power in a Time of Crisis." *Convergence*, November 29, 2022. https://convergencemag.com/articles/building-resilient-organizations-toward-joy-and-durable-power-in-a-time-of-crisis.

Mitsilegas, Valsamis. *The Criminalisation of Migration in Europe: Challenges for Human Rights and the Rule of Law.* London: Springer, 2015.

Mulinari, Diane. "Postcolonial/Decolonial Traditions: Intellectual Challenges to Sociologies of Absences." Seminar given January 25, 2023, Antiracism Seminar Series, Department of Sociology, Stockholm University.

Simon, Jonathan. *Governing Through Crime: How the War on Crime Transformed American Democracy and Created a Culture of Fear.* Oxford: Oxford University Press, 2007.

Stumpf, Juliet. "The Crimmigration Crisis: Immigration, Crime and Sovereign Power." *American University Law Review* 52.2 (2006) 367–419.

Tazreiter, Claudia, et al. "Spectres of Subjugation/Inter-Subjugation/Resubjugation of People Seeking Asylum: The Kyriarchal System in Australia's Necropoleis." In *Regulating Refugee Protection Through Social Welfare: Law, Policy and Praxis*, edited by Peter Billings, 68–90. New York: Routledge, 2023.

Tazzioli, Martina. "Crimes of Solidarity: Migration and Containment Through Rescue." *Radical Philosophy* 2.1 (2018) 4–10. https://www.radicalphilosophy.com/commentary/crimes-of-solidarity.

Walia, Harsha. *Border & Rule: Global Migration, Capitalism, and the Rise of Racist Nationalism.* Chicago: Haymarket, 2021.

Weber, Leanne. "The Welfare Policing of Asylum Seekers as Necropolitics." In *Regulating Refugee Protection through Social Welfare: Law, Policy and Praxis*, edited by Peter Billings, 47–67. Routledge, 2022.

Woude, Maartje van der, et al. "Crimmigration in the Netherlands." *Law and Social Inquiry* 39 (2014) 560–79.

3

All You P*k*s F**k Off Home

Amjid Khazir

The first time I heard the vile chant "All you P*k*s f**k off home," I was just too young to comprehend what it meant and why it was offensive. To understand why such words were abusive and racist, or where such language, hateful attitudes, and behaviours came from, would genuinely take me many more years. Of course, I was ignorant by age, and those who expressed the words were ignorant by choice, but the sense of unease, dread, and tension is something I will never forget, and to this day I worry for those experiencing the same if not far, far worse abuse and hate.

From that first, or at least by memory one of the early experiences of racism, to the work that I do now, the sense of disappointment and deflation I feel from the human capacity to hate and abuse will never leave me. However, as the saying goes, "Whatever does not break you, makes you stronger," such instances, trials and tests, in a typical resilient Northeast England fashion, and true to a "hard-working" Pakistani nature, make me even more committed to fight for equity, social cohesion, and for the dignity of all people in the face of ignorance and hate. I will aim to do everything I can for hate not to succeed, and furthermore, this ambition feels like a calling to me, in that my life's experiences and ambitions seem to have guided me towards finding ways to tackle hate and encourage humanity towards a path of peace, unity, and thriving co-existence.

This chapter will explore my experience of racism and my endeavours to tackle it by promoting social cohesion through education, film, sport, and wider activism. Intrinsic to my motivation is my faith, as a Muslim, whereby it is demanded of me to respect all people and beyond respect, to never speak ill or abuse other people, because of the religion or nation they belong to. At Prophet Muhammad's (peace be upon him) final sermon to the people of Makkah, he said: "There is no superiority of an Arab over a non-Arab, or of a non-Arab over an Arab, and no superiority of a white person over a black person or of a black person over a white person, except on the basis of personal piety and righteousness." In the Qur'an, we are told by Allah: "O mankind! We created you from a single (pair) of a male and a female, and made you into nations and tribes, that ye may know each other (not that ye may despise each other). Verily the most honoured of you in the sight of Allah is (he who is) the most righteous of you. And Allah has full knowledge and is well acquainted (with all things)" (Q 49:13).[1]

With these inculcated drivers and ambitions, grounded in faith, social experience, and hope, I will aim to provide context to my own upbringing as a "child of immigrants" and through my present and future ambitions I will speak about my work at Media Cultured, my membership of A World of Neighbours (AWoN), and our collective objectives to tackle hate, racism, and violence.

FROZEN IN TIME

Growing up in Middlesbrough, an industrial heartland town in the northeast of England, we played football every day, like seriously—every single day! One day, as we once more filled the school playing fields directly opposite my home, with cries of "pass, shoot, and get in," we were doing what boys of any colour, race, religion, or age across the town were doing, passing time playing football. All together with my older brothers, extended cousins, and friends, we had no substitute care, opinion, or cause in the world, aside from scoring more goals, staying outside as long as we could, and ultimately going home, to suffer from leg cramps at night, and being marked out by bruised shins the next day.

---

1. I am using the translation by Yusuf Ali, available at https://quranyusufali.com.

Amongst this mix of boys, we ranged from five-year-olds all the way to fifteen years of age. We were mainly brown boys of Pakistani heritage, and our friends from Beckon Hill School who were mostly white (themselves likely of Irish descent and something I only realized many years later) made up the teams and required numbers for a game. At times, we would even play Pakistanis v. Whites, which looking back now was both a peculiar and quite interesting dynamic.

So, to the day in question, some of the older boys amongst the group, upon first eyeing in the distance two older white males entering through the gates from the furthest entrance to us, staggering across the field, trudging in, in a drunken state, instantly stood and watched with keen interest. The older boys seemed to be promptly aware, it was as if they were on the lookout to see what—if something or anything—might occur next. They obviously, looking back, were experienced with such events. I noticed their change in mood and the overall atmosphere, I obviously also knew something was now wrong, but what?

Instinctively, I grabbed the ball, fearing that these "strangers" may try to steal our football, a new Mitre Delta which our father had recently bought for us. This was me at six or seven, only football mattered.

The ball was not of any interest to the two strangers, who from a distance seemed like they were in their late teens or early twenties. Their concentration and attention were on all of us, a group of young mostly brown boys, dressed in tracksuits and shorts, using, as standard, our jumpers as goalposts, and the only thing that differentiated us from any other similar group of boys, across the town or country doing the same thing, was the colour of our skin.

As the two diminutively provocative strangers got closer and closer, we saw their gaze was undeniably fixed upon us, but the path they were on was not; they seemed to be taking a route parallel to us, in a direction that was used to shortcut across the field rather than directly towards our location on the pitch. This veering off was somewhat of a relief but the trepidation and anxiety didn't seem to take the same turn. Call it a primal instinct or defence mechanism, but we all knew something was wrong and, true to those feelings, our fears and senses were soon proven right.

As the distance between the two parties gently grew, with the only real sound being the blustery wind, suddenly the air and tension were cut and interrupted by a distorted version of an old nursery rhyme called "Knick Knack Paddy Whack, give a dog a bone." The strangers vocalized the final phrases being all you "P*k*s F**k Off Home." They continued singing this awful, racist song until they eventually completed their short detour.

Gratefully on this occasion, this was as bad as it got, the reprobates slowly left the field and we went back to playing football after defensively smiling it off whilst the older lads said a few choice words back. The next vocal address to disturb us was the equally terrifying sound of the mother of one of our friends walking over to the large metal fence that surrounds the field, to tell us all that it was time to come home for dinner.

Home of course being across the street, not a country many thousands of miles away.

In the years ahead, there were many more occasions where I would hear such racist language and songs, and suffer racist abuse, not only from strangers but also from so-called friends (schoolmates) and even at certain points teachers. I wasn't alone in this, it was the norm, but none of this was more than a moment of differential interruption to my day—I would quite literally ignore it, respond in kind, or just take it and move on. Having been told by my parents to effectively turn the other cheek, that's what I would do.

Things changed for me personally as I got to being a teenager myself and I was no longer attending the school opposite my home but a senior school a couple of miles away. At Hall Garth Comprehensive it wasn't just the local lads that I knew growing up, but a far broader range of kids from across a wider part of the town; many of these kids came from what were either predominantly Asian or predominantly White areas of the town.

Using racist language as "banter" was part of the norm for some but ultimately, regardless of territorial or demographic differences, we all got on and I began to now play football for my school team too. Again, hearing racist language from opposition players wasn't a surprise, but the acknowledgment of what it meant to be racially abused came to mean more to me. I had begun to understand my identity, and whether it was just part of growing up, listening to certain types of music (hip-hop), or becoming self-aware more generally, suddenly the words began to enrage me, and not only me, but there was also now a certain resolution to not let being racially insulted or otherwise insulted to pass, neither from me nor my friends.

The sheer fact that nature itself led me to be of a tall and athletic build was a factor too, but most of my Asian friends were of the same mindset and physical build also. We no longer feared the consequences of being approached by white lads, we certainly weren't going to turn the other cheek, but rather than let any insulter casually walk away, we would chase them down to resolve our grievances and stand our ground.

This dynamic stayed with me through my time at school, college, and Teesside University. I was Muslim, Pakistani, British, Asian, and Proud. I loved my country, my hometown, and my "back-home" town too. The relevance of my identity, belonging, political and social discourse to my wider worldview had developed to a point where I could now take down and dismantle a racist diatribe verbally and could more than often avoid physical confrontation, if the situation allowed.

THE WORLD CHANGES

Moving forward, we are in the late nineties and I am settled at my local university, not only self-aware but surrounded by consciously aware people of all backgrounds from across the country who rejected racism, would call it out, and treat, overall, one another with love, respect, and curiosity. During my time at university, I also worked in a local restaurant and later as a taxi driver. This meant that racist abuse and experiences of such were never far away. The "uni life" and the "street life" were two very, very different worlds; the dissimilarity was literally night and day, or more aptly rich and poor.

And then, on one September afternoon, in 2001, not just mine but everyone's world changed forever. As Al-Qaeda attacked America, we all watched as two planes were flown into the twin towers in New York, and another into the Pentagon. Mass murder was broadcast live on our TV screens. Suddenly, it wasn't only the colour of your skin that was the problem, it was your religion too. I and a group of about a billion and a half other Muslims were firmly put—and to this day remain—under the threat of notice, menace, abuse, intrusion, and attack.

A few days after 9/11, I recall that I'd gone for a haircut and my barber, someone I consider a friend, while the haircut took place and our "barber shop" conversations developed, blurted out, "They should bomb the f**king Palestinians, they were behind the attacks"—to which I retorted, both swiftly and vehemently, "What the f**k are you on about." A very loud and public disagreement ensued, but ultimately, we "agreed to disagree" when the owner and manager of the shop asked us to stop, in fear that other customers may join in and we could have a real problem in the shop. Once again, the tension was palpable and it almost felt like being on the school field, only this time there was no football, but a barber with very sharp scissors in his hands.

Up to this point in my life, such conversations and discourses that stirred up feelings and caused uncomfortable situations had separated "uni life" from "street life." But now from the halls of academic discussions to barber shops, taxis, grocery stores, and restaurants, the mood and interpersonal talks became morose, temperaments and attitudes changed, and the student bodies' curiosity became more intrusive and at times highhanded rather than intrigued.

"What do you believe, do you condemn terrorism, do you support the invasion of Afghanistan, what about the war on terror, do you know any terrorists," and these were just questions from my so-called friends. The hardened looks on the streets weren't just from drunken strangers anymore, they seemed to be everywhere. It wasn't the odd random "you don't belong here," or "why don't you f**k off back home," it was now becoming a more regular and normal occurrence, not just for me, or Muslims, but for Sikhs or anyone who looked remotely Muslim, Pakistani, or Arab.

It had to be back to turning the other cheek because you simply can't fight everyone, and you can't debate everyone either. So, what does one do, how do I take account of co-religionists hijacking not only planes but my religion, how do I make sense of the world and find a way that tackles both extremism and Islamophobia? A way that avoids violence for all and encourages education and harmony. How do I get back to that place where losing a football was the biggest concern, not watching the world and the people in it become ever more mired in hate, abuse, and violence?

CHANGE THE WORLD

My response was to look for a pre-emptive way that helped prevent young people from racism and radicalization. As the UK government and social media companies introduced a panic button to safeguard young people from paedophiles online, I wondered why such measures were not being put in place to protect communities from far-right content, or why videos of beheadings that were being published online out of Iraq during the war were not being given the same attention. This content was and still is readily accessible, but to me seemed like obvious recruitment and grooming propaganda.

In my mind, this "extremist" content was equally capable of being used to prime young, vulnerable, and potentially isolated people into violence and into places where they would be exploited. So, I took my concerns to my local council, then the police, and was eventually after many months and many meetings invited to meet with the government at the UK Home Office in London in 2009. I took this opportunity once again to relay my concerns about social media, the impact of the war on terror on social cohesion, and why I felt government policy was making matters worse not better.

However, I wasn't there to just criticize. I wanted to suggest solutions, and I did. I felt we could counter rising hate, racism, and extremism through alternative content and films and by delivering them in workshops at schools, colleges, universities, and mosques, or what the government themselves had listed as "at risk" institutions. These workshops and accompanying provisions could be used to train teachers about the pathways to extremism and encourage young people in safe spaces to recognize, reject and report content or views that were encouraging violence, looking to abuse, and pitting one group against another.

Ultimately, I had said what I came to say, and without any government funding or backing; it was just words, utterances that those who had listened to me responded nicely to but ultimately ignored. Maybe I was too critical, maybe I seemed too eager, or maybe I was just a bit unprepared, whatever the reason, the proposal, and concerns I had raised were noted but I was told thank you for coming and effectively "We'll be in touch." I have never since had any contact or dealings with the UK government on these issues, or specifically with the people from that meeting, and firmly believe that successively elected figures have meant well but caused more harm than good with much of UK policy towards these issues and even worse through implementation.

At that time, I felt I had done my part, and still maintained that improved future policies and programmes can prevent further issues and promote social cohesion. So, I felt my positive but limited contribution was enough. I couldn't have been more wrong. Just two years after meeting the UK government, the impact of extremism, racism, and hate once again became far more personal to my family, and this time, with tragic, heart-breaking consequences.

SALT OF THE EARTH

In June 2011, the night preceding a march by the far-right English Defence League group in our hometown, my uncle Mohammed Zabir, a father of seven, a devoted husband, one of my father's three younger brothers and all-round wonderful man, was assaulted by a passenger who had climbed into his taxi. Just after midnight, at the end of this taxi journey, the assailant, whilst sitting directly behind the driver's seat, struck my uncle with a beer bottle over the back of his head. The assailant then jumped out of the vehicle, and ran away, but was then reported to have returned, by sprinting towards my uncle, who had by this time moved out of the cab, bloodied, and dazed, and met him with a fierce "drop kick," straight on my uncle's chest, leaving him with even more severe injuries. Six weeks after this horrifying incident my uncle Zabir died. He had suffered a massive heart attack and was unable to recover. At only 56 years of age, we lost a true pillar of our family.

My uncle's death left the entire family heartbroken, but to then realize the attacker himself was of mixed heritage, a son of a black man and a white woman, was even more distressing and perplexing. It was alleged that on the evening of the attack, with community tensions, heightened by the upcoming march, this seventeen-year-old assailant had been convinced, radicalized, and ultimately driven towards this act of violence by his peers, who had convinced him that the march was "about Muslims, not blacks or racism." Ahead of the taxi journey, this young man had spent an evening in the pub celebrating his upcoming 18th birthday and would then eventually be found guilty of the charge of "section 18, wounding with intent," and would serve a short sentence in a young-offenders institute as he was not able to be tried as an adult.

From that moment and to this day, and with the work we in Media Cultured do every day, we look to honour the memory of my uncle, and all those who have suffered at the hand of racism, fascism, extremism, Islamophobia, antisemitism, and anti-immigrant bigotry by tackling it head-on. From the impact of intolerance and abuse I witnessed 30+ years ago, to every new report, we see on our screens today the rise of hate and increased polarization is all around us, and just as we stood proud in the face of it previously, we do so now.

My work takes me to schools, colleges, sports clubs, and a range of public spaces where we can use our films, educational workshops, and stakeholder networks to bring people together to counter all forms of racial and religious prejudice. We support, empower, and educate young people so that they can understand exactly what hate is, where, how, and why it is spread, and what they can do to recognize, reject, and report it. We work with the likes of the Premier League, police forces, and international partners, including the United Nations to deliver powerful alternative narratives that build resilience to the growing polarising "us versus them" ideologies.

In doing this work we have seen incredible, inspirational, and committed young people, and organizations begin to not only understand the impact of racist notions but demonstrate through their own activities amazing ways to support emerging communities and social cohesion. By developing critical thinking and actions, we impart a social and cultural understanding, and importantly show that we may have diverse colours, creeds, and beliefs, but "diversity" makes us all stronger. If we can learn to accept our differences and embrace the core values, our common human traits will cause the extremist messaging to fail.

Our films, education programmes, and events have won numerous awards, and our BRACE (Building Resilience and Championing Equality) workshops are internationally accredited, allowing us to work in corporate training spaces and with academia. Here we can strip back what are often tick-box diversity targets and tokenistic platitudes, to impart to the attendees the reality of the challenges around social cohesion, and the systemic and structural challenges that migrants, asylum seekers, and people of colour face.

These safe spaces allow for conversations to take place that are often held in silos and where the group dynamic is often one that fails to challenge ignorant, ill-informed, and prejudiced takes on a range of subjects. Whether it is conspiracy theories regarding COVID, age-old tropes about how "the Jews run the world," or the more recent ones such as "Muslims are taking over," or how "immigrants and asylum seekers get a free house and a new car," to the completely ridiculous positions that "refugees are a clandestine army being brought in to reinforce the great replacement"—or are a "weapon of mass migration."

I am grateful that our work is received as well as it is, and I genuinely pray that there will no longer be a requirement for this work to take place at all, anywhere in the world. That no matter your colour, creed, race, religion, or status, no individual would be the victim of hate, abuse, and violence. I pray that we can create a world in which peace is finally built and that all conflicts are resolved, once and for all.

This idealism may be a hope too far, for some, but I firmly believe that all we lack is the people to deliver the same message of social unity, again and again, and where time constraints within a workshop setting are challenging, the amplification of the core message can be delivered consistently within our social circles, through our sports, film, art, gaming, and social media outlets.

Without being overbearing or exasperating, we can communicate key messages that dismantle the tropes, collapse the conspiracies, and provide real fact-based information that clearly, measurably, and demonstrably defeats hate. To achieve this, it is important that we all sincerely appreciate that true pluralism means this information will always be grounded on differences of opinion, markedly dissimilar moral and ethical baselines, and sometimes passionate points of disagreement.

With all that said, no theological, historical, political, social, or cultural difference will ever vindicate abuse, and violence towards any other human being. If, as Nelson Mandela said, "education is the most powerful weapon in the world" and as Ibn Rushd states, "ignorance leads to fear, fear to hate, and hate to violence and suffering" then we must find means and models that steadfastly and effectively educate, remove ignorance, and ultimately stop hate, racism, and abuse. From that young boy who was confused by random strangers shouting abuse, from the shifts in my understanding of my own social and political identities, to losing my beloved uncle to racism, to engaging politically, working voluntarily at grassroots levels, making films, delivering workshops, consistently and gratefully being in a space where I can make a difference, I am truly grateful and sincerely hopeful that we can change the world and defeat racism.

Seeing inspirational stories from around the world of young people rising to unify against abuse, watching in awe as my friends and colleagues deliver incredible academic insights, community programmes, and educational solutions to hate and division, and being part of AWoN through which, as a global network of practitioners, academics, people of faith and good conscious, we come together to support the most vulnerable and promote social cohesion, is truly empowering and humbling for me at the same time.

I/we won't be leaving our homes any time soon to relocate at the behest of any racist individual or policy, and furthermore, we will make sure that those who are displaced, on the move, or are a minority in their community are never defeated, removed, or abused. We will stand up for those too young and helpless to help themselves and we will always stand up to those who do the abusing.

There are more of us (uniters) than them (dividers), and goodwill, will always win, in the end.

4

Race, Religion, and Refugees in Europe

Past and Present

Anya Topolski

THE SOCIETAL CHALLENGE, as stated by the European Union Commission President, Ursula von der Leyen, in her June 17, 2020, speech to the European Parliament, is clear. "I am glad to live in a society that condemns racism," she said "but we should not stop there. The motto of our European Union is: 'United in diversity.' Our task is to live up to these words, and to fulfil their meaning."[1] The political challenges, as laid out in the EU's recent "Anti-Racism Action Plan," are also clear.[2] But is it possible to prevent racism if we do not fully understand it? To do so in Europe, means we must investigate racism's entanglement with religion.[3] This chapter aims to present such an investigation.

In what follows, I provide a working-definition of racism in terms of dehumanization which challenges the often-held view of racism which arose in Europe in, and in response to, Nazi racism against Jews. To undergird this working definition, I offer two historical vignettes that show

---

1. Leyen, "We Need to Talk About Racism."
2. See European Commission, "EU Anti-Racism Action Plan 2020–2025."
3. Goldberg, "Racial Europeanization"; Meer, "Racialization and Religion"; Klug, "Limits of Analogy"; Romeyn, "Anti-Semitism and Islamophobia"; Lentin, *Why Race Still Matters*; Baar and Kocze, "The Roma and Their Struggle"

how race and religion are entangled. This brings us to the writings of philosopher Hannah Arendt, a Jewish refugee. Arendt, who experienced the violent exclusion of state racism, maintains, as do many academics and activists today, a false binary between race and religion. This false binary is facilitated by the concept of secularism which enables, and often implicitly serves to legitimize, the structural exclusion of states against refugees. It is this binary, I suggest, that has to be countered both in the academy and activism.

RACISM IN EUROPE—IS EUROPE POST-RACIAL?

The approach which I take here is to try to define the logic of racism. Inspired by decolonial scholarship, I focus on what "racism" does, which is to dehumanize "others," and thus define its logic as one of dehumanization. As such, when I use the term "racism," I am referring to one of the ways we describe the effects of this dehumanizing logic. Dehumanization, as those who work with refugees know better than most academics, does not always explicitly refer to the question of the humanity of others, but comes in different forms and formats. Moreover, as the category of "the human" has changed throughout history, so has the practice of dehumanization. This is the core of a racial logic which, when combined with institutionalized power, has the potential to exclude and eliminate difference. To identify the effects of the exclusion and elimination of difference, we look to history for an observable pattern, without forgetting that this racial logic operates both explicitly and implicitly.

One of the explicit reasons for using the term dehumanization is to challenge the assumption that racism is a secular phenomenon based on "scientific" criteria. This misconception has led to a solely biological conception of racism in which race is conceived of as immutable. Not only is this based on a simplification of Nazi racism, which was both cultural and natural, it also serves to create a false binary between "race" and "religion."[4] This false binary is very present in contemporary discourse about racism. It is said that Islamophobia is not a form of racism because it is based on religion, which is a choice, where racism is based on races, which do not exist in post-racial Europe. As such Islamophobia is reduced to a form of religious discrimination. Being Muslim, regardless of one's practice, is taken to be a matter of personal belief based

---

4. Topolski, "Good Jew, Bad Jew"; "Race-Religion Constellation"; "Rejecting the Rhetoric of Uniqueness."

on individual choice. However, the term "religion," like that of race, is a highly contested and constructed concept with a complex genealogy.[5] The way I use it here, religion refers primarily to the dynamic and often contradictory theological logic of the Roman-Catholic Church which had the power to name and demarcate what was, and was not, included as a "religion." In this vein, it also entangled with the modern discourse of secularism which serves to name what is, and is not, to be included in today's secular public sphere.[6]

In using the term dehumanization, then, I reject the opposition between nature/fixed and culture/flexible, which grounds the binary between race and religion. By focusing on its logic, the masking effects of this binary are unveiled. A dehumanizing logic, even prior to the term race or racism, operates when one group denies the full inclusion of another group into a political community, based on a particular assemblage of markers of difference. Since the long nineteenth century, these markers of difference have been based on biology or phenotype (antisemitism and anti-Black racism) and sought "scientific" legitimacy. But the race-religion constellation establishes that these markers of difference vary across time and space.[7] They cannot be limited to phenotype.

Prior to the sixteenth century, these markers of difference were based on a Christian theology that viewed non-Christians as lacking a soul, reason or rationality, and civilisation, among other things. While many of these markers of difference were invisible, theological laws made them visible by, for example, requiring Jews and Muslims to wear prescribed items of clothing as in Canon 68 of the Fourth Lateran Council from 1215. The race-religion constellation makes visible a continuity between the past and present: the exclusion and dehumanization of Jews, Muslims and other non-Christians from the political community. The pattern of exclusion revealed by the race-religion constellation is not accidental. It is part of a hidden pattern or logic that scholars must continue to uncover in order to understand contemporary forms of dehumanization.

---

5. Asad, *Genealogies of Religion*; Taylor, *Secular Age*; Anidjar, *Semites*.
6. Butler et al., *Power of Religion in the Public Sphere*.
7. Topolski, "Race-Religion Constellation."

RACE, RELIGION, AND REFUGEES IN EUROPE'S PAST—A SIXTEENTH-CENTURY VIGNETTE

In the sixteenth century, the Latin Church faced at least two challenges, which it perceived as threats to its power: an internal schism from Protestants and an external enemy with the colonization of the Americas that challenged the notion that Europe was the centre of the globe. During this period, the term "race" first became used in relation to the idea that true Christians had pure blood (*limpieze de sangre*), free of either Jewish or Muslim impurity.[8] This is a clear example of the entanglement of religion and phenotype which served to legitimate the dehumanization of non-Christians, both in Europe (Jews and Muslims) and in the colonies (non-white non-Christian peoples). During the time of the Inquisition, the state expulsed Jews and Muslims from the Iberian Peninsula—including those that had previously converted to Christianity.

If we look beyond Europe, we see yet another entanglement of race and religion in the colonization of the Americas, an entanglement documented in the 1552 Valladolid debates. The central concern of this theological debate between Bartolomé de las Casas (1474–1566) and Juan Ginés de Sepúlveda (1494–1573), organized by the Church, was about the nature of the beings living beyond the border of the Christian world—are they animal, human or something else?[9] This question was in fact a theological one—do these beings have souls and can they be "saved," or not and thus can be enslaved or exterminated. For de las Casas, "Indians" do have a soul whereas for Sepúlveda they don't. For both theologians, Africans, unlike the "Indians" had seen the light of Christ but had rejected it (like Jews and Muslims) and chosen rather to continue their courtship with the devil.

The conclusion of the Valladolid debates regarding Africans also affected those perceived as Arab or Semitic Muslims in the Iberian Peninsula. While the Jews had been forced to flee Spain in the fifteenth century, leaving behind all their property, it was only in the sixteenth century that converted Muslims were likewise forced to do so. In this period, the anti-Saracen rhetoric of the Crusades was reframed in terms of the same soul/non-soul binary present in the Valladolid debates.[10] According to

---

8. Hannaford, *Race*; Eliav-Feldon et al., *Origins of Racism in the West*.

9. Shohat and Stam, *Race in Translation*; Maldonado-Torres, "Race, Religion, and Ethics."

10. Wynter, "Unsettling the Coloniality."

the logic of the times, Muslims in Europe, like enslaved black Africans in the colonies, had rejected Christianity, the true religion, serving to justify expulsion, colonization, and possibly extermination.

At this same time, much is happening in Europe which points towards the state formation around the race-religion constellation. In addition to the production of "pure blooded" states in the Iberian Peninsula, northern Europe—by means of the religious wars—also formed religiously homogenous states. These religious wars were likewise legitimized in terms of dehumanization based on salvation and thus operated according to a racial logic, albeit prior to the modern period when the term "race" is coined. These theological and political conflicts constructed an exclusionary binary between who is saved and who is damned which intersects with the binary between white and black bodies thereby defining who was fully human. These conflicts led to the expulsion and murder of hundreds of thousands of those identified as non-Christians.

A solution to the political and physical violence in Europe, which led to the death of over ten million people between the sixteenth and early eighteenth century, was first conceived of in Augsburg in 1555. The Peace of Augsburg established the paradigm of *cuius regio, eius religio*, which means "whose realm, his religion." This new paradigm of political communities was formally institutionalized at the Peace of Westphalia in 1648, which led to the structuring of new states in the form of nation-states. Nation was thus first defined by one's religion which was fundamentally linked to one's soul and therefore humanity. This political peace, which created sovereign states with distinct theological-political constellations, enabled many of the non-Catholic denominations of Christianity to be accepted, at least in theory, as forms of Christianity which was judged the only true religion. There was, however, no "peace" for those groups in Europe that were not in possession of any acceptable form of "true" religion, in other words for non-Christian "peoples." These peoples were most often viewed as barbarians, uncivilized and lesser beings—all forms of dehumanization.

Another part of the above story that is often masked, is its entanglement with the production of the first group of people to be called refugees. (One could argue that 1492, with the expulsion of Jews and Muslims from the Iberian Peninsula was a previous wave—although the term was not coined then.) The term "refugees" comes from the French term "refuge," to seek refuge, referring to those non-Catholics expelled from France, a Catholic state, because they were Huguenots—most of whom were forced to seek refuge abroad. Refugees are thus, at least etymologically, persons excluded from a particular nation-state because of their religious denomination. Nonetheless the Huguenots eventually found a place to welcome them. It is worth noting that this connection between refugees and religion, which I claim is co-constitutive of racial exclusion, is by no means limited to the past. According to Gatrell, a refugee scholar:

> Long before 1900, political disorder and war compelled vanquished or politically obdurate groups and religious minorities to seek refuge elsewhere. In 1492, Spain brought centuries of Moorish rule to an end and enforced Catholic conformity, causing 200,000 Muslims and Jews to flee. German Protestants who were expelled from the Palatinate in the seventeenth century made their way to Kent where they languished in vast tented settlements before proceeding to Pennsylvania. One million Huguenots left France rather than convert to Catholicism following the Revocation of the Edict of Nantes in 1685. Revolution in Haiti in 1791 caused white plantation owners to flee; some of them ended up in an isolated part of Cuba called Guantánamo Bay.[11]

If it is the case, as Gatrell implies, that the production of refugees is entangled with that of religious exclusion, then making visible the race-religion constellation is also important for scholarship on refugees today.

RACE, RELIGION, AND REFUGEES IN EUROPE TODAY— A TWENTIETH-CENTURY VIGNETTE

In *The Origins of Totalitarianism* Arendt demonstrates how nineteenth-century states required homogeneity to establish and maintain "the nation."[12] The tragedy Arendt identifies at the heart of the nation-state is that it cannot sustain itself without excluding others. She describes in excruciating detail how this process occurs, a process which sadly today is increasing in frequency.

At present, there are over one hundred million forcibly displaced people (thirty-five million official refugees, five million applying for asylum, sixty million internally displaced).[13] Most of their names, stories, and identities are erased. They are tragically defined as a problem,

---

11. Gatrell, *Making of the Modern Refugee*.
12. Arendt, *Origins of Totalitarianism*.
13. UNHCR, "Figures at a Glance."

reduced to numbers, dehumanized. It is with regret that I argue that many so-called liberal secular democratic states are also race-states, and that the law enables this structural exclusion. While I appreciate this is less explicit than in race-states, such as the Nazi state, it nonetheless is a reality that must be made visible in order to be challenged.

Racism, a form of dehumanization, based on the socially constructed hierarchical category of "race," denies the basic fact of human plurality, that is, that all human beings belong to humanity and that this earth must be shared, a position Arendt upholds in *Eichmann in Jerusalem*.[14] A racial hierarchy is constructed by way of a mapping of the human, lesser human, sub-human and often non-human that is materialized through institutions with political power. How this hierarchy operates is clear from Arendt's analysis of the reality of dehumanization. Arendt herself finds the roots of race thinking in Thomas Hobbes, a seventeenth-century thinker:

> Hobbes at least provided political thought with the prerequisites for all race doctrine, that is, the exclusion in principle of the idea of humanity. . . . If the idea of humanity of which the most conclusive symbol is the common origin of the human species, is no longer valid, then nothing is more plausible than a theory according to which brown, yellow, or black races are descended from some other species of ape than the white race, and that all together are predestined by nature to war against each other until they have disappeared from the face of the earth. . . . [As such] Race, is politically speaking, not the beginning of humanity but its end.[15]

Arendt thus recognizes that racism is fundamentally related to the question of humanity, and more specifically to the process of dehumanization which denies some "people" inclusion in the idea of the human.

What she does not seem to recognize is that this category is not limited to a biological or secular one. Race, as a social construct, is made material when transformed into an organization principle for a state—but, and here I disagree with Arendt, it is by no means one limited to the nineteenth century. What Arendt fails to recognize is that racism has its roots in Europe, and not as she claims in "the Dark continent," unless of course Europe is the "Dark continent."[16] The vignette above made

14. Arendt, *Eichmann in Jerusalem*, 279.
15. Arendt, *Origins of Totalitarianism*, 157.
16. Arendt, *Origins of Totalitarianism*, 186.

this point. Furthermore, the Shoah, despite its appalling horrors, is not exceptional—it is part of a much longer pattern of racially justified exclusions and genocides. As such the problem is not only the coupling of nation and state but also the particular way in which the state has been conceived of in the West as co-constituted by race and religion. The latter cannot embrace plurality and thus requires some form of "racial" exclusion to maintain itself.

In her analysis of the paradox of human rights, Arendt was one of the first to conceptualize the constitutive relationship between the nation-state and the production of refugees.[17] Citizens, often unaware of their privileges, take the particular post-Westphalian connection between state and nation to be natural. Most refugees, often out of desperation, also tend to accept this as it is only via the nation-state that it is possible to appeal for protection, for recognition of their human rights. While there are exceptions, neither group engages with the paradox of human rights Arendt identified in her analysis of totalitarianism. Citizens, at least those who feel they fully belong, have no real motive to question the state. The stateless most often do not have the luxury of this type of questioning—instead their time is spent trying to integrate or assimilate and justifying these actions by further affirming the exclusionary frame of the "nation" to which they desire to belong. Arendt empathized with the tragedy of the *parvenu* willing to do anything to assimilate. These *parvenus* were willing to become anybody, to do anything, to not be perceived as Jewish because, in a race-state, the latter meant that they were not human. This again makes clear the link between antisemitism, a form of racism, and dehumanization which is only possible when one categorically excludes some groups from the idea of humanity.

According to Arendt, it is the *pariahs* that recognize this paradox and have painfully realized that it is only if one accepts that to be Jewish is also to be human that one challenges the frame created by the state to justify their exclusion.[18] In "We Refugees," Arendt theorized that belonging and inclusion by means of assimilation, that is by denying *who* one is, was problematic.[19] It is precisely because Arendt so explicitly identified this structural injustice that it is unfortunate that she failed to see the constitutive relationship between the race-religion-state that not only

---

17. Arendt, *Origins of Totalitarianism*, 267–304.
18. Arendt, *Jew as Pariah*, 63.
19. Arendt, *Jewish Writings*, 270–71.

produces "the refugee" but also creates the category of excluded others, who are then dehumanized (or othered which means their humanity is not being put into question) by means of the race-religion constellation. As such, the race-religion constellation complicates our understanding of the refugee *per se*.

In the European context, then, the refugee is always racialized because the nation-state is constructed via religious exclusion that is linked to modern notions of race. This brings to light a form of racialization of refugees that Arendt did not acknowledge. It is also helpful for thinking about why the racialized other can become a stateless person within the borders of her own country. In other words, Arendt fails to appreciate that the Westphalian state required this constitutive other to be excluded to solidify its own unity and borders, and that racialized religious categories are the primary means of exclusion. I believe that her oversight is rooted in her failure to fully deconstruct the notion of secularism and her acceptance of a position known as Jewish exceptionalism, although clearly not in the same fashion as Zionism does. By way of conclusion, I want to explore this blind spot as I believe it remains hegemonic in contemporary scholarly and political discourse.[20]

THE SECULAR MASK—LIFTING THE VEIL

At times, Arendt seemingly accepts the rather naïve notion that religion is opposed to secularism, which masked the race-religion constellation. This is most evident in her definition of the term antisemitism. In the 1967 preface to *The Origins of Totalitarianism* she stated:

> Antisemitism, a secular, nineteenth-century ideology—which in name, though not in argument, was unknown before the 1870s—and religious Jew-hatred, inspired by the mutually hostile antagonism of two conflicting creeds, are obviously not the same thing; and even the extent to which the former derives its arguments and emotional appeal from the latter is open to question.[21]

While the "arguments" justifying antisemitism and religious Jew-hatred are different, the former political and the latter theological, Arendt fails to question their entanglement or the term secular itself. From the perspective of the state, there is no significant difference between antisemitism

---

20. Gaffney, "Memories of Exclusion."
21. Arendt, *Origins of Totalitarianism*, xi.

and religious Jew-hatred: both are means to maintain state homogeneity. Perhaps due to her often-uncritical Eurocentrism, Arendt accepts the idea that there is a significant difference between the secular modern (nineteenth century) and the religious pre-modern (eighteenth century) Europe. This view disconnects Europe's past from its present, as if there has been a paradigm shift rather than, as I suggest, a masked pattern of racial-religious exclusion that is constitutive of the state.

Antisemitism, while coined in 1870 to refer to Jews only, is by no means a secular concept. By accepting it as secular, even if only in name, it seemingly legitimates its disconnection from centuries of structural Christian power and privilege to exclude and exterminate non-Christians, institutionalized in the state that preceded it. This is an example of an opposition enabled by assuming that the secular is opposed to Christianity rather than its masked continuation. The secular, as both Christian and non-Christian scholars argue, is a continuation of a Christian project which often maintains Christian power structures and privileges in the guise of neutrality or the proclaimed (rather than realized) separation of state and church.[22] Gil Anidjar, who is perhaps the most far-reaching critic of the mirage of the secular, puts his finger on a blind spot shared by Arendt as well as many of us today.

> Christianity turned against itself . . . while slowly coming to name that to which it claimed to oppose itself: religion. . . . Christianity invented the distinction between religious and secular and thus made religion. It made religion the problem rather than itself. . . . Secularism is a name Christianity gave itself when it invented religion.[23]

Without denying the fact that for many Christianity has been a "force for good," and its inclusive discourse of universal salvation, the reality is that its power, while changed, has not ended with the rise of the secular but rather has been further hidden. This is what Sven Lindqvist, writing on the colonization of Africa and Australia, calls the ambiguity of Christianity: it played a role in both initiating and empowering genocide as well as trying to prevent it.[24]

---

22. Gauchet, *Disenchantment of the World*; Asad, *Formations of the Secular*; Wynter, "Unsettling the Coloniality"; Taylor, *Secular Age*; Anidjar, *Blood*.

23. Anidjar, "Secularism," 52–77.

24. Lindqvist, *Dead Do Not Die*.

Arendt, although a *Jewish* refugee and victim of state racism, affirms the secular myth which relies on a problematic binary between religion/secular, a binary that is used to justify assimilation, racism, and dehumanization—past and present. I contend that the discourse of secularism masks the race-religion constellation and thus state/structural Christian power and privilege. In other words, the discourse of secularism covers up the fact that the game rules that apply to Christians, whether practicing or secular, were established to institutionalize structural Christian power and privilege, as well as other related forms of supremacy, and as such they are rigged against all constructed others making it impossible to win—that is, impossible to fully belong. Real belonging, which requires appreciation of alterity (symbolic and material differences) as well as formal legal inclusion, is structurally impossible as the nation-state requires the othering, exclusion and potential expulsion of this difference to maintain its essential homogeneity; that is, the state requires some form of racism—whether religious, cultural, or biological. The other, as other, is marked by precarity, both in material and ideal terms, and is perpetually vulnerable to being dehumanized, "racialized," and eventually expelled.

We, today, continue to share Arendt's secular blind spot in that we fail to recognize that the rules for "Christians" (and post-Christians, secular or atheist), do not apply to non-Christians. Furthermore, we fail to see that these structural disadvantages and exclusions also apply to several other groups, past and present, such as Roma/Sinti, Muslims, and people of colour. This is equally true today if one is willing to ask painful questions. For example, why is there such a discrepancy between acceptance rates of Christian vs Muslim Syrian refugees?[25] The presumption is of course that shared religious backgrounds will make integration/assimilation easier—but why would that be so in a supposedly modern and secular society? While in theory Arendt recognized that genocide could affect other excluded groups, her ability to identify past examples, does force us to question how much she refused to think/see because of her blind spots—and more importantly, what are our own blind spots?

One of the consequences of Arendt's secularism blind spot relates to her account of how the nature of seeking refuge, and the definition of a refugee, has changed. She states that "a refugee used to be a person driven to seek refuge because of some act committed or some political

---

25. Hackett, "Favouring Christian Over Muslim Refugees."

opinion held. Well, it is true we have had to seek refuge; but we committed no acts and most of us never dreamt of having any radical political opinion. With us the meaning of the term 'refugee' has changed."[26] Arendt assumes a distinction between seeking refuge because of one's words and deeds versus having to seek refuge because of the facticity of one's being. This exclusionary binary is based on the binary between culture and nature challenged by the race-religion constellation. The problem has never been the "other," whether Jews, Muslims, etc., practicing or not, the problem was that the nation-state needed to exclude to sustain itself—which is why it dehumanizes a particular group of people making them seemingly superfluous.

While Arendt misjudged the situation of Jewish refugees as exceptional, the reality she describes is tragically not exceptional. The experiences she describes of having lost their homes, wanting a place in the world, wanting to belong and willing to become whatever they believed was needed to attain that goal, is painfully common. Arendt appeals for us not to judge Jews harshly—an appeal I would affirm in relation to all of Europe's unwanted others—because as she rightly says, "If we tell the truth and be just human beings, . . . [we are] nothing . . . since we live in a world in which human beings as such have ceased to exist for quite a while; since society has discovered discrimination as the great social weapon by which one may kill men without any bloodshed."[27] The weapon she describes is dehumanization—a status of humanity in which one is rootless, superfluous and disposable. Thus, while the Nazi state was violent, this same means of dehumanization—less visibly violent (to those who are not marked as different or those not willing to see it) is present in contemporary nation-states. While there are no doubt elements which are unique to each form of racism, and to each nation-state, the history of refugees—past and present—demonstrates the entanglement of race-religion and state.

So, what does this mean for refugees themselves, and for their allies, whether activists, academics, or policy makers? We must begin to unveil the hierarchical structures of secular liberal democracies, structures that prevent the real inclusion and flourishing of refugees. Structural change, which is what is needed, takes time, and requires change both in relation to ideas and politics. This means we need to work collectively on

---

26. Arendt, "We Refugees," 55.
27. Arendt, *Origins of Totalitarianism*, 65.

the ground and via governments. On the level of ideas, I would argue it is essential to understand that race and religion are entangled concepts, past and present. This reality needs to be acknowledged to appreciate that refugees are very often denied protection from racism, claiming that instead they suffer from religious discrimination, or vice versa—and that this denial happens on the level of discourse as well as via legal and social institutions. We must all work to make everyone more aware of the racialized reality of refugees in Europe. This also requires that we challenge, daily, the dehumanization of refugees. The entanglement of race and religion has real material effects on refugees in the rhetoric used to dehumanize them and in their reception in different nation states, and that this happens in what appears to be secularized liberal democratic nation-states. For too long we have allowed ourselves to live under the illusion that Europe has, after the Shoah, transcended its racist past—this illusion must be unmasked.

BIBLIOGRAPHY

Ahmed, Nazir. "Islamophobia and Antisemitism." *European Judaism* 37.1 (2004) 124–27.

Anderson, Benedict. *Imagined Communities: Reflections on the Origin and Spread of Nationalism*. New ed. London: Verso, 2006.

Anidjar, Gil. *Blood: A Critique of Christianity*. New York: Columbia University Press, 2014.

———. *The Jew, the Arab: A History of the Enemy*. Stanford: Stanford University Press, 2003.

———. "Secularism." *Critical Inquiry* 33.1 (2006) 52–77.

———. *Semites: Race, Religion, Literature*. Stanford: Stanford University Press, 2007.

Arendt, Hannah. *Eichmann in Jerusalem: A Report on the Banality of Evil*. London: Penguin, 2006.

———. *The Jew as Pariah: Jewish Identity and Politics in the Modern Age*. Edited by Ron H. Feldman. New York: Grove, 1978.

———. *The Origins of Totalitarianism*. New York: Harcourt Brace Jovanovich, 1973.

———. "We Refugees." In *The Jewish Writings*, edited by Jerome Kohn and Ron H. Feldmann, 264–74. New York: Schocken, 2007.

Asad, Talal. *Genealogies of Religion: Discipline and Reasons of Power in Christianity and Islam*. Baltimore: Johns Hopkins University Press, 1993.

Ashcroft, Bill. "Language and Race." *Social Identities* 7.3 (2001) 311–28. https://doi.org/10.1080/13504630120087190.

Baar, Huub van. *The European Roma: Minority Representation, Memory, and the Limits of Transnational Governmentality*. Amsterdam: F&N Eigen Beheer, 2011.

Baar, Huub van, and Angela Kocze. *The Roma and Their Struggle for Identity in Contemporary Europe*. New York: Berghahn, 2020.

Bethencourt, Francisco. *Racisms: From the Crusades to the Twentieth Century*. Princeton: Princeton University Press, 2014.

Bracke, Sarah. "Religion and Race: A Story of Conceptual Entanglement." Keynote Lecture presented at the *On the Edge? Centres and Margins in the Sociology of Religion*, British Sociological Association, Sociology of Religion Annual Conference, University of Leeds, July 12, 2017. https://www.uva.nl/profiel/b/r/s.a.e.bracke/s.a.e.bracke.html.
Bunzl, Matti. *Anti-Semitism and Islamophobia: Hatreds Old and New in Europe.* Chicago: Prickly Paradigm, 2007.
Butler, Judith, et al. *The Power of Religion in the Public Sphere.* Edited by Eduardo Mendieta and Jonathan VanAntwerpen. New York: Columbia University Press, 2011.
Delanty, Gerard. *Inventing Europe.* New York: Palgrave Macmillan, 1995.
Delanty, Gerard, and Chris Rumford. *Rethinking Europe: Social Theory and the Implications of Europeanization.* London: Routledge, 2005.
Eliav-Feldon, Miriam, et al. *The Origins of Racism in the West.* Cambridge: Cambridge University Press, 2013.
Emerson, Michael O., et al. "Studying Race and Religion: A Critical Assessment." *Sociology of Race and Ethnicity* 1.3 (2015) 349–59. https://doi.org/10.1177/2332649215584759.
European Commission. "EU Anti-Racism Action Plan 2020-2025." *European Commission*, September 18, 2020. https://commission.europa.eu/strategy-and-policy/policies/justice-and-fundamental-rights/combatting-discrimination/racism-and-xenophobia/eu-anti-racism-action-plan-2020-2025_en.
Feldman, Stephen Michael. *Please Don't Wish Me a Merry Christmas: A Critical History of the Separation of Church and State.* New York: New York University Press, 1997.
Gaffney, Jennifer. "Memories of Exclusion: Hannah Arendt and the Haitian Revolution." *Philosophy & Social Criticism* 44.6 (2018) 701–21.
Gatrell, Peter. *The Making of the Modern Refugee.* Oxford: Oxford University Press, 2013.
Gauchet, Marcel. *The Disenchantment of the World: A Political History of Religion.* Princeton: Princeton University Press, 2001.
Gidley, Ben, and James Renton, eds. *Antisemitism and Islamophobia in Europe—A Shared Story?* New York: Palgrave Macmillan, 2017.
Goldberg, David Theo. "Racial Europeanization." *Ethnic and Racial Studies* 29.2 (2006) 331–64. https://doi.org/10.1080/01419870500465611.
Goldenberg, David M. *Black and Slave, the Origins and History of the Curse of Ham.* Berlin: de Gruyter, 2017.
Hackett, Sarah. "Favouring Christian over Muslim Refugees Is Bad for Everyone." *Conversation*, September 15, 2015. https://theconversation.com/favouring-christian-over-muslim-refugees-is-bad-for-everyone-47440.
Hannaford, Ivan. *Race: The History of an Idea in the West.* Washington, DC: Woodrow Wilson Center, 1996.
Hay, Denys. *Europe: The Emergence of an Idea.* New York: Harper and Row, 1966.
Heng, Geraldine. *The Invention of Race in the European Middle Ages.* New York: Cambridge University Press, 2018.
Heschel, Susannah. "The Slippery Yet Tenacious Nature of Racism: New Developments in Critical Race Theory and Their Implications for the Study of Religion and Ethics." *Journal of the Society of Christian Ethics* 35.1 (2015) 3–27.

Iogna-Prat, Dominique. *Order & Exclusion: Cluny and Christendom Face Heresy, Judaism, and Islam, 1000–1150*. Translated by Graham Robert Edwards. Ithaca, NY: Cornell University Press, 2002.

Kelley, Shawn. *Racializing Jesus: Race, Ideology and the Formation of Modern Biblical Scholarship*. London: Routledge, 2002.

Klug, Brian. "The Limits of Analogy: Comparing Islamophobia and Antisemitism." *Patterns of Prejudice* 48.5 (2014) 442–59. https://doi.org/10.1080/0031322X.2014.964498.

Lentin, Alana. *Why Race Still Matters*. Chichester: Wiley-Blackwell, 2020.

Leyen, Ursula von der. "We Need to Talk about Racism." *European Commission*, June 16, 2020. https://ec.europa.eu/commission/presscorner/detail/en/speech_20_1114.

Lincicum, David. "F. C. Baur's Place in the Study of Jewish Christianity." In *The Rediscovery of Jewish Christianity from Toland to Baur*, edited by F. Stanley Jones, 137–66. Atlanta: Society of Biblical Literature, 2012.

Lindqvist, Sven. *The Dead Do Not Die: "Exterminate All the Brutes" and Terra Nullius*. New York: New Press, 2014.

Mahmood, Saba. *Religious Difference in a Secular Age: A Minority Report*. Princeton: Princeton University Press, 2015.

Maldonado-Torres, Nelson. "Race, Religion, and Ethics in the Modern/Colonial World." *Journal of Religious Ethics* 42.4 (2014) 691–711. https://doi.org/10.1111/jore.12078.

Marchand, Suzanne L. *German Orientalism in the Age of Empire: Religion, Race, and Scholarship*. Cambridge: Cambridge University Press, 2010.

Mastnak, Tomaz. *Crusading Peace: Christendom, the Muslim World, and Western Political Order*. Berkeley, CA: University of California Press, 2001.

Meer, Nasar. "Racialization and Religion: Race, Culture and Difference in the Study of Antisemitism and Islamophobia." *Ethnic and Racial Studies* 36.13 (2013) 385–98.

Moore, Robert I. *The Formation of a Persecuting Society: Authority and Deviance in Western Europe 950–1250*. 2nd ed. Chichester: Wiley-Blackwell, 2007.

Olender, Maurice, and Arthur Goldhammer. *The Languages of Paradise: Race, Religion, and Philology in the Nineteenth Century*. Cambridge, MA: Harvard University Press, 2008.

Pagden, Anthony, ed. *The Idea of Europe: From Antiquity to the European Union*. Cambridge: Cambridge University Press, 2002.

Pocock, John Greville Agard. "Deconstructing Europe." *History of European Ideas* 18.3 (1994) 329–45.

Romeyn, Esther. "Anti-Semitism and Islamophobia: Spectropolitics and Immigration." *Theory, Culture & Society* 31.6 (2014) 77–101. https://doi.org/10.1177/0263276413519482.

Rubio-Marín, Ruth, and Mathias Möschel. "Anti-Discrimination Exceptionalism: Racist Violence Before the ECtHR and the Holocaust Prism." *European Journal of International Law* 26(4) (2015) 881–99. https://doi.org/10.1093/ejil/chv058.

Schenker, Hillel, and Abu Zayyad Ziad, eds. *Islamophobia and Anti-Semitism*. Princeton: Markus Wiener, 2006.

Shohat, Ella, and Robert Stam. *Race in Translation: Culture Wars around the Postcolonial Atlantic*. New York: New York University Press, 2012.

Taylor, Charles. *A Secular Age*. Cambridge, MA: Harvard University Press, 2007.

Topolski, Anya. "The Dangerous Discourse of the 'Judaeo-Christian' Myth: Masking the Race–Religion Constellation in Europe." *Patterns of Prejudice* 54.1–2 (2020) 71–90. https://doi.org/10.1080/0031322X.2019.1696049.

———. "A Genealogy of the 'Judeo-Christian' Signifier: A Tale of Europe's Identity Crisis." In *Is There a Judeo-Christian Tradition? A European Perspective*, edited by Emmanuel Nathan and Anya Topolski, 267–84. Berlin: de Gruyter, 2016.

———. "Good Jew, Bad Jew: 'Managing' Europe's Others." *Ethnic and Racial Studies* 41.12 (2018) 2179–96.

———. "The Race-Religion Constellation: A European Contribution to the Critical Philosophy of Race." *Critical Philosophy of Race* 6.1 (2018) 58–81.

United Nations High Commissioner for Refugees (UNHCR). "Figures at a Glance." UNHCR, n.d. https://www.unhcr.org/uk/figures-at-a-glance.html.

Vial, Theodore. *Modern Religion, Modern Race*. Oxford: Oxford University Press, 2016.

Voegelin, Eric. *Race and State*. Translated by Ruth Hein. Columbia, MO: University of Missouri, 1997.

Vries, Hent de. *Religion: Beyond a Concept*. New York: Fordham University Press, 2008.

Wynter, Sylvia. "1492: A New World View." In *Race, Discourse, and the Origin of the Americas: A New World View*, edited by Vera Lawrence Hyatt and Rex Nettleford, 5–56. Washington, DC: Smithsonian Institution, 1995.

———. "Unsettling the Coloniality of Being/Power/Truth/Freedom: Towards the Human, After Man, Its Overrepresentation—An Argument." *CR: The New Centennial Review* 3.3 (2003) 257–337. https://doi.org/10.1353/ncr.2004.0015.

5

Reality Checking the Economics of Migration

Why Refugees Aren't Fiscal Burdens

Peo Hansen

OVER A FEW SUMMER DAYS, as I was putting the finishing touches to my book *A Modern Migration Theory*, my daughter developed a pain in her left foot after having twisted her ankle.[1] As the pain persisted, we went to see a doctor. In the waiting room at the local clinic, I took note of the fact that seven of the ten doctors in the corridor had foreign names, three of which were Muslim. I have seen doctors from Iraq, Romania, and Syria at this clinic, which was no coincidence given that Iraqi and Romanian doctors make up two of the largest groups within the cohort of foreign-born doctors in Sweden. More than 30 percent of all doctors in Sweden are born abroad,[2] and in the case of Iraqi doctors most of them arrived as refugees in the noughties. My daughter was examined by a doctor from Germany who swiftly referred her to the main hospital for an X-ray.

We took a taxi to the hospital, and here as well the person servicing us was foreign-born, maybe from Syria. Around half of Sweden's taxi drivers are foreign-born and the great majority have come as refugees. The driver dropped us off at the emergency room entrance, and from

---

1. Hansen, *Modern Migration Theory*.
2. OECD, *Recent Trends in International Migration*.

there we had to ask for directions to the X-ray department. We were helped by a doctor and a nurse who came walking our way. Judging from their ID badges it seemed as if the doctor was from an African country and the nurse from a Middle Eastern country. In all likelihood, the nurse who took care of my daughter in the X-ray department was also from a country in the Middle East. Close to 15 percent of the nurses working in Sweden come from other countries.[3]

Luckily, the X-ray indicated no fracture, and so we headed for the bus stop to go home. There was a bus parked by the pavement, but the driver told us that it would take a while before it would depart. With my daughter in some pain, we decided to take a taxi again. This time our driver might have been from Somalia; the same probably applied to the bus driver. Over a half of those working as bus and tram drivers in Sweden are born in another country, and, needless to say, almost all of them have come as refugees. I think I have made my point. But I should mention too that we also passed by a team of cleaners in the hospital. The pattern repeated itself, and no coincidence in this case either. 60 percent of the cleaners in Sweden are foreign-born, and, yes, the majority have refugee background.[4] They clean Sweden for very low pay, and they continued to fulfil this essential public function during the COVID-19 pandemic.

My daughter and I had an excursion into the Swedish reality. In this reality, people who have come as refugees carry out vital work without which the Swedish society and economy would cease to function. Close to 30 percent nationally, and about 55 percent in the Stockholm region, of those working in the Swedish elderly care are foreign-born—practically all of them have a refugee background.[5] Although it refuses to acknowledge this fact in the public debate, in a report from 2018 even the Swedish government[6] concedes as much: "Without the foreign-born women and men, the elderly care would face significant problems in fulfilling its task."

Again, this is the reality, and the numbers are there for everybody to see. Yet this reality persistently fails to register in national and European debates on asylum and migration. Instead of broadcasting the real benefits that refugees and labour migrants bring to EU countries and, from

---

3. OECD, *Recent Trends in International Migration*.
4. See Statistics Sweden, "Pizza Makers"; "Yrkesregistret med yrkesstatistik 2018."
5. Wigzell et al., *Vård och omsorg om äldre*, 47.
6. Socialdepartementet, *Framtidens äldreomsorg*, 16.

there, enact policy to improve migrants' often precarious situation, the political establishment has done the opposite. It has made sure to soak and trap the European Union in a toxic debate over an alleged plethora of negative effects of migration—though "highly skilled" migration is sometimes spared.[7]

Integral to this is the ubiquitous *cost perspective* on migration, which makes up one of the most powerful shields against the EU's migration reality. This perspective, or narrative, is the main focus of this chapter.

THE COST PERSPECTIVE ON MIGRATION

As I describe in great detail elsewhere,[8] not only politicians but also researchers today agree that refugees admitted to the European Union constitute a net cost and fiscal burden for the receiving societies. Whereas researchers draw this conclusion from a seemingly neutral accounting exercise—refugees are said to contribute less in taxes than they receive in welfare assistance—politicians and the media eagerly use this "economic science" to justify and explain restrictive asylum policies. To be sure, politicians and researchers may judge low-earning and low-skilled labour migrants to be both necessary and affordable, but *only* on the condition that their access to welfare provisions is restricted. This does not apply to refugees, however. Since refugees cannot work and pay taxes from day one and since they may have children, refugees will initially always depend on welfare assistance. By definition, therefore, they are deemed fiscal burdens.

From the perspective of research, this is just a scientific fact, and so research cannot be held accountable for being complicit in stoking the sentiment that refugee reception and low-earning migrants jeopardize the welfare state and that, consequently, refugee prevention constitutes a prerequisite for the fiscal viability of the welfare state. As one expert in the field puts it: "The lower the skills and earnings of migrants in the

---

7. Although the Ukrainian refugee crisis would change the tone of both governments and the EU in the spring of 2022, this only applied to the "European" refugees from Ukraine. With time, however, EU governments have also become more and more prone to emphasize the "costs" also for the Ukrainian refugees. "Almost ten months after the invasion," the *Financial Times* commented in December 2022, "the warm welcome [of Ukrainian refugees] is giving way to fatigue as Europeans are pressured by rising inflation and government budgets come under strain" (Kazmin et al., "Migration Fatigue").

8. Hansen, *Modern Migration Theory*, 23–48.

host country, the greater will be the strictly economic case for restricting some of their welfare rights in order to minimize the fiscal costs for existing residents."[9] The "strictly economic" serves to indicate that the issue at hand is neither grounded nor decided within the realm of political choice. Rather, economic laws of fiscal sustainability are said to constrain what is politically feasible.

According to world-renowned economist Branko Milanovic, "The arrival of migrants threatens to diminish or dilute the premium enjoyed by citizens of rich countries, which includes not only financial aspects, but also good health and education services." Yes, you read right, migrants working in the health services are supposedly diluting "the premium enjoyed by citizens of rich countries." Admitting low-earning migrants therefore "requires withholding some civic rights," Milanovic asserts, "We can debate the sharpness of the trade-off, but cannot deny its existence."[10] In Milanovic's quest to figure out ways to "pay for increased migration," such withholding of rights to migrants—or "discriminatory treatment," as he terms it—are both necessary and beneficial to all. Migrants, Milanovic suggests, "could also be made to pay higher taxes since they are the largest net beneficiaries of migration."[11]

Finally, here's another representative scholarly view, published in a recent issue of the International Organization of Migration's (IOM) journal *International Migration*:

> The refugees represent a fiscal burden for the host countries at least short and medium term. Under these conditions refugee migration is unable to help to alleviate the aging related fiscal burden of the host societies, on the contrary, it contributes to its worsening. Thus, when the majority thinks that refugees represent a fiscal burden (they "take out more from the public purse than they pay in"), they are not wrong this time. It is not possible to argue against this with solid empirical evidence. Naturally, the moral (and legal) obligation argument for accepting the refugees is still valid but it couldn't be underpinned with further economic reasoning. The moral obligations and the economic benefit are in conflict here.[12]

---

9. Ruhs, *Price of Rights*, 46.
10. Milanovic, *Global Inequality*, 152.
11. Milanovic, "There Is a Trade-Off."
12. Gál, "Fiscal Consequences of the Refugee Crisis," 352.

As communicated in the quote, "the majority [is] not wrong this time," implying that, though majorities may be wrong most of the time, on the issue of refugees they are not. Here, the majority opinion is in agreement with science. The political parties on the extreme right have always had this piece of "economic science" tattooed into their party programmes and flagship slogans. Here is an instance when Europe's extreme right cannot be dismissed as populists or as being guilty of simplifying complex issues. As asserted in the quote, the factuality of refugees constituting a "fiscal burden" "is not possible to argue against . . . with solid empirical evidence." And since a fiscal burden, per definition, is synonymous with something very negative in the public debate, we should not be surprised if politicians and the public take those making up the burden—the refugees—to be undesirable too.

In response to this, the proponents of the cost perspective simply say that to mask or hide the truth about refugee migration—or any other migration deemed costly—goes against the scientific ethos and that it would make for an even worse place to begin integration. Many would add that tampering with the truth will only aid the anti-immigration populists—a particularly common retort from mainstream politicians and scholars who want to mark their distance from the extreme right. Since so few challenge the basic principles and maths of the cost perspective, it has gained an air of unassailable truth. But those who claim that they side with accuracy in order to avoid playing into the hands of the anti-immigration right do something even worse than allowing the cost assumption to stand unchallenged. They give it new life and credibility by insisting it be acknowledged *in advance*. It is like starting a discussion about equal pay by insisting that we acknowledge that women are a fiscal burden on men because women pay less in taxes—and that trying to diminish or hide this "fact" only plays into the hands of the sexists.

A MODERN MIGRATION THEORY

My purpose, however, goes much further than debunking the cost perspective's detrimental impact on migrants' integration and inclusion. Employing the descriptive macroeconomic framework provided by the scholars within Modern Monetary Theory (MMT), it is also to demonstrate that the cost perspective fundamentally builds on a flawed economic conception.[13] Much of this is attributable to the heavy imprint

---

13. See, e.g., Ehnts, "Eurozone is Fully Committed"; Mitchell et al., *Macroeconomics*.

of the orthodox "sound finance" doctrine on migration research and policy—the assumption that governments face a budget constraint much in the same way as households, municipalities, and businesses. This orthodox "sound finance" economics and its household accounting thus mistakes state spending for being precisely that: analogous to household spending. Here, therefore, spending amounts to little more than a cost, in the same way that a household looks at its outlays—i.e., as something that subtracts from the household's income, savings or borrowed money. Consequently, the money spent on refugees would have to be made up for through tax hikes, "risky" borrowing or by removing funds from other areas, such as welfare benefits intended for needy citizens.

For countries that issue their own currencies, however, none of this applies. Since the central government is the monopoly issuer of the currency, it follows, both in logical and in concrete terms, that it necessarily has to spend or lend the currency (via the banking system) into existence before it can collect it back in taxes. If this was not the case, there would be no money to pay taxes with. Such governments are thus the exact opposite of municipalities, businesses, and households, all of which have to collect, earn, or borrow the money before they can spend it; they are mere users of money, not issuers. Hence, and as MMT explains, currency-issuing governments are not revenue-constrained. This means that taxes collected by the central government are not used to fund government spending as they are when collected by currency-using bodies such as municipalities or constituent states in federations (or as in the eurozone prior to ECB's adoption of the Pandemic Emergency Purchase Program).[14] Central government taxes fulfil other indispensable functions and purposes. By constantly removing a large chunk of money—and thus spending power—from the private sector, taxes work as a powerful anti-inflationary measure while at the same time moving resources from the private to the public sector. Taxes also work as an instrument regulating income and wealth distribution, and they are used to promote or discourage certain industries, professions, and behaviours. And there are, of course, other purposes that central government taxes can be made to fulfil—but revenue for spending and saving for future spending do not form part of them. Again, as the monopoly issuer of the currency, the government can always spend its own currency.

---

14. See Ehnts, "Eurozone is Fully Committed."

As MMT also demonstrates—and as the historical pandemic-spending corroborates—money spent never disappears, and this, of course, applies to all monetary systems everywhere. This is so because all central government spending, by definition, must end up somewhere and hence be collected by someone.[15] Spending by the central government is thus synonymous with income in the non-central government sector—as such, spending always equals income. Or, as Wray puts it: "Aggregate spending creates aggregate income."[16] In the scholarly literature on the fiscal impact of migration as well as in fiscal policy-making, this irrefutable fact is never considered, which, when one comes to think about it, is strange indeed. Had it been seriously pondered, I suspect the whole notion of the potential unsustainability of refugee spending would have had to be reconsidered. In other words, what is so bad or dangerous about households, businesses, and municipalities receiving net incomes?

REAL RESOURCES, FINANCIAL RESOURCES

What may be even more serious is that scholars and policy-makers also fail to understand why we need to distinguish between real resources, such as labour, and financial resources. Reflecting this failure, researchers cannot grasp the value and indispensability of the labour performed by those 60 percent of cleaners in Sweden who are born abroad. Instead, they conceive of these workers as fiscal burdens. Their tax contributions fall below average and so they are said to receive more in government welfare spending than they pay in. By always being in the red, so to speak, these workers will neither be able to redeem the costs for their initial stay in the country during which they did not work and pay taxes at all. Of course, if refugees work as doctors, they will be able to offset such alleged costs, and they may also be able to offset additional costs, such as their children's schooling. But, if they work as cleaners, they remain perpetual net costs. According to this logic, then, Sweden would have been better off without the cleaners who came as refugees.

This is silly and absurd reasoning. To deem people as fiscal assets or fiscal burdens depending on whether they pay above or below the average for tax payments is to misunderstand society. Not everyone can earn above-average incomes, as, by definition, some will be above whereas some will be below. What purpose does it serve to consign those who

15. Wray, *Modern Money Theory*, 18.
16. Wray, *Modern Money Theory*, 18.

earn below "average" to the status of costs and burdens when, as everyone ought to know too, society is impossible without them? What would society be like if no one worked in food production, if no one cleaned, cared for children and the elderly, drove the buses, or worked as assistant nurses? The COVID pandemic is, of course, another case in point. As one study about essential workers during the pandemic concluded:

> The overarching picture is that of a migrant workforce that acts as an integral part in keeping basic and necessary functions of European societies working amidst periods of forced closure. It is worth stressing how, among migrants, the low skilled workers are especially over-represented in a number of key occupations that are vital in the fight against COVID-19, underscoring their often neglected value within European economies.[17]

As I have already indicated, the real resource contribution from the foreign-born nationals to the Swedish society has been nothing less than astounding (Hansen 2021). With fewer Swedish-born workers joining the labour force than leaving it, the entire net addition of working age people in Sweden has, since 2008, consisted of the foreign born. Between 2010 and 2017 the number of working age (16–64) Swedish-born people dropped by over 150,000 while the number of working age foreign-born grew by some 360,000 people.[18] In this period, Sweden was thus able to increase its working age population by more than 200,000. This growth will pick up even more until 2025, when the foreign-born share of the working age is set to hit 27 percent, as compared to 18 percent in 2010. Because of this, Sweden is the only country in the EU (and beyond) that has *not* seen an increase in the median age over the last decade. The figures for 2017 illustrate this well. Here, the labour market added 94,000 jobs, of which 75,000, or 80 percent, went to foreign-born workers.[19] According to the Swedish Public Employment Service (SPES 2018), this pattern is likely to continue.

Crucial, too, is that refugees in Sweden have disproportionately ended up in smaller, rural municipalities. Many of these municipalities appreciate refugees as vital in making local communities liveable again, helping to reverse a decades-long vicious spiral of depopulation, declining local tax revenue and welfare service retrenchment. Thanks to

---

17. Fasani and Mazza, *Immigrant Key Workers*, 11.
18. Almérus et al., *Arbetsmarknadsutsikterna hösten 2018*.
19. Almérus et al., *Arbetsmarknadsutsikterna hösten 2018*, 26.

refugee reception, municipalities that were closing schools are now opening them as well as building new ones.[20]

Concerning fiscal policy, during the three years the Swedish central government increased spending massively to manage the reception of 163,000 refugees (2015–2017). In 2015, and for many years prior to that, Sweden had been the largest recipient, proportionally speaking, of asylum seekers in the EU. Most of the funds went to the municipalities that received the refugees. But the government made sure to inform the public that the spending was a necessary evil that would impact negatively on the Swedish economy and welfare state—this was the message that was repeated by the government over and over again. In addition, practically all economic expertise warned in unison of economic and financial damage, urging the government to trim spending and introduce austerity measures to avoid deficits and debt accumulation.

But while Sweden's central government, its economic experts and the media were busy worrying about the expenditure column and the future fiscal balance, many rural and depopulating municipalities away from Stockholm were busy welcoming this expenditure as income. Thanks to the refugee spending by the central government, 2016 ended up being one of the best fiscal years ever for Swedish local governments, with practically all the country's 290 municipalities running surpluses.[21]

The central government spending to the municipalities financed the reception of refugees and their initial integration. In and of itself this increased public consumption enormously; and it stimulated investment and employment, which greatly boosted overall economic growth. But since much more money was transferred than was needed for the immediate refugee concerns, municipalities were able to attend to other things too, such as welfare needs, schools and infrastructure. Besides impacting positively on the health of welfare services, in many municipalities state refugee funds also enabled municipalities to invest, save and pay down debt.[22]

The admission of refugees—that is, *real* resources—together with the generous addition of financial resources from the central government thus proved to be a hugely virtuous combination for scores of depopulating municipalities in Sweden. With this we also see the nullification of

---

20. See Hansen, *Modern Migration Theory*.
21. SALAR, *Ekonomirapporten*, 36–50.
22. See further Hansen, *Modern Migration Theory*, 13–170.

what scholars and centrally located politicians claim to be an inescapable and indisputable trade-off between refugee spending and welfare spending—between the reception of refugees and strengthened welfare for all. Right before our eyes, then, Sweden had built a real-world model—however reluctantly—that was capable of receiving large numbers of refuges while at the same time investing in welfare. Instead of the misconceived trade-off between migration and welfare, or the alleged choice that must be made between welfare spending and refugee reception, the Swedish case demonstrated that it is exactly the other way around. Spending on the refugees, the non-citizen newcomers, became a way of rediscovering the viability of welfare for all.

HUMAN RIGHTS ARE NOT A SACRIFICE

When politicians sound the alarm over refugee costs, claiming that these threaten the fiscal sustainability of the welfare state, they do so from the comfortable place of being able to cite research. No accusations of populist fakery here. But most of the time they do not have to cite research. The notion that there is a trade-off between refugee migration and the welfare state is simply common sense in the public debate. The debate is not whether this is actually accurate; everybody agrees that refugees involve costs for taxpayers. The debate is, rather, whether these *costs* are deemed affordable or not. It is clear who is winning this debate in terms of policy outcomes; asylum policy is becoming increasingly restrictive, and the residence and social rights for those refugees who still manage to enter the European Union are being curtailed. No EU member state wants to share the "refugee burden."

But it is a strange debate, because the losing side, or those defending refugee rights, almost always contend that human rights never should be allowed to be subjected to cost–benefit analyses. Given that no one is questioning the assumption that refugee reception indeed constitutes a cost, this position is understandable. Under these circumstances, human rights proponents will always lose a cost–benefit debate over refugee reception. But as I have explained, this assumption is inaccurate: refugee reception is not *costly*. Rather, it amounts to a beneficial addition of real resources, as illustrated in the snapshot of the Swedish reality above. The government spending on refugees, for its part, will do what government spending always does: it will end up as income in other sectors of the economy—that is, as income for municipalities, businesses and others involved and employed in the management of refugee reception and integration. Those advocating human rights, therefore, do not have to concede the mistaken orthodox assumption that refugees are costly. Nor do they have to think of "the economy" as the enemy. Receiving refugees in the EU is not an economic or fiscal sacrifice.

But let me be clear: I am not saying that Sweden or the EU as a whole should admit refugees *because* it benefits Sweden and the EU. Sweden and the EU should admit refugees to honour their human rights obligations and commitments. On the economics of it all, there is no argument. In admitting and investing in refugees—that is, *real* resources—societies in Sweden and the EU can only benefit.

BIBLIOGRAPHY

Almérus, Annelie, et al. *Arbetsmarknadsutsikterna hösten 2018: Prognos för arbetsmarknaden 2018–2020*. Stockholm: Swedish Public Employment Service (SPES), 2018. https://mb.cision.com/Public/1326/2705029/b4f5e3d10346631e.pdf.

Ehnts, Dirk. "The Eurozone Is Fully Committed to Modern Monetary Theory (MMT)." *Brave New Europe*, April 4, 2020. https://braveneweurope.com/dirk-ehnts-the-eurozone-is-fully-committed-to-modern-monetary-theory-mmt.

———. *Modern Monetary Theory and European Macroeconomics*. Abingdon: Routledge, 2017.

Fasani, Francesco, and Jacopo Mazza. *Immigrant Key Workers: Their Contribution to Europe's COVID-19 Response*. IZA Policy Paper 155. Bonn: Institute of Labour Economics (IZA), 2020. https://docs.iza.org/pp155.pdf.

Gál, Zsolt. "Fiscal Consequences of the Refugee Crisis." *International Migration* 57.5 (2019) 341–54.

Hansen, Peo. *A Modern Migration Theory: An Alternative Economic Approach to Failed EU Policy*. Newcastle: Agenda, 2021.

Kazmin, Amy, et al. "Migration Fatigue: Europe Braces for New Influx of Ukrainians." *Financial Times*, December 11, 2022. https://www.ft.com/content/cf00788c-2799-4d4e-9158-666d1a31ca26.

Milanovic, Branko. *Global Inequality: A New Approach for the Age of Globalization*. Cambridge: Harvard University Press, 2016.

———. "There Is a Trade-Off Between Citizenship and Migration." *Financial Times*, April 20, 2016. https://www.ft.com/content/2e3c93fa-06d2-11e6-9b51-0fb5e65703ce.

Mitchell, William, et al. *Macroeconomics: A Modern Money Theory Approach*. London: Red Globe, 2019.

Organisation for Economic Co-Operation and Development (OECD). *Recent Trends in International Migration of Doctors, Nurses, and Medical Students*. Paris: OECD, 2019.

Ruhs, Martin. *The Price of Rights: Regulating International Labour Migration*. Princeton: Princeton University Press, 2013.

Socialdepartementet [Ministry of Health and Social Affairs, Sweden]. *Framtidens äldreomsorg—en nationell kvalitetsplan.* Skr 2017/18:280. Stockholm: Government Office of Sweden, 2017.

Statistics Sweden. "Pizza Makers Have Largest Share of Foreign-Born Persons." *Statistikmyndigheten SCB*, March 7, 2019. https://www.scb.se/en/finding-statistics/statistics-by-subject-area/labour-market/employment-and-working-hours/the-swedish-occupational-register-with-statistics/pong/statistical-news/the-swedish-occupational-register.

———. "Yrkesregistret med yrkesstatistik 2018." *Statistikmyndigheten SCB*, March 5, 2020. https://www.scb.se/contentassets/b49d7efc2653457f8179f18461d2bf38/am0208_2018a01_sm_am33sm2001.pdf.

Swedish Association of Local Authorities and Regions (SALAR). *Ekonomirapporten, maj 2017.* Stockholm: SKR, 2017.

Wigzell, Olivia, et al. *Vård och omsorg om äldre: Lägesrapport 2019.* Stockholm: Socialstyrelsen, 2019. https://www.socialstyrelsen.se/globalassets/sharepoint-dokument/artikelkatalog/ovrigt/2019-3-18.pdf.

Wray, L. Randall. *Modern Money Theory: A Primer on Macroeconomics for Sovereign Monetary Systems.* 2nd ed. New York: Palgrave, 2015.

6

"Sabina, You Must Promise Me You Won't Tell My Father"
Stories of Social Work

Sabina Esp

I am a practitioner. A social worker residing in the city of Östersund, in the north of Sweden. I am not used to sharing stories, and it doesn't come easy to me. How do I choose which stories to pick? How do I dress them in words for a reader? How do I find the time to write?

I didn't anticipate that writing these stories would have such an effect on me. I've needed to take many breaks, and each writing session has left me heartbroken for hours afterwards, having to revisit dark moments and memories. Because the way I manage to persevere is through focusing mainly on the possibilities. And here I am sharing the challenges.

I know these stories are important to share. Through A World of Neighbours, I am learning that more and more. And the people I am writing about agree—even though it's been hard for them to read what I have written. They persevere through forgetting.

So, I give you five stories. Filled with tears, sorrow, grief, and anger. Loss of trust and rights, loss of support, dignity, and faith. Five stories of real people and real events. From my perspective. Together, these five stories also shape a story of one of many social workers and the challenges we are facing.

"SABINA, YOU MUST PROMISE ME YOU WON'T TELL MY FATHER"
A LETTER FROM THE MIGRATION AUTHORITIES

It had been yet another long week at the shelter. I was longing for my new coworker to start next week and not having to do all of this on my own anymore. Sure, I did get the occasional support from other diaconal employees within the parish but the overall and daily management including staffing was still all on me. Two months earlier when I accepted the position to start up and run the shelter for homeless refugee[1] youth, I immediately said it wouldn't be enough with just myself. And my superiors agreed, and so did the municipality who provided the funding. But recruitment always took time.

I had promised my partner to be home by 6 p.m. tonight. There had been so many evenings lately, when I had called him to say that I would be late. Again. Before going to work early this morning though, he said that he really wished for me to be home at a sensible time because he saw I needed the rest. We agreed he would cook dinner to be ready by six, all I needed to do was show up.

Today had been hectic and heavy loaded and I was just about to wrap things up when Azim shows up at the door. He is asking for his letter that I had texted him about. I hand the letter over to him and we say goodbye as he continues down the corridor to his room.

Azim is eighteen years old and I have known him since back in 2015 when he arrived, then only fourteen. At the time I worked as a manager for the municipality running foster housing for unaccompanied refugee minors, and Azim had been one of them. It had been a meaningful job but in 2017 I decided to hand in my resignation. Swedish migration legislation had changed drastically in just two years. We had closed our borders, confined people before forcefully deporting them, rejected applications of asylum where the same reasons for a permit had previously been accepted. Me and my colleagues in the management team had to perform severe cutbacks since our financing had been cut in half by the government. Many of those members of staff we recruited back in 2015 and 2016 now had to go even though we still had loads of children and youth to foster and care for.

One day our accountant complimented me for all my great efforts in performing these cutbacks and how good my figures looked. I took a deep breath and shared with him that the previous week, a refugee boy

---

1. I choose to refer to them as "refugees" because that is how they see themselves. However, the authorities have denied them refugee status.

from a neighbouring municipality had jumped off a bridge. He was a classmate and dear friend to several of my youths. The night before I had gone with some of my girls to put flowers and light a candle by the riverbank where the boy's body had floated to land.

I wanted to hear nothing on how good my figures looked. There were so many young lives at stake, and I didn't become a social worker just to store children. They needed friends, love, care, fostering, guidance, hope for the future. I came to realize I couldn't do this job anymore. My boss had full understanding when I decided to hand in my resignation. My employees too, but the words of one of them will always stick with me. "Ok Sabina, I understand you can't stand up for this anymore. But what if we get a manager who *can* stand up for this, wouldn't that be worse?"

I felt like a quitter. After my resignation I decided to take a break from social work, and for half a year I worked as a waitress at a restaurant. And one day I got a phone call from a priest. They needed a project manager, urgently, and had been recommended my name. And now here I was. With Azim and others of my wonderful youths. Doing what I became a social worker to do—helping people.

I locked the office door. For a short while I stood by the entrance, deciding if I should leave or go to check on Azim. The letter was from the migration court of appeal. The time was now 5:20 and it would take me twenty-five minutes to get home. I had fifteen minutes to spare. I knock on Azim's door. He is sitting on the floor reading the letter. He hands it over to me and I crouch next to him. "The Migration Court of Appeal does not grant leave to appeal. The Migration Court's ruling therefore stands."

He asks me what to do next. I don't have an answer. Azim starts to cry; I am fighting to keep my own tears back. I sit down and wrap my arms around him. He talks about how going back to Afghanistan is not an option. How a life on the streets in Europe would be way better.

Azim had so many words and so many tears. And the clock was ticking away. At home I had my partner cooking for me, waiting for me. And here I had Azim, needing me.

I tried to be as gentle as I could, saying to Azim I had to leave. We agree to continue the conversation the next day. As I stand up, Azim says to me that he promises to leave the shelter as soon as possible. That he knew the rules and that I wasn't allowed to let him stay once his judgement had been final in three weeks' time. I didn't know how to respond.

"SABINA, YOU MUST PROMISE ME YOU WON'T TELL MY FATHER"

Because it was true—the municipality who provided the funding, was very clear that one of their terms was that all youth staying at the shelter needed to have a legal status. Azim soon would not. But where would he go? He had no one.

I got home just on time. Me and my partner had our dinner and were chatting away about our upcoming holiday. My partner said I seemed distraught. And yes—I couldn't help thinking about Azim and all the others at the shelter. Them having so little, me having so much. Sometimes I felt guilty for not doing enough and not giving them more of my time. My refrigerator was always full, I had restaurant dinners, nights at the movie theatre and holidays abroad. I lived with my loved ones, not having to worry about neither my nor their security. Still, I left Azim alone when he needed someone next to him.

Other times I felt guilty towards my partner for running late. Or towards both him and me, for being home but still not having left work. Was I ever going to feel adequate, sufficient, enough?

BORDER POLICE AT THE SHELTER

It was cold and dark as me and my partner exited the cinema that evening. My phone had been on silent, and I discovered I had several missed calls from my co-workers. It had to be an emergency—they knew not to contact me whilst off duty.

"The border police are here. There's seven of them."

My heart started to race from the words of my colleague. Never in my mind would I have expected the police in our city to come looking for undocumented people at a shelter run by the church. And seven of them?

The ten-minute drive to my shelter had never felt so long before. As I was driving, I quickly scrolled through the Messenger thread we had with the sixteen youths residing in the shelter.

"Ali and Mohammad, stay away! The border police are here!"

"Amed, Mosa and Qadir—lock yourself in your rooms!"

"Jump out of the window! Run!"

Ali, Mohammad, Amed, Mosa and Quadir were all undocumented. Four of them had arrived back in 2015 as unaccompanied minors, like almost all of the youths at the shelter. Most were from Afghanistan. Prior to 2015, almost all unaccompanied minors from Afghanistan were granted subsidiary protection and permanent residence permits. Now almost all of them got their asylum applications rejected. But some of them got a temporary permit dependant on studies and work—but there were many requirements to be met. You had to have arrived in Sweden prior to November 24, 2015. You must have waited at least fifteen months for a decision on your asylum application. You must have been at least eighteen years old at the time of the decision for your asylum application. And more. You had to understand all the regulations to be sure you made no mistakes. I remember how so many weighty referral bodies were outrageous when the law came into place. "The limit has been reached for what is acceptable in terms of how legislation can be designed," was expressed by the Swedish legal council—a governmental body. And here I was, in the midst of those laws and their consequences for individuals. Having had to become somewhat of a local expert trying to navigate them.

Ali had arrived November 28, 2015. Mohammad on December 6. Amed had been waiting for only 13 months before he got a decision. And at the time when the migration authorities decided on Qadir's case, he was at the age of 17, 364 days, and 18 hours.

Returning to Afghanistan was not an option for any of them. As many others had done before them, they were planning on fleeing to another European country. In France for example they considered the situation in Afghanistan too severe to deport young people to. Sometimes they didn't even send someone back to Sweden despite of the Dublin Agreement, since the French authorities knew Sweden would deport them to Afghanistan.

Just before I entered the shelter, I sent a message to another Messenger group, consisting of volunteers providing accommodation in their homes to undocumented youth.

"The border police are at the shelter. Everyone, stay safe."

As I entered the shelter a co-worker was already meeting me, she had seen my car rolling up. She was panicked.

"They're here for Mosa and they're sitting with him now. They don't seem to know he has a daughter."

Mosa was nineteen years old when he arrived in Sweden back in 2015. I had given him shelter as an exception, since my project was supposed to support only those who had arrived as unaccompanied minors. But the previous summer when the last official refugee camps in our region were closing, he was desperate to stay in the area. A friend of him had given him my number. It turned out he had a baby girl born here in Sweden. He and the mother of the child had been deeply in love, but the baby was not planned for. And the mother couldn't care for her, and

Mosa didn't know how to care for the baby on his own—especially not when residing in a bedroom he shared with four other men at the refugee camp. So, when the social welfare office recommended for the baby to be put in foster care from birth, both parents agreed.

Since Mosa moved into my shelter I had spent many hours with him, teaching him about Swedish custody regulations, the rights of his daughter and himself, helping him with his contacts at the social welfare office. Ever since his daughter was born, he had met with her once or twice a week. She had no contact with her mother and her father was her only family besides the foster family. Mosa's daughter was everything to him and he was hoping that as soon as he would get his residence permit, and he could get a job and his own place to live, he and his baby girl would be able to start living as a family.

But as so many other refugees from Afghanistan, his asylum application was rejected. Again and again. And now here we were, with the border police having orders from the migration authorities to proceed with a forced deportation.

And no, they didn't know he had a daughter. They wanted proof of this, and I went to my office to fetch Mosa's files. Two of the policemen read through all the documents, learning about this toddler at risk of losing her father. Once they had read it, one of them started explaining to me that it didn't make a difference. They still had orders from the migration authorities to deport him. For some very long seconds I could do nothing but look the policeman in the eyes. I couldn't help shaking as I opened my mouth.

"I don't know how to ask you this. Maybe it's not even a question. I am Swedish too, just like yourself. And this is not my Sweden. My Sweden doesn't deport Afghan refugee youth. My Sweden doesn't break families apart. You as policeman never had to do this before. What happened to humanity and solidarity? Sweden where we are now, is broken! Don't you agree?"

"All I can say," he replied, "is that we have a rule of law in Sweden, and our job as the police is to maintain that rule of law. We are just doing our job."

That night they decided not to take Mosa with them but instead have him report weekly to the police station. But there were so many other youths they took by force, placed for months in confinement before deporting them to Afghanistan. I can't think of how their lives are today. If they are alive. And hearing those words from the policeman, "We are just doing our job," I felt that I lost even more of the fragmented shivers of faith I had once had for Swedish values and principles.

"EVERY GIRL HAS A RIGHT TO A LIFE IN DIGNITY," THEY SAY

"Sabina, I have had a meeting with our temporary vicar. We agree that our financial help to these families must stop. You need to inform them about this. Do you need any support in doing so?"

She was my new boss, the fourth one I had had since the project had started two and a half years earlier. Our current vicar was the third one.

I understood her. I had tried to raise the need for sustainability in the support and services my project could provide to people in need, but given the organizational circumstances we often found ourselves needing to prioritize putting out fires. Decisions were often taken ad hoc, and my proposal for a long-term strategy had been put in somebody's drawer to be looked at "when it's a bit less hectic for the parish."

There were so many unmet needs, and so few resources.

"No, it's ok, I'm fine. They will understand."

As I exited her office and stepped out in the corridor, I saw posters on the wall from one of the previous campaigns run by Act Church of Sweden, the international aid and development organization within the Church of Sweden. "Every girl has the right to a life in dignity," the poster said, with an encouragement to contribute economically to this cause, enabling Act to make improvements for many girls across the world.

I wondered if people knew how many girls we had here in Sweden—neighbours to all of us—*not* living a life in dignity. Not having the right to support. And now I was about to tell some of these girls and their families that neither our parish could support them in what they needed the most.

A DOCTOR'S APPOINTMENT

"Do you have faith in God?" I ask twenty-year-old Abdul next to me in the passenger seat, as I am taking him to his doctor's appointment.

I was still not used to asking questions about God since I had been taught through Swedish culture that our spiritual identity is something we keep private. And in my previous positions within municipalities, these questions would have been really "outside the box." When receiving a new unaccompanied refugee minor to our group homes, we would initially ask about religious inherency and inform what kind of religious communities and services were available. Then finishing the sentence with: "If you want to know more, please ask us." After that we would leave the child with the responsibility of raising matters of spiritual and existential needs, desires, identity, and health. Just like most secular Swedes are left on their own with them.

The difference, however, as I have learnt through my recent commitment with diaconal work and foremost through the young people themselves as soon as I dared to ask them, is that many who come to Sweden already have a strong religious identity. However, as a child this may not always be a priority, and in their home countries parents would take responsibility for this through their overall upbringing. Being left alone with this is new to many of them.

The beaming summer sun made the whole lake sparkle as we crossed the bridge.

"Yes, I have faith in God. But I feel like I am sitting very far away from God. And that maybe God has forgotten about me."

At the doctor's office I try not to intervene and only be there as a support. But the conversation with the doctor was almost about to end without Abdul having raised the true matters to why we had made the appointment. I ask for his permission to share these reasons, and he says yes.

We stayed with the doctor for another hour. Together we could speak of all the anxiety, the insomnia, the headaches, the fears, and the stress. How his friends had reached out to me with their perceptions of him as very depressed and sometimes disillusioned, almost on the verge of psychotic. Me suspecting Abdul to have some sort of intellectual disability, himself sharing what difficulties he encountered in everyday life. Failing at school, failing at work, failing in most responsibilities and demands being put upon him.

We ended the session with the doctor remitting him to a psychiatric team for further investigations. We left the clinic, me probably more relieved than Abdul. Because he didn't understand what I had already known for a long time—that a diagnosis confirming an intellectual disability, would be the only chance for him to be granted protection status and the possibility to continue to live in Sweden. Or else, he too would face deportation to Afghanistan where he had no relatives to support him and care for him.

I was grateful that Abdul had finally given me the permission to book that appointment, having tried to support him for several years—first through the municipality, now through the church. At the same time, he was only one of many thousands of young refugees across Sweden, all of them having their asylum applications rejected and met with demands for school graduation and work within six months for their permission to stay in this country. Many of whom were homeless. And while I was grateful to spend my working days supporting those living in my town, my heart was breaking from the knowledge that so many of these young people across the country were left abandoned and all alone in all their struggles, not having anyone to fight for and with them.

"DON'T TELL MY FATHER"

As I entered the café, I saw that Zara was already there. Her face lit up and she came to greet me with a big hug. This was the first time I had seen her covering her long dark hair with a veil. Her older sister usually did so, but never Zara.

We both ordered a cup of tea and sat down at a table by the window. We started chit-chatting about life in general and I decided to share what was on my mind.

"I think this is the first time I see you wearing a veil?"

Zara paused for a few seconds. She then starts by sharing that she is not comfortable with it at all. That the veil gets in the way and that she is having difficulties learning how to fasten it properly. But that her cousins in her home country had started questioning the pictures she shared on Instagram. Saying she was too lightly dressed, that she should cover herself, that she might get into trouble if she was ever to return to Iran.

"First, I didn't care," she said. "I don't want anyone to say what I can and can't do. But as you know, we got another rejection on our asylum application. I'm soon turning eighteen and will just like my older sister get a status as undocumented and have even less rights. And now I am starting to feel scared. What if we can't stay here? What if I must return?"

I didn't know how to respond and for a moment we were both just silent.

"What does your father say about you wearing a veil?"

"He asked me why," she replied, "but I just said I wanted to try for a while. And then he just said it's my choice . . . I can't tell him the real reason; it would make him so sad."

I will never forget the first time I met her father. How his eyes were filled with grief and fear, how his shoulders were weighed down with worry and burdens no parent should have to carry. The future of his children was out of his hands, and he was not even able to provide for them anymore. During their asylum period he was allowed to work, but that permit had just been withdrawn. He was also declined migration allowance since the authorities claimed he could have saved money from his previous earnings. They didn't accept his argument of having to pay for rent, since staying in Östersund and paying rent was "his own choice." The year before when the migration services closed all offices and camps in our region, they had been offered a new camp on the other side of the country. But since he had a job and could afford a small apartment, he thought that staying in Östersund was the best for his family. Him being able to continue working, and his children continuing school. Especially since his oldest daughter of eighteen, already undocumented and unwanted, would no longer have the right to attend school unless she stayed at her current one.

But no. According to the migration authority, paying rent was his own choice. So now they were not granted an allowance, and he was not allowed to work. What would they eat?

They had a good life in Iran. He was a contractor with his own business, they had a beautiful house he had built himself, and they had two cars. Materially speaking they were doing good—he had started work at the age of eleven and never quit. But as his oldest daughter reached puberty, their community started to try to push him and his wife into betrothing her, finding her a husband. She was only thirteen years old. And he knew that being an Afghan refugee girl in Iran, she would have no other future than to be somebody's wife. Nor would her two younger sisters. So, he and his wife decided the family should leave. They wanted a different future for their daughters, a future of freedom and human rights.

And here she was in front of me, one of these very daughters. This time dressed in a veil. She was seventeen years old and had lived in Sweden for six years now. She had never worn a veil before, she didn't want to wear a veil, and still she found herself forced to cover up.

"Sabina, you must promise me you won't tell my father."

7

The Vigil

*On Silence, Grief, Sight, and the Power of Belief
A Conversation with Anna Hjälm*

Aude Sathoud

In the beginning was silence—

I type as Jenin's night explodes under the airstrikes conducted by the Israeli army during the most dramatic military operation led in the West banks those past two decades.

In the beginning was silence—

I reflect as some sing (ashore) while others sink (at sea). They call it one of the deadliest shipwrecks to have taken place by Greek coasts in the last years until survivors share how coastguard forces' rope toppled the boat.

In the beginning was silence—

I guess as French streets burn and youth screams in the aftermath of yet another police murder. They call it an act of self-defence until video recordings reveal how a seventeen-year-old young man presenting no threat to two armed policemen was shot dead in the chest.

In the beginning was silence—

Anna and I wonder as we speak remember, as I later write this text, memory of a conversation through time and space, grief, hope and wordlessness, at the beginning of the summer 2023, between The Hague, Athens, Paris and Jerusalem.

As we meet for the first time, each on our side of the screen, Anna Hjälm is sitting in Jerusalem, in her office of the Swedish Theological Institute of the Church of Sweden, which she now heads, after working as the Programme Director of A World of Neighbours for three years. In between a meeting to set the Institute's budget for the coming six months, two peace demonstrations, a briefing with the Archbishop and some marmalade-making, Anna finds a moment to look back, reflect, remember out loud—so that I hear. For some two hours we do not see pass, we trace back to the beginnings—Sweden, 2015. Together, we search for the right words and attempt to weave a story she wishes she could have told along with Dirk Ficca—who is there, somehow, we know and feel as she recalls. *How to make space for the absence?* we wonder all throughout. *How to render the voice of those we miss?* Those who passed away as much as those whom we left behind—or were left by. Those with whom we cross paths—for a walk or a waltz. For a day or for life. Those whose voice still echoes, years after. Those to whom we keep on talking, at night, and sending letters. How to write not only after or about but from our grief? Wander around the holes they leave? How does one testify of the invisible? Of the unbearable, perhaps? How does one write about silence? The ineffable of violence? How does one keep their eyes open when the rest of the world looks away? How does one carry on seeing, without or after words, persists in being—there? Believing. From dusk, till dawn.

This is the recollection of our vigil.

SIT DOWN AND LISTEN, AS THE WORLD SPINS AROUND

In 2015, former Archbishop of the Church of Sweden, Antje Jackelén was just beginning her mission when she witnessed the arrival in Europe of an increasing number of asylum-seekers, notably fleeing the war in Syria. Almost all congregations of her Church, and along with them so many other religious communities, throughout the country and beyond, found themselves at the forefront of their reception and support. She quickly realized that this movement was not merely changing the Church in quantitative and operational terms—the need for more volunteers on the ground, but transforming it at a deeper level, in its intervention and thus place and meaning within civil society. "She had a quick understanding that this would create interreligious encounters and work beyond urban centres, all the way up to the outback of the North—not that it had not existed before, but this was on a grander scale," Anna explains. "Her ambition, once acknowledging the significant work undertaken by religious actors with people on the move, and for the coming coexistence and resilient society, was to find a way for the Church of Sweden to support it, not only within but possibly outside the borders of Sweden as well." It is to Anna Hjälm, who had been working in interreligious and conflict contexts in Sweden and the Middle East with the Church of Sweden for the past years, that the Archbishop turned to make her wish a reality. "And she said 'You can also have one of my strongest tools.' It was Dirk Ficca," Anna smiles.

Trained as a geographer, Anna took on her mission as a new research field. The first year thus was one of long hours of readings and field visits to meet with people working in Greece, Italy, Poland, Hungary, Germany, England and Scotland. "We followed what I call the snowball method I would use when going on fieldwork for my own research. We would find one committed and skilled individual, ask if they would agree to both meet us and help us connect with the best people they knew of in their area. And usually people know. They know exactly." And we do, indeed. Later, as Anna and I keep on thinking, try to put words on that typical feeling we get when encountering A World of Neighbours practitioners, I remember Rouddy. After spending a few days with him on Lesvos, I wrote how meeting him felt like reuniting with a lifelong friend already. "The people who join the network," Anna later writes, "somehow recognize each other. They recognize the commitment and want for a better world." We go back to seeing, I think to myself and smile. That is how it starts, before any uttered word, sometimes. Standing side by side, seeing eye to eye—at the world as it is and, perhaps, even more, as we know it can be.

Listening to tenths of workers supporting people on the move throughout Europe, Anna and Dirk attempted to answer a simple question:

> What can we do and what can we not do? We had one goal: to make the world better, specifically for those people. Now, we needed to find how. What became clear quite quickly to us both is that we wanted to focus on receiving communities, more often than not composed of people with migrant and refugee background themselves, and to work at the local level. That is when we started talking of practitioners. The people we aimed

at supporting were not the ones at the head of organizations, but those who had one foot on the ground and another in a formal position from which they could influence their community. Meeting with and listening to them all, we tried to understand what they were doing, how and why they were doing it. Only then could we start asking about their needs and the ways we, with the limited resources we had, could support them. That was the process—starting with "save the world" and then narrowing it down to, "What do we have resources to actually do and where could we put our efforts into?"

Surprised with and upset by the little acknowledgement and funding of European and national institutions for the support work of religious organizations—even more so the Muslim ones, Anna remembers being all the more impressed with the commitment, compassion and understanding of all the practitioners she and Dirk met on the way. "Not only were so many people doing excellent work, but there were so many people doing excellent work in so many different ways, at every level and hierarchical position, and in sometimes very challenging conditions." Anna keeps a special memory of their passage in Hungary, whose anti-immigration context has not ceased to deteriorate ever since. "That is one of my most heartbreaking memories, witnessing the challenges and risks undertaken by practitioners there," Anna shares.

> That resulted in us going back to Sweden and saying, "Look, this is a special case, this is a truly special situation. We need to do something here"—perhaps even more as the Church of Sweden than as A World of Neighbours. We thus came back a few months later, with the Archbishop and her closest advisor, to visit the practitioners we had met. We wanted them to know that someone—the Archbishop of the Church of Sweden, knew what was—and still is going on in Hungary, hoping that this would give them some strength and some understanding that they are not forgotten.

Some years later, in May 2023, Budapest was chosen to hold A World of Neighbours' second annual meeting.

I SEE AND HEAR YOU NOW, AND I WILL NOT FORGET

From then on, something became very clear to Anna in regards to her intimate and political situation—and thus role, responsibility and mission in such a moment.

> I don't want to come to someone, newly arrived in Sweden or Hungary, who may have been on the move for years, with the enormous amount of trauma they bear, and ask, "So how is life here?" We are not only talking of the anxiety of being sent back, but of the constant fear for one's family and friends left behind too. I can't fly in and fly out and ask a question that might turn someone's life upside down. What I can do, however, is to turn to the person working with them. While they might also experience secondary trauma, practitioners still are, most of the time, in a better position to speak. That is when it became very clear to me—we have different roles here. Mine is to listen to the practitioners. There is this famous line about the one who comes with empty hands and thus can help another to carry—sometimes, being a witness is as important.

Reflecting on our conversation, later on, Anna remembered her encounter, in 1995, with a survivor of the siege of Leningrad, during the Second World War. Fifty years later, as Sarajevo was under siege, she had asked him about his thoughts.

> He told me there was one major difference between those trapped in Leningrad in the first years of the 1940s and those suffering in Sarajevo as we were speaking. He said, "They know we know. They can call and hear news. They know we, on the outside, know they are in there. In Leningrad, we did not know. We thought maybe those on the 'outside' had forgotten all about us. Or maybe thought we were all dead. Or, we thought, maybe they were all dead. . . . But in Sarajevo they know, that they are not forgotten." There is a power in being a witness, I think. In insuring that someone, left in a horrible situation, in despair, knows they are not forgotten—that another knows. Maybe that is also what we do in a vigil? We sit together, not because it changes anything—the one we lost is still lost to us—but because at least we pay respect to a life lived, a memory kept, a suffering lived through. And because we together witness not only the loss but the remembrance.

And it may be just that, I tell Anna in a smile—what we attempt, what we are meant to do, sometimes. As simple and obvious as it may sound, such a humble and lucid position is rare—even more so in the humanitarian-capitalist tradition of the "Western saviour," who is there to help, solve, do—while more often than not standing from a systemic position of oppression. How do we make sense of this, I wonder, us whom hold the power-to-help insofar as we hold the power-to-harm in the first place? How do we think and act, still? How to undo and allow? It may begin by sitting down. Dare to stay quiet and listen—to languages we do not know of, the unspoken.

"Sometimes the only thing that can be done is to be silent," Anna goes on,

> because there is either nothing you can say or no word able to change anything in the moment. And I think, maybe, or I am sure, actually, that faith-based organizations, or people of faith, are better equipped for that—just because we are, in a sense, better trained in collective silence. We do it together, in prayer or in other sorts of religious practices and moments. Many of us, working within churches or religious communities, are those towards whom people turn when there are no more words—when you have lost the relative, when you're grieving or when you're just giving up.

I remember Brussels, AWoN's first annual meeting, as Anna speaks. I tell her how I felt, then, that the most important had not been so much in all our talking, planning, organizing as much as in our lying in the grass, quiet, looking at the sky and climbing trees. That may be what Dirk was envisioning, we reflect, when he would repeat—"our goal is people." Going back to the ground and bodies as an horizon, a political strategy—this may be another originality of A World of Neighbours. Starting with and growing through collective action and encounters, without waiting for authorizations, to achieve a common goal—making the world more breathable.

LAMPEDUSA, LESVOS, GAZA—BORDERLINES

Anna grew up in the remote areas of northern Sweden. She studied geography in one of the northernmost universities, close to the polar circle periphery—a location she cherishes to this day as "both a playground for invention, due to the lack of governmental control and responsibility, in some sense, but also as a place attracting little attention and public eye"— realm of the invisible, that is. Where one can both exist—or be erased.

> That is what I recognized in Greece, and then in so many other locations. Asylum-seekers, refugees and migrants are always geographically marginalized, meaning pushed aside—out of sight, out of mind, into the periphery of the country. In Greece,

of course, the islands are the periphery, but the eastern part of continental Greece as well, in Thessaloniki and its surroundings, for example, where we went. We saw the same in Germany, when we visited a Coptic Orthodox monk who ran a refugee centre in some countryside that used to be a training camp for the army. This, which had been purposefully settled in a place where there is no community, was then chosen to be turned into a refugee camp. A few weeks back, listening to the Swedish news, I heard that some idea from the government was to open detention centres for refugees and migrants in the far north. It again is this systematic geographic pushing aside, moving of refugees and migrants into the periphery. This can both be the geographic periphery at the scale of the country or out of the city centres, into those areas where no one from the majority community ever has to go. Seeing it through my geographical glasses, it appears as a major challenge, and something you need words for to understand, perceive. Gaza is the obvious example, where no one can ever go, more or less, that is completely cut off from all sorts of interaction. I've been here so many years, I've never been able to go to Gaza. One of my colleagues, who is a Palestinian, was in Gaza in 2014 the last time—and she has family there! It is almost impossible to enter. Refugee camps are in the outskirts of the cities, behind walls or beyond the main roads, so that no one ever has to see the misery that's going on there—apart from the many, many people who have been living there for generations.

How to account for the unseeable (and yet so *seeable*)? I wonder out loud. The life that is—captured, harassed, forb(h)idden behind the wires and walls of the camps of Gaza, Lesvos, Lampedusa. The nameless bodies on the oblivion of which our proud and loud *democracies* are built. I remember Arendt, to whom I so often go back to—since Athens. Her tragedy of those who live in the margins, with no papers nor place, no rights nor state, that is—"only humans," bare life, shadows and absences.

"Unfortunately, I think that the next step in that process," Anna goes on,

starts when well-established communities themselves, who see, have seen, who know, do not—cannot speak up, because of the risk of some kind of double-punishment. Some Muslim communities in Eastern Europe, for example, who are indigenous to those countries, are part of the society, may not engage in direct support of people on the move because that would increase their own visibility and put them at risk of attacks from the right. That is very scary in a democratic society, when people or groups start self-moderating in such ways.

The genius of modern states, if we think with scholars such as Michel Foucault, lies just there, indeed, in their ability to incorporate violence so that individual's self-discipline, regardless of the laws—which, meanwhile, still increase in repressive intensity.[1] Their power resides in our somatic knowledge of the limit, our inherited memory and trauma of transgression, punishment and stigma. Hence the necessity of the return to embodied collective action and healing, micropolitics of breach-opening. For what do we expect, then? I ask Anna, what are we waiting for? The walls to get higher, the curfews to multiply? The state-of-emergency to last so long that it becomes normal—as has been the case in so many countries those past years?

> I think that's a very valid question. What do we think will change? What do we think or even expect our politicians will do? Where are we going with this? And if we're not going anywhere with it, will we just keep on closing the gates and pretending these people do not exist? It's easy to give up to that idea of the impossible, that feeling of powerlessness. Maybe that is also part of the work and strength of A World of Neighbours, in the connection it creates and nurtures between practitioners, to be, once again, a reminder. For that narrative is just not true. It is not true that we do nothing. The combination of destructive narratives asserting both "we should not put so much efforts into supporting people on the move" and "no one does anything about the situation of people on the move" is wrong and harmful. We need to let people know that—because it gives hope! The civil society and faith-based organizations give hope!

Anna insists before sharing a few last thoughts.

ON HANDS AND POEMS—A SILENT FINAL DANCE

"I am also much of a word person," Anna says as she shows me the many notes she has written down all around her desk.

> Those are just single phrases, a few words, sometimes, that, for some reason, speak to me and to which I feel the need to think more about or write on. One of them I particularly would go

---

1. See, e.g., Foucault, *Discipline and Punish*.

back to with A World of Neighbours is a spoken word poem by Palestinian-American artist and activist Suheir Hammad, do you know her? One of her pieces was such a big help when I felt like this was too big, thinking, "We are too few, this network is amazing but we would need to be four thousands more." In those moments, the absolute commitment she expresses in this poem was a beautiful reminder. The first lines read:

I will not
dance to your war
drum.
I will not dance to your drummed up war.[2]

What it means, to me, is that resistance starts in saying, "No, I will not stand, I will not accept your narrative—of xenophobia or fear." It also points out and reminds us that some conflicts are not real, some are "made to be" by those seeking a fragmented society. I constantly come back to that—what we can do is to share other stories. We have seen other things. We've heard each other. We have met people who told us about the work that they do, the travels they have made to come to Europe. The least of our responsibilities, then, is to commit to not giving up—to commit to not being part of dancing to the war drums.

"This is not a crisis to handle. This is human life. Once acknowledging this, you shift from a crisis management narrative to a coexistence narrative or maybe even just human narratives." This shift in perspective, this emancipation from the far-right turned hegemonic narrative of "migrants" envisioned a fantasized mass—faceless, nameless, useless, I remember vividly, from my first days in Athens. Coming back from the Bosnian border, where she had taken part in a Walk of Shame organized by Rikko Voorberg for the first time,[3] a fellow Norwegian practitioner, Signe Myklebust, had shared with me how she had been struck at "how different people were, from one another." There had come the dreamer, the racing cars lover, that woman who, devastated after a pushback, had slowly gotten back on her feet, that family looking after a dog so kindly—as many faces and stories drawing lives and beings. "Not knowing any of

---

2. Hammad, "What I Will."

3. Rikko Voorberg reflects on the "Walk of Shame" in his chapter in this book. More information can be found at https://walk-of-shame.eu.

them makes you think of them as a group—'migrants,'" Signe had concluded, "but people are different."

But migrants are people.

"This is not a crisis that will pass," Anna gently smiles.

> This is being human. There are no lonely worlds. You just happen to see them now. And I think that, in this sense, belief constitutes a somewhat disruptive activity. Part of what we believe, indeed, or part of being a religious person, is actually accepting that I am not in full control. That can be scary, of course, but it can also be so empowering, saying, "Look, no, I do not know the end of this." I enter this situation, not knowing if I have the right tools, if I will find the right words or even if I can change anything. I do, however, believe that a different world, a different situation, is not only possible but doable. We are humans, these are my hands—and I will tear them into change if I can.

Following A World of Neighbours' first annual meeting in Brussels, in May 2022, a few of us practitioners joined Rikko on another Walk of Shame to the northern France refugee camps of Dunkirk and Calais. Coming back, I wrote a poem which I remember as I close this chapter and, once again, from afar, thank Anna—for her vision, her time, her reflections. For allowing me to witness and relate her silent conversation with Dirk Ficca.

AND THE END OF THE WORD

I am exhausted. Can feel it my eyes every one of my move my brain in slow motion—still I write. Nothing. I do not want to tell—or I can't. There are so many waves there is so little space within and still I can't. And still there is no word. To say. And I was wondering what was this void beyond what will be left survive in the silence after my apocalypse when there is no word else

But us.
But us.
But.
I sat there and listened
To the wind
Sunflower seeds
To the sea that will sink
To the last daisy
Strawberries

To the son who came first
Who stood up on his head
To the sun of our death
She put ice in my hand
And we hugged and we laughed did not know each other
And he prayed to some God
And we were holding hands
And I was standing there
Outside of language
And we danced, too
I guess
For when the word will end
When there is no word else
Our bodies will remain
Our soul in the forest
For when it is time to leave
The water deep and still
You may remember us
And the sunflower seeds
And repeat in your head your mouth full of tears—yet
They were there
We were here
There.
We
.

BIBLIOGRAPHY

Foucault, Michel. *Discipline and Punish: The Birth of the Prison.* Translated by Alan Sheridan. New York: Vintage, 1977.

Hammad, Suheir. "What I Will." *TED* (blog), December 8, 2010. https://blog.ted.com/text-of-what-i-will-by-suheir-hammad.

Part II

The Call

8

Arriving with Empty Hands

A Theological Case for a Post-Help Praxis

RIKKO VOORBERG

If you have come here to help me you are wasting your time, but if you have come because your liberation is bound up with mine, then let us work together.

—LILLA WATSON, INDIGENOUS AUSTRALIAN

THIS QUOTE HAS BEEN HAUNTING me ever since I read it.[1] I am a Dutch theologian and initiator of artistic and activist initiatives. In 2019, I was asked to join a discussion on the topic of activism and help for refugees. A fierce debate was going on between those that wanted to help as much as they could and others who were fighting for political change. The focus was the infamous Camp Moria, the "Human Rights Graveyard" as the graffiti reads on the concrete wall in front of the camp.

---

1. This is an edited version of a lecture delivered at a conference of the European Academy of Religion in Bologna in June 2022.

Camp Moria, the "Human Rights Graveyard." Photo: Rouddy Kimpioka.

Is it still ethical to keep handing out food and water and the occasional paracetamol when you cannot protest against the hellhole this camp has become, out of fear that you will be thrown out of the camp? Just before the discussion started, a friend gave me that quote by Lilla Watson. Can I listen to this quote, can I make this first step? And how should we approach this appeal? Strategically, spiritually, or personally? I can include beneficiaries of my intended "help" into the board of my organization, but will that do? And what do the spiritual sources of the great religions, for example, tell us about helping and receiving? Wasn't Abraham a migrant himself, a stranger in a strange land? How come most religious organizations identify with the "helpers," who are trying to follow their religious motivation by reaching out to those in need, instead of seeing the actual people in need as their most probable source of spiritual awakening? Prophets are usually outcasts, not leaders of help organizations.

WHY ACADEMICS SHOULD BE ACTIVISTS TOO

In this chapter, I will make a case for a post-helping praxis and as a sidenote: the power and maybe even the necessity of a certain kind of activism for the researcher and academic. That may sound a bit bold, but keep reading and see if you agree. As some sort of public theologian with a master's degree in political theology, based in the very secular city of

Amsterdam, I organized all kinds of artistic and activistic interventions in the public square. It was a personal existential search for the truth and the power of the Christian values that I was born and raised with, and that I studied for all those years at the Theological University. Would these values count for anything in a post-Christendom society? The theatrical and activist initiatives received both high praise and firm critique, from religious as well as secular voices, nationally and internationally. All of these initiatives were rooted in indignation and curiosity; indignation about our common inability to be human together and a curiosity to what would happen if we already started to embody the things we hope for, even if it was only symbolically. Could another world be possible and can we make the idea of "hope" tangible? Supposedly, Augustin says, "Hope has two beautiful daughters: Anger and Courage. Anger at the way things are, and Courage to see that they do not remain as they are."

Anger is a difficult emotion to handle, but it's the only one of the four basic emotions (fear, sadness, happiness, and anger) that tries to make a change. Often in destructive ways, but that doesn't have to be the case. Mother Hope can teach Anger to be constructive, and her sister, Courage, can help us to be bold enough to try to do it.

So, in 2012, together with church people and anarchists, we squatted a church in order to host 120 undocumented people that were protesting outside in the middle of winter against government regulations. And together with fellow artists, we turned a nasty protest against mosques in the Netherlands into an involuntary sponsor event for those same mosques. It was a simple recipe; a fascist group announced that they would make a Ramadan-BBQ-tour. They planned to have barbeques with pork in front of the mosques to protest the existence of these places of worship in the Netherlands. We asked everybody in the Netherlands to donate a certain amount of money per protester that turned up, or per piece of meat on the barbecue. The bigger the barbecue would be, the more money would go to that particular mosque. The part of this action I liked the most was delivering the cheque to each of the targeted mosques. We were welcomed with great gratitude. It wasn't the money; it was the feeling of standing together as Dutch people from different faiths against hate and Islamophobia. One of the mosques, we couldn't reach by phone or email to make an appointment. So we just walked in, took our shoes off and went down the corridors and up staircases until we found a group at the back of the building. One person came out to send us away, probably thinking we were tourists. After we told them about our initiative, they invited us in for tea and sweets. We had to tell them about the action, from start to finish, because they had missed all the media upheaval! We had a good laugh together.

At one of the targeted mosques. Personal photograph.

Early in 2015 three of my friends and I visited Lesbos. We had heard about refugees arriving there—scores of people and organizations followed. We organized caravans of cars to Brussels, the Hague and even Athens, offering our government to help them to relocate refugees from the dark, isolated camps in the south of Europe to the Netherlands in order to finish their asylum procedures in more humane circumstances. Can this be called a form of theology? I firmly believe it can, as long as you do this praxis as a form of research. I will explain in more detail later, but it means that this "doing" is not the outcome of your (theological or humanitarian) thinking, but putting yourself in the situation to slowly come to understand by perceiving, physically, emotionally, mentally, and spiritually—to learn from this immersion what it is that faith is about. This is arguably how initiatives such as these are an example of "doing theology."

THE PROBLEM OF HELPING

In 2020, five years after the first NGOs and grassroot organizations came to the island of Lesbos to help out, we took some time to reflect on the help that was given. One of the painful conclusions was that help often doesn't, in fact, help. That helping a person in need, especially regarding refugees at the borders of Europe, often serves the needs of the helper. That helping was often, as the saying goes, "oiling the wheels of injustice." We brought tents and food to refugees who were asking for freedom, we were protesting in our government cities for those who felt completely forgotten in the no man's land far away from these cities of power. Did we listen, did *I* truly listen?

Bosnia, 2020. A shivering and exhausted Afghan refugee is making a fire in the demolished camp near the border of Croatia. He has just been pushed back by European funded militia. He offers us a cup of tea and tells us the story of how he tried to cross into Croatia, how he was robbed by the police, beaten, and returned without his jacket in the midst of the Balkan winter. But the worst thing was, he told us while pouring the tea, the moments when volunteers handed out food but did not look at him while doing so. "Sometimes I want to throw it back at them. I'd rather go hungry than receive food in this way." It was a poignant illustration of the dire need to be *seen as a human being*. The whole concept of helping is problematic, also from a theological perspective.

DEHUMANIZATION

The label for the effect of European migration policies on people on the move (refugees and migrants) is "dehumanization." The question has to be how *re*-humanization can be achieved. Not the re-humanization of people, but more precisely: the re-humanization of connections between European residents and people on the move. Moments of re-humanization happened when volunteers, helpers, and activists emptied their hands, took time off from their duties to simply sit by the fire, accept a cup of tea or some food, and spend time together. The act of doing nothing, the reversal of roles from helper to receiver, proved over and over to be a key.

Another key element in re-humanization was the conversation about the shame Europeans felt when they were confronted with the effect of migration policies. A key factor in rehumanization and restoring relationships, we realised, was the conscious decision to admit the feeling of shame, and openly talk about it to peers and to victims. It feels stupid but to tell victims of European borders that you are ashamed about your government acting in such a way on your behalf, proves more often than not to be helpful. It's the victim that sometimes starts to believe that he or she is crazy to feel all this anger, frustration and sadness. Opening up about this shame sometimes helps to confirm the feeling of the victims that they are treated unfairly. In relationships between friends or lovers, feelings of shame are often denied; we rather blame someone else than to admit that we failed, or we rather do all kinds of sweet things to make up for things we didn't even dare to admit to the other. It's true that shame can cause people to isolate themselves, but that doesn't mean we should avoid the feeling altogether. Shame can be the emotion that fits the situation and then you better open up about it—by doing so relationships can be restored, and so can the feeling of being human.

We developed an initiative called the Walk of Shame, inviting Europeans to join us to the borders of Europe with nothing but empty hands and an open heart. To spend time with people on the move, share whenever appropriate how ashamed we were about the dehumanizing policies of our governments, and eat and drink together if we would be welcomed in as guests. It may sound counterintuitive, but the testimonies of refugees and Europeans prove over and over again how life-changing and healing this form of "not-helping" can be.

A POST-HELP PRAXIS

The Jesuit Refugee Service, a Catholic international organization, has banned the idea of help from their mission statements. They write: "JRS seeks to accompany, serve, and advocate the cause of refugees and other forcibly displaced people, that they may heal, learn and determine their own future."[2] The director of the Jesuit Refugee Service puts it this way: "We try to place special emphasis on being with and doing with, rather than doing for. We want our presence among refugees to be one of sharing with them, of accompaniment, of walking together along the same path."[3] It is this concept we are exploring with A World of Neighbours too.

The postmodern tradition of Radical Theology with people like John Caputo and Peter Rollins is theologically helpful in this regard.[4] It critiques the tradition of God as the metaphysical problem-solver. That particular God is dead, they argue, echoing the Nietzschean declaration.

---

2. https://jrs.net.

3. Smolich, "Accompaniment and Welcome."

4. For example, see Rollins, *Fidelity of Betrayal*; *Idolatry of God*; Caputo, *Weakness of God*; *What Would Jesus Deconstruct*.

They point out that God in Jesus joined our earthly lives, shared suffering and death—and rose from this death only to leave this earth shortly after. Theology and church, mosque and synagogue shouldn't line up with CEOs and gurus, promising to remove the pain. The world is in need of people who can sit with the pain and stay there as long as necessary. Martin Luther said that theology and faith can be summed up by three words: meditation, prayer, and wrestling, *meditatio, oratio* and *tentatio*.[5] Real theology is a painful encounter with shortcomings, it's the desperation of the human condition—in all with which we turn to God and God turns to us—to be in this together. The vision is not a world of light, but a world in which light is shed on the painful things hiding in the dark. That's not a solution, but it can help.

IT'S NOT ABOUT RESULTS

On February 15, 1966, Jim Forest, theologian and peace activist, writes a desperate letter to his friend, the noted mystic Thomas Merton. Opposition to the war in Vietnam is growing, but the American effort is becoming grimmer. Forest writes:

> What can we do? What can we undertake that we have not already done? I don't want to sound desperate. I haven't given up on this work of ours yet. But I really feel like an ant climbing a cliff, and even worse, because in the distance the roar of an avalanche seems to sound. There is no exit, so I don't bother to look for one.[6]

Thomas Merton writes in reply:

> Do not make yourself dependent on the hope of results. When you are doing the kind of work you have taken on, essentially apostolic work, you may have to face the fact that your work will be seemingly worthless and may even produce no results at all, or even results contrary to what you expect. As you get used to this idea, you begin to focus more and more, not on the results, but on the value, the accuracy, the truth of the work itself. And there too a great deal has to be gone through, as gradually you struggle less and less for an idea and more and more for specific people. The range tends to narrow down, but it gets much more

---

5. See Luther, "Preface to the Wittenberg Edition."
6. For the correspondence, see Forest, "Thomas Merton's Letter."

real. In the end, as you yourself mention in passing, it is the reality of personal relationships that saves everything.[7]

Helping doesn't necessarily require personal relationships, but rehumanization does. And there's a key to be found in theology, at least I found it in Christian theology. It has to do with suffering, to find the courage, the hope, and the anger to immerse yourself into the darkness, to not be afraid of "death" in whatever form it comes. To find life in "hell"—whether it's the hell of Moria, Bosnia, or the one that your neighbour is living in. It's the sharing and the caring, whatever the outcome might be. That's another way of having faith. The previous Archbishop of Canterbury, Rowan Williams, says the following about the church (and he could have said it about all religious and faith institutes): "The Church exists to connect people at the level of their hunger for a new world."[8] The main question in the church should not be whether you are safe in the hands of God, it's whether God (or goodness) is safe in your hands. This is a turning upside-down of any consolatory version of faith—and rightly so, I would say.

It is important to note, however, that this may sound a little bit heroic, or tough. But it absolutely isn't, at least it doesn't feel that way. It's difficult, emotional, and often puts you in awkward situations. Every time I show up with a group from the Walk of Shame at some squatted building or walk up to people at some random bus-stop in Bosnia or Serbia, I don't have a clue what to say. "Hi, I'm Rikko, how are you?" It's strange, because the more usual encounters have a specific purpose: journalists who want a story, helpers with food or clothes to share, police who want to check on people or chase them away. Now it's just you, for no other reason than making a connection, as if you were neighbours. It's a giant leap across the invisible gap between permanent residents and people on the move, the irregular and regular, those perceived as "legal" and those perceived to be "illegal." How strange it is to show up, as someone with papers and wealth, maybe invited in maybe not. Showing up "empty handed" is a strange thing to do, even at a friend's dinner party. Even more so in this situation. But it does bring change. The only thing people on the move really need is a legal place to be, or safe ways to travel. If they would have that, they wouldn't need my water, food, or clothes. The only thing these people really need, I can't give to them. Because the

---

7. See, again, Forest, "Thomas Merton's Letter."
8. Williams, *Being Christian*, 34.

politicians that rule in my name, are not able or willing to treat people on the move humanely. Helpless is what we are, and we need to admit it and not cover it up with tokens of help. We arrive with some sort of helplessness, sharing beautiful moments of connection by small bonfires in forests and deserted factories that are full of people from all around the world. We leave with helplessness again, only staying in touch by social media. But I have to learn to trust these men, women, and children from Afghanistan, Iraq, Eritrea, Syria, Turkey, and so many other places when they tell me how important these moments of connections are, that these are true re-humanizing moments.

I would like to conclude with this: If academics, researchers, activists, and journalists are looking for truth, as they should, then their research has to be rooted in more than words, it has to form personal relationships with those in need, it has to be about the doing itself—not as a result of research but *as* research. Faith without works is dead, the Apostle James says. Well, maybe the same can be said of academics and maybe every vision, plan, scheme, and concept. Let justice be the call that draws us out from our safe spaces into uncharted territory, into a place of reconciliation and cooperation. A post-help praxis is in need of courageous people who dare to empty their hands and open their hearts and spend time with those who suffer.

BIBLIOGRAPHY

Caputo, John D. *The Weakness of God*. Bloomington: Indiana University Press, 2013.

———. *What Would Jesus Deconstruct: The Good News of Postmodernism for the Church*. Grand Rapids: Baker Academic, 2007.

Forest, Jim. "Thomas Merton's Letter to a Young Activist." *Jim and Nancy Forest* (blog), October 18, 2014. https://jimandnancyforest.com/2014/10/mertons-letter-to-a-young-activist.

Luther, Martin. "Preface to the Wittenberg Edition of Luther's German Writings (1539)." In *Martin Luther's Basic Theological Writings*, edited by Timothy F. Lull and William R. Russell, 39–42. Minneapolis: Augsburg Fortress, 2012.

Rollins, Peter. *The Fidelity of Betrayal: Towards a Church Beyond Belief*. Brewster, MA: Paraclete, 2008.

———. *The Idolatry of God: Breaking Our Addiction to Certainty and Satisfaction*. Brentwood, TN: Howard, 2013.

Smolich, Thomas H. "Accompaniment and Welcome: The Jesuit Refugee Service and its Pastoral Role." *Society of Jesus*, n.d. http://www.sjweb.info/documents/cis/pdfenglish/199909006en.pdf.

Williams, Rowan. *Being Christian: Baptism, Bible, Eucharist, Prayer*. London: SPCK, 2014.

9

Finding One's Place at a Busy Intersection

The Methodology of the A World of Neighbours Practitioners' Network

Ryszard Bobrowicz

In January 2020, the first phase of the A World of Neighbours (AWoN) project was coming to an end. After 2 years of intense site visits, including meetings with 150 actors in 11 countries and 5 working groups, the project organized a pre-summit in Malmö, gathering all kinds of stakeholders in one place—from refugees to decision-makers, from practitioners to policymakers, from scholars to church-leaders. The goal was clear—to find the best path forward for the project, that could provide lasting improvements for people on the move and those supporting them—both at the day-to-day and structural levels.

At the time, three paths emerged that sought "to strengthen and envision the work of receiving communities—with refugees and migrants and to enhance the interreligious and civil society infrastructure of Europe in service to the journeys and aspirations of 'people on the move.'"[1] A Swedish "living laboratory" was supposed to find new ways of coming together at the local level, especially in terms of inter-faith praxis. The practitioners' network was supposed to support those that are

---

1. AWoN Practitioners' Network Overview (internal document).

at the intersection between people on the move and all other stakeholders. The planned 2022 summit was supposed to make a global statement and encourage stakeholders at all levels to learn from the lessons of post-2015 work and the other two sub-projects.

Little did we know that just three months after the summit, we would have to radically adapt our plans due to the COVID-19 pandemic. And yet, the call was clear—the virus did not magically suspend all other challenges. It did not provide safe homes for people on the borders. It did not create safe conditions for those seeking asylum. It did not make the waters calm for those fighting for a better life. It did not decrease the burden for those working with accompaniment or social cohesion. Quite the opposite, it redirected the attention, and often also funding, from people on the move, making their situation even more dire and the job of practitioners even harder.

Thus, adapting to the situation, AWoN has continued the project and doubled down on the idea of a practitioners' network. While our colleagues took the initiative in the other two sub-paths (living laboratory and the summit), together with Dirk Ficca we have developed a methodology for the practitioners' network. This chapter will describe its different aspects: from the reasons for the network, through its structure, the process of recruitment and initiation into the network, to its evolving outcomes.[2] In other words, the chapter will show how we tried to find a comfortable space for practitioners in the middle of a busy intersection—the place where migration practitioners find themselves, as grass-root workers directly working with people on the move and receiving communities, mediating between them and all other stakeholders.

THE REASONS

In the initial mapping of stakeholders in the refugee relief, AWoN distinguished five key stakeholder groups: people on the move, receiving community, media, policy- and decision-makers, as well as practitioners (see figure 1).

---

2. It must be noted that the methodology described below considers primarily the initial phase of the network. Since then, it transformed into a standalone organization run completely by the practitioners themselves, who adapted the process to their needs. In this way, the methodology remains dynamic. The following description will provide insights into how it all started.

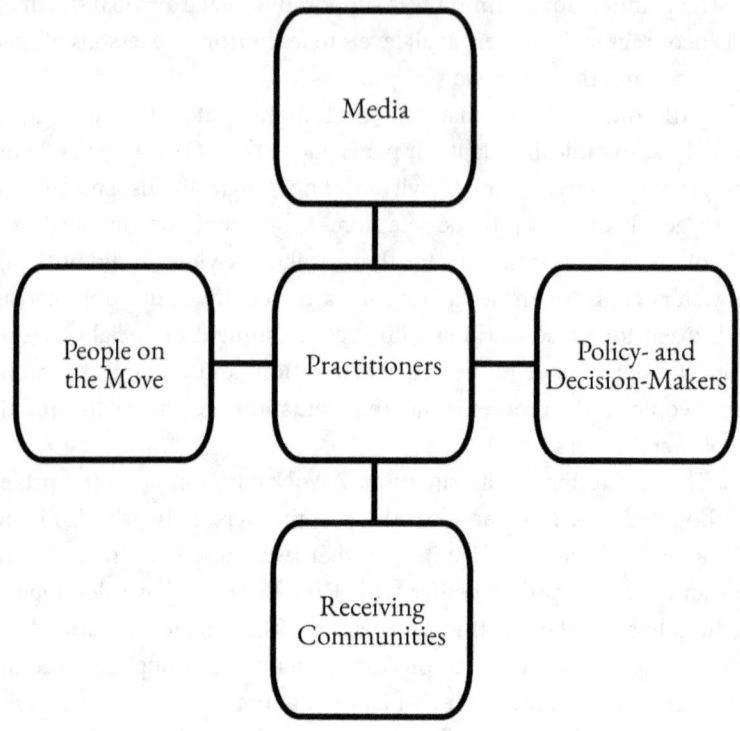

Figure 1: Key Actors

At the core of AWoN's vision is a change that "rests in the transformational character of the living, humanizing and mutually-transforming encounter with, and accompaniment of, 'people on the move.'"[3] Practitioners are at the centre of such encounters, as they have one foot on the ground, working with people on the move on an everyday basis, and one in the local, regional, national, and/or international processes taking place in the host countries. They often play the mediating role between all other stakeholders in the migration process, on top of taking care of their primary tasks.

And yet, they also struggle significantly with issues such as severe resource limitations, lack of know-how and structural support, emotional

---

3. AWoN (internal notes).

distress, compassion fatigue, and burnout.[4] They work in increasingly hostile environments that often vilify them and criminalize their efforts.[5] Their collaborative opportunities are also often limited by the need for exchanges at the leadership level, rather than on the grounds.

We experienced this firsthand during the various meetings with practitioners—while they poured their hearts into their work on an everyday basis, the piling challenges were making them extremely tired and frustrated. They sacrificed their own well-being to make sure that others have it. And that had its costs. Since then, some of the people we have met no longer work with people on the move. Not because they no longer care about them, but because they could no longer sustain the level of engagement required by the work.

Thus, the idea for the practitioners' network was developed to mitigate these challenges. By directly connecting practitioners from different organizations, countries, contexts, profiles, and faiths in agreement with their institutional contexts, we hoped to create a community of practice that could more efficiently share resources and know-how, provide them with a stronger position and voice, and support each other emotionally and structurally, decreasing the risks of compassion fatigue and burnout. It would also create a space for developing new models of inter-faith collaborations and encounters through inter-faith praxis rather than dialogue. The four key fundamentals in developing the idea for the network were:

- Employing an asset-based approach, drawing on the goodwill and aspirations of people, communities, existing models, and structures, as its *raison d'être* and organizing trajectory.

- Engaging in capacity-building activities in support of a movement as it already exists and is evolving, and not in creating new institutional and formal structures.

- Nurturing a social infrastructure, by identifying, enlisting, and mobilizing the people who share the vision, and are committed to the work: namely, in a network of relationships and collaboration among refugees, migrants, receiving communities, grassroots

---

4. García-Carmona et al., *Migration to the EU*; Brendel et al., "Impact of Work-Related Barriers"; Mavratza et al. "Professional Quality of Life."

5. Hussein et al., "Experiences of Migrant Social Work"; Canning, "Managing Expectations"; Puzzo et al., "Impact of Cultural Intelligence."

120　PART II │ THE CALL

practitioners, institutional leaders, and well-placed champions of the movement.

- Enlisting a cadre of network practitioners committed to building, cultivating, and sustaining a "community of practice" among grassroots practitioners.[6]

STRUCTURE

One of the key assumptions in the development of the network was to limit its structural elements to a minimum. Instead, the network was supposed to utilize as much of the existing resources and structures as possible, providing only coordination and support where lacking. At the same time, it was important to bring to the table all important stakeholders.

Figure 2 shows the initial vision for the network. The most central element of the network was constituted by sixty "network practitioners," carefully selected practitioners who would devote approximately one day per week to the network, working on behalf of the broader network of practitioners and receiving communities as well as institutional partners. They would be supported, trained, and equipped with collaboration tools by the small central office, which would play primarily a coordinating role. The network practitioners would collaborate with other stakeholder representatives, including the researchers, cultural institutions, and affiliates from countries not included in the initial twenty-two.

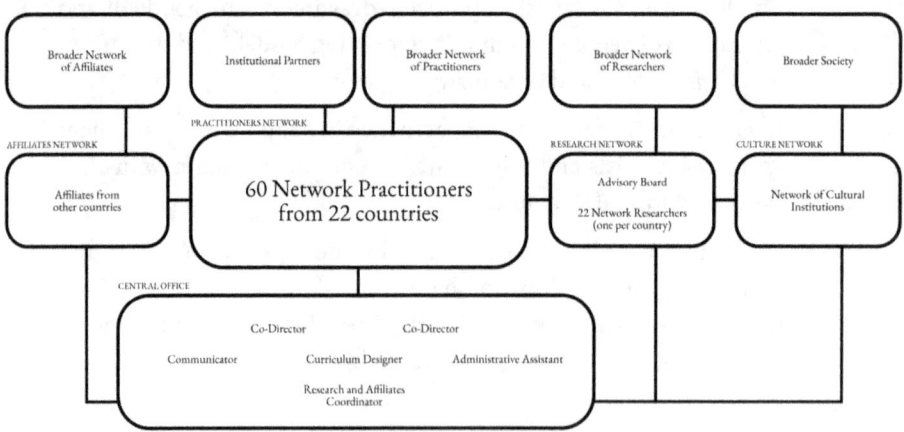

Figure 2: Initial vision for the network's structure

6. AWoN (internal notes).

Although since then the network evolved into a standalone organization and is structured slightly differently (the central office consists of a small working team, supported by an executive board), the practitioners remain in the centre and collaborate with the team of researchers and affiliates. The central office is also now run completely by practitioners, who are supported by experts on the advisory board.

RECRUITMENT

Recruitment was the first step in establishing the network. When looking for network practitioners, we attempted to spread them in terms of competencies, geography, work profile (especially, whether practitioners work directly with accompaniment or indirectly with social cohesion), migration background, gender, and faith tradition to ensure adequate diversity within the network. Out of the sixty network practitioners, we hoped that forty would be supported by their organizations, while twenty would receive funding from us.

As the network would have a high trust component, we decided to split the recruitment into cohorts of ten, to establish smaller initial communities that could get to know each other much better. We also decided to not open the call, but instead begin with an application by invitations only, relying on the broader network established in the previous phase of the project, and grow the practitioners' network through a snowball effect.

After the invitation and positive response from the practitioner (and, if supported by them, the practitioner's organization), they were invited to prepare a formal application, consisting of a short survey on them and their professional career, as well as a letter of interest. This was followed by an online interview and consultations with selected references.

While the above procedure might seem close to a regular job application, the letters we received and the interviews we conducted were nothing like them. Every single time an individual practitioner provided us with a glimpse into their personal worlds—the individual paths that led them to this line of work, the joys and sorrows of people they met, the challenges faced by them, the individual approaches the practitioners extended to them, the innovative solutions they came up with. As interviewers, we were greatly enriched by these conversations, that will stay with us for the rest of our lives.

If the needs of the practitioner and the network aligned, they were invited to commit to becoming a network practitioner. The initial commitment was for three months (an exploratory agreement), the duration of the exploration period, during which they could see whether they could benefit from the network and benefit the network in return. If, after the initial commitment they were still interested, they would be invited to commit to a long-term collaboration (a partnership agreement).

The commitment to the network consisted of three main elements: offering an equivalent of eight hours or one day a week to the network, attending the annual gathering of the network, and helping to set the agenda for the European Summit. The term "equivalent" was crucial in the consideration of the practitioner's involvement. It was not supposed to add to their work, but rather make them consider how their everyday work could align with the network's goals.

THE EXPLORATION PROCESS

The three-month exploration process was designed to create a small, cohesive, initial community for the practitioners to later engage with other cohorts. It was supposed to provide a strong support network, create a space for reflection on different aspects of their practice, provide them with tools for operating in the network, and create stronger bonds between the individual practitioners included in each cohort.

The exploration process was designed based on two main pedagogical approaches: a community of practice and collaborative learning.[7] A community of practice is, in short, a group of people with shared practical interests who meet regularly to reflect together on their challenges and insights. Practitioners, as the term suggests, are engaged in the common practice but do not always have time and space to reflect upon it and exchange experiences with others. While some form of communities of practice existed for centuries, they received significant theoretical interest in the field of pedagogics recently, which allowed us to build on their best practices, especially how to structure them and how to sustain them long-term.[8] The goal was for the communities of practice to remain in

---

7. At this stage, we received very helpful advice from the Chicago-based Goldin Institute, for which we are extremely grateful.

8. For more, see, e.g., Hoadley, "What Is a Community of Practice?"; Li et al., "Evolution of Wenger's Concept"; Palincsar et al., "Designing a Community of Practice."

place, although with less intensity (e.g., a meeting once a month) after the exploration process too.

Collaborative learning turns the regular teaching model on its head. Instead of a single teacher/trainer providing instruction for the other students, every participant takes up the role of a teacher and student at the same time. As Cornell University's Center for Teaching Innovation describes it:

> Collaborative learning can occur peer-to-peer or in larger groups. Peer learning, or peer instruction, is a type of collaborative learning that involves students working in pairs or small groups to discuss concepts or find solutions to problems. Similar to the idea that two or three heads are better than one, educational researchers have found that through peer instruction, students teach each other by addressing misunderstandings and clarifying misconceptions.[9]

This works especially well for groups with larger professional experience, as they already possess sizeable knowledge in their respective field of practice.

The exploration process consisted of three elements, repeated weekly, aimed to take approximately four hours per week: materials for self-paced reflection (one hour), weekly group meetings (two hours), and one-on-one meetings (one hour). All activities took place online, with the use of Zoom. Each of the thirteen weeks of the explorative process was devoted to a different topic:

Week 1: Introduction

Week 2: Personal Assessment

Week 3: What is Your Context?

Week 4: Assessing Current Realities

Week 5: Sphere of Influence

Week 6: Thinking Through Narratives

Week 7: Practitioner's Profile

Week 8: Well-Being & Self-Care

Week 9: Scope of Work

Week 10: Building Collaboration

---

9. Center for Teaching Innovation, "Collaborative Learning."

Week 11: Communication Strategy

Week 12: Personal Video

Week 13: Evaluation

A week before the meeting, the practitioners received a dossier which provided some reflection materials for the week's topic, most often followed by a short, written reflection exercise. They also received information on one-on-one pairings for the week. The practitioners were asked to reach out to their pair and schedule a one-hour call during which they were supposed to find one skill, idea, or resource they could benefit from each other and discuss the reflection exercise.

The two-hour group meetings were, after the first two sessions, run by a different practitioner each week until evaluation. They started with a short reflection by the leading practitioner, followed by a brief check-in on the last week's practice by each of the participants. This was followed by a pair exercise, plenary reporting, and a group exercise on the week's theme before concluding remarks were drawn. A script was prepared to provide structure to the meetings, support the leading practitioner, and keep meetings within strict time limits. External guests were invited from time to time to provide additional expertise when needed and introduce a bit of variety into the format. With the growth of the cohorts, the practitioners from previous cohorts started to serve as experts for the subsequent cohorts.

As with the interviews, the group meetings offered transformative encounters for all involved. The richness of the conversations, and the collective perseverance and creativity were insurmountable. The one-to-one meetings, however, received the most positive feedback. Practitioners reported that, if they could choose only one element in the whole programme to maintain, they would choose the one-to-one meetings.

EVOLVING OUTCOMES

At the outset of the practitioners' network development, we listed a set of goals for the network as follows:

- To strengthen religious communities as receiving communities for refugees and migrants;
- To strengthen, affirm, and network practitioners;

- To strategize how refugees, migrants, and practitioners can have a seat at decision-making tables at all levels, in partnership with religious communities and practitioners;
- To enhance the individual and collective moral voices for the protection and self-determination of refugees and migrants;
- To resource religious communities and practitioners in influencing migration policy through direct (advocacy) and indirect (societal norms, democratic participation, partnership with civil society) methodologies and vehicles;
- To promote positive societal and cultural narratives regarding refugees, migrants, and their inclusion in the broader society;
- To foster conditions for an inclusive and cohesive society, reflected in relations, values, norms, and practices;
- To envision, model, and work towards a diverse, socially cohesive, and welcoming Europe.[10]

As one of the network's founders, it is not up to me to judge to what extent we have achieved these goals. It is a work in progress in any case. Nonetheless, the existence of this book testifies at least to the fact that we were successful in networking practitioners with each other and with other actors, and that we try to enhance their moral voices and promote positive societal and cultural narratives regarding people on the move. With the combined stories and the discussion between researchers and practitioners, we also attempt to envision a model for a socially cohesive and welcoming Europe. The individual practitioners also testified to the usefulness of the network in their everyday practice, especially in decreasing the sense of isolation, lessening the mental burden of the work, and providing a space for collaboration with others whom they would never meet.[11]

But the outcomes are constantly evolving. The curriculum of each subsequent cohort was adjusted based on the feedback provided in the evaluation session of the previous cohort. A more local version of the network has been trialled in Sweden to see whether the model can be efficient also on a smaller scale. Other potential applications of the model were also discussed and might be implemented in the future.

10. AWoN Practitioners' Network Overview (internal document).
11. AWoN Prospectus (internal document).

At the end of 2021, we lost the charismatic leadership of Dirk Ficca, whose sudden death necessitated a much quicker transformation of the network into one led by practitioners for practitioners. A year and a half later, I can say with great satisfaction that the practitioners stood up to the challenge and the network evolved into a standalone organization run fully by migration practitioners. The first annual meeting in Brussels in June 2022 provided the necessary foundations for the establishment of the network and divided the work. The second annual meeting finalized the preparatory works.

As part of the preparatory works, a group of practitioners took the lead on adapting the network's methodology to its operating conditions, resources, and needs. The core elements remain in place—both group meetings and one-to-one meetings are a part of what is now called "home groups." A community of practice and collaborative learning are still the core assumptions in how they are structured. But they also innovate—they have changed the frequency of the group meetings, they have a greater mix of established and new members, and they have streamlined the exploratory process. A digital platform is also being prepared to enable practitioners a greater degree of creative freedom in engaging in collaborative learning, collective projects, and more specialized communities of practice too. At the outset, after three cohorts were initiated, we hoped to organize regional meetings throughout the year, beyond the annual meetings, but the limitations posed by the pandemic did not make it possible. Hopefully, these will be a possibility in the future, as they were meant as an outreach activity to local receiving communities too.

BIBLIOGRAPHY

Brendel, Hannah, et al. "The Impact of Work-Related Barriers on Job Satisfaction of Practitioners Working with Migrants." *Social Sciences* 12.2 (2023) 98. https://www.mdpi.com/2076-0760/12/2/98.

Canning, Victoria. "Managing Expectations: Impacts of Hostile Migration Policies on Practitioners in Britain, Denmark and Sweden." *Social Sciences* 10.2 (2021) 65. https://www.mdpi.com/2076-0760/10/2/65.

Center for Teaching Innovation, Cornell University. "Collaborative Learning." *Center for Teaching Innovation*, n.d. https://teaching.cornell.edu/teaching-resources/active-collaborative-learning/collaborative-learning.

García-Carmona, Marina, et al. *Migration to the EU: A Survey of First-Line Practitioners' Perceptions During the Covid-19 Pandemic*. Vienna: Perceptions Project, 2021. https://project.perceptions.eu/wp-content/uploads/sites/24/2021/09/PERCEPTIONS-Report-A4-Migration-to-the-EU-A-survey-of-first-line-practitioners-perceptions-during-the-COVID-19-pandemic.pdf.

Hoadley, Christopher. "What Is a Community of Practice and How Can We Support It?" In *Theoretical Foundations of Learning Environments*, edited by Susan Land and David Jonassen, 287–300. New York: Routledge, 2012.

Hussein, Shereen, et al. "The Experiences of Migrant Social Work and Social Care Practitioners in the UK: Findings from an Online Survey." *European Journal of Social Work* 14.4 (2011) 479–96. https://doi.org/10.1080/13691457.2010.513962.

Li, Linda C., et al. "Evolution of Wenger's Concept of Community of Practice." *Implementation Science* 4.1 (2009) 11. https://doi.org/10.1186/1748-5908-4-11.

Mavratza, Theokliti, et al. "Professional Quality of Life in Greek Health Professionals Working with Refugees and Migrants." *Materia Sociomedica* 33.2 (2021) 94–99. https://doi.org/10.5455/msm.2021.33.94-99.

Palincsar, Annemarie Sullivan, et al. "Designing a Community of Practice: Principles and Practices of the GisML Community." *Teaching and Teacher Education* 14.1 (1998) 5–19. https://doi.org/10.1016/S0742-051X(97)00057-7.

Puzzo, Gabriele, et al. "The Impact of Cultural Intelligence on Burnout among Practitioners Working with Migrants: An Examination of Age, Gender, Training, and Language Proficiency." *Current Psychology* 43 (2024) 4443–57. https://doi.org/10.1007/s12144-023-04641-x.

10

Responsible Research Projects within a World of Neighbours
Decolonizing Research Ethics

Majbritt Lyck-Bowen

The aim of this chapter is to outline how I and the researchers I work with from A World of Neighbours (AWoN) understand research ethics and how we apply them in the projects we carry out with practitioners from the network. Research ethics is basically principles and guidelines for how research should be carried out in a responsible way. It concerns all decisions researchers make from the moment the research is first thought of, to the time when the impact of the research is known. This chapter will argue that in addition to rethinking how key ethical principles should be applied, researcher's positionality, reflexivity and enabling practitioners to become equal partners must be at the core of this process.

MOVING BEYOND A UNIVERSAL UNDERSTANDING OF RESEARCH ETHICS

The foundations for modern day research ethics were laid in response to World War II with the United Nations' adoption of the Universal Declaration of Human Rights (UDHR). The aim of the declaration was to help ensure that fundamental human rights are universally observed and respected. As pointed out by Mohamed Msoroka and Diana Amundsen, there are many links between the UDHR and contemporary dominant research ethics.[1] Researchers' fundamental commitments to recognizing the dignity of every human being and not harming or endangering human life are based on Articles 3 and 6 of the UDHR which declare that: "Everyone has the right to life, liberty and security of person," and that: "Everyone has the right to recognition everywhere as a person before the law." Furthermore, two of the key principles in research ethics, "informed consent" and "voluntary participation," are based on Article 19 of the UDHR that states that "Everyone has the right to freedom of opinion and expression; this right includes freedom to hold opinions without interference."

The 1964 Declaration of Helsinki turned the principles of the UDHR into universal ethical research guidelines aiming at protecting the rights of human beings participating in research world-wide. At the centre of the declaration is the commitment of the researcher to prioritize the wellbeing of research participants over all other interests. The declaration also states that research participants must be informed about the key aspects of the research. Based on this information participants must freely agree to participate in the research and they have the right to withdraw this consent at any time or to refuse to participate at all without facing any negative consequences. Preferably participants' consent must be documented in writing, otherwise it must still be witnessed and recorded. Finally, all research projects must also be reviewed and approved by an independent research ethics committee.

As researchers working for AWoN, we fully recognize the important links between the UDHR and research ethics and the overriding importance of not harming research participants and receiving the approval of an independent research ethics committee. However, we strive to challenge the universality of Western-based research ethics and the claim that they should be applied the same way regardless of the social, political, cultural and religious contexts. Instead, we believe in the importance of decolonizing research ethics. As highlighted by Ranjan Datta decolonizing research means critically questioning the underlying assumptions that underpin how we do research and challenge the assumption that Western knowledge, opinions, and methods are superior.[2] It means plac-

---

1. Msoraka and Amundsen, "One Size Fits Not Quite All."
2. Datta, "Decolonizing."

ing research participants' and communities' voices and understandings at the centre of the research process and breaking down the barriers between participants and researchers. It also means adapting and applying our Western based research ethics in ways that benefit the research participants and the communities we are engaging with and that maximize the impact of their knowledge.

RESEARCHER POSITIONALITY AND REFLEXIVITY

As pointed out by Gabrielle Russell-Mundine, an essential first step in the process of decolonizing research is critical researcher reflexivity.[3] To understand the function of researcher reflexivity we must first turn to another important concept, namely researcher positionality. According to Andrew Holmes, positionality refers to the researcher's worldview as well as the position they adopt in the research project and its political and social context.[4] He argued that an individual's worldview "concerns ontological assumptions (an individual's beliefs about the nature of social reality and what is knowable about the world), epistemological assumptions (an individual's beliefs about the nature of knowledge), and assumptions about human nature and agency (individual's assumptions about the way we interact with our environment and relate to it)."[5] Our worldviews are influenced by a mix of factors such as our life experiences, our ethnicity and nationality, our religion and culture, our gender and sexuality, our political stances and our socioeconomic positions. Holmes also contended that establishing the positionality researchers adopt in a given research project, means identifying how the researcher is located in terms of what is being researched, who is taking part in the research and the research process and context.[6]

The importance of critical self-reflection, which means examining one's own motives, feelings, and reactions and how they influence the way one thinks and acts in different situations, for ethical practice is well established. Similarly, researcher reflexivity requires that we as researchers think carefully about how our own worldviews affect our position within research projects and impact on research processes including how we understand and apply research ethics. Considering that AWoN is a

---

3. Russell-Mundine, "Reflexivity in Indigenous Research."
4. Holmes, "Researcher Positionality," 1.
5. Holmes, "Researcher Positionality," 1.
6. Holmes, "Researcher Positionality," 2.

multireligious network and that much of the research includes religious aspects, it is especially important that we as researchers consider our religious positionality.

According to a study by Catherine Pavia, there are two main ways in which researchers' religious positionalities affect the research.[7] Firstly, religious positionalities act as terministic screens, a concept originally introduced by Kenneth Burke. Burke argued that the terminologies researchers utilize consciously or unconsciously affect what they see and perhaps more importantly what they do not see.[8] This means that they might pay more attention to particular questions, behaviours, and interpretations and disregard others. As an example, if a research project uses the categories Muslim, Jewish, or Buddhist, it might pay more attention to similarities and differences between religions and consciously or unconsciously discount that moderate believers within all religions might have more in common than moderate believers might have with more radical believers within their own religion. Burke also contended that terms combine some issues leading to identification but also separate other issues leading to distancing.[9] This means that researchers' religious positionality might make them identify with participants because of the similarities they share rather than distancing themselves from participants because of their differences. This might have both positive and negative consequences for the research process. As an example, if a Christian researcher interviews a Christian participant, their shared religious identity might make them connect more easily. However, it might also lead the researcher to listen less carefully or ask fewer clarifying questions that might reveal differences because she assumes that her understandings are the same as the participant's because of their shared religious identity. Secondly, Pavia also contended that researchers' religious positionality might affect their attempts to represent their participants' beliefs fairly.[10] She suggested that: "Representing this diversity and complexity requires careful attention to participant selection; increased participant collaboration, from research design and throughout the process of writing up the

---

7. Pavia, "Taking Up Faith."
8. Burke, "Terministic screens."
9. Burke, "Terministic screens."
10. Pavia, "Taking Up Faith."

data; and the perspectives of multiple outside readers on research data and written drafts."[11]

As researchers we are committed to continuously and reflexively thinking about all these issues and questions regarding how our worldviews affect the way we understand and apply research ethics to help ensure that we uphold the highest ethical standards in a context appropriate way throughout the research process. We will approach each research project with curiosity and open minds and we will carefully consider how our worldviews influence what we choose to research, and how we design research processes, including which concepts and theories we use as the foundation for our research and which research methods and methodologies we apply and how we apply them. Considering the significance of equality and inclusivity, we will also always think carefully about which participants we include and exclude from our research projects and how we can fairly and equitably include all participants' voices in our data analysis.

RELATIONSHIP BETWEEN RESEARCHERS AND PRACTITIONERS

Carefully considering our relationship with research participants is another important part of decolonizing research ethics. As argued by Vivetha Thambinathan and Elizabeth Kinsella, when research participants come from different cultures such as is often the case in research conducted within AWoN, it is not enough that researchers acquire some prior knowledge about the research participants and context and try to carry out the research in a culturally sensitive way.[12] Instead, for cross-cultural research to be carried out ethically, it needs to be constructed in collaboration with research participants to help ensure that the wealth of knowledge of research participants are not only apparent in the research data but also in the development of the theoretical framework and the research process. Basically, to decolonize research ethics we as researchers need to be open to reimaging our views on existing concepts and theories and ways of designing and carrying out research. This means talking with the practitioners about how we should define key concepts such as "integration" and "people on the move" and which assumptions

11. Pavia, "Taking Up Faith," 355.
12. Thambinathan and Kinsella, "Decolonizing Methodologies in Qualitative Research."

we should use to underpin our research. Inclusion also means that as researchers we should always deal constructively with disagreement. Practitioners within AWoN already play a vital role in initiating research projects since they identify issues they want the researchers to focus on. However, we as researchers must also continuously strive to enable practitioners to become co-creators in designing the research and including them in decisions about issues such as who should be included in the research and how data should be collected and analysed.

One of the most important challenges in this participatory way of designing and implementing our research project is the imbalance of power between researchers and practitioners. There are many factors that contribute to this imbalance. Firstly, as stressed by Barbara Israel et al., power relationships between researchers and research participants are shaped by wider social inequalities determined by identity markers such as education, class, and race.[13] As emphasized by John Gaventa and Andrea Cornwall, it is also often difficult to change the notion that researchers are the "experts" with social power to determine what constitutes valuable knowledge.[14] In addition, as highlighted by Bill Cooke and Uma Kothari, as researchers we are also the ones that apply for funding for the research projects, ultimately making us responsible to the funding bodies and giving us control over how the funding is spent.[15] Furthermore, it is also important to acknowledge the imbalance of power within the group of practitioners based on the practitioners' experience, gender, language proficiency, religion, nationality, and position within the network. Inspired by post-colonial feminism,[16] we will consciously and regularly pause the research process and make time for exploring, questioning, and evaluating ways in which we can challenge these power imbalances. Inclusion and equality are central concepts within the network, and we will continuously strive to ensure that all contributions from all the people involved in the research are equally valued and that knowledge is always co-created.

As argued by Andrea Armstrong et al., trust is another vital component of participatory research because of its importance for building

---

13. Israel et al., "Challenges and Facilitating Factors."
14. Gaventa and Cornwall, "Power and Knowledge."
15. Cooke and Kothari, "Participation."
16. Darroch and Giles, "Decolonizing Health Research."

and maintaining interpersonal relationships.[17] However, developing and sustaining trust between researchers and practitioners is challenging because it often takes longer to develop than academic and funding timelines permit.[18] There are also often substantial differences in needs and expectations between the stakeholders in the research projects that cannot always all be met because of a lack of resources. As researchers we appreciate that trust between us and the practitioners can be fragile and needs continuous nurturing not only during but also in between research projects. This necessitates prolonged researcher engagement with the network that go well beyond individual research projects. We are also well aware that we can help build and maintain trust by showing love and compassion for one another and treating each other with dignity and respect. It is also essential that we have an ongoing dialogue with the practitioners about the research projects, that we are transparent about the benefits and risks of taking part in the research, and that we feedback the findings to the network in a timely and inspiring manner. An important part of this process is also to make our research action-orientated, aiming at constructively addressing issues and challenges raised by the practitioners. Finally, as emphasized by Moyra Keane, it also means engaging with the practitioners outside the research agenda in activities such as training, workshops, and social events.[19]

DECOLONIZING KEY ETHICAL PRINCIPLES

A vital part of decolonizing research ethics also includes re-examining and rethinking the key ethical principles from the UDHR-based research ethics framework and how they should be applied with the practitioners.

One of these key principles is that people participating in research must not experience any harm and must be treated fairly with dignity and respect. Decolonizing research ethics means including the practitioners in identifying potential ways that taking part in research projects might affect them. It includes having open, honest, and ongoing conversations with the practitioners about how and to what degree risks of harm can be mitigated, and their understandings of what it means to be treated fairly with dignity and respect in a given research project. It also means being open and ready to significantly change or terminate a research project,

---

17. Armstrong et al., "Trust and Temporality in Participatory Research."
18. Armstrong et al., "Trust and Temporality in Participatory Research."
19. Keane, "Research Ethics and Diversity of Worldviews."

if there is deemed to be a risk of any harm to the practitioners or the researchers if the research continues.

Another key ethical principle is obtaining informed consent from all participants in the research. Informed consent is meant to ensure that all participants understand the basic aspects of the research project and their role in it before they decide on whether or not to take part in the research. Participants are typically provided with information about the purpose(s) of the research, who is funding and carrying out the research, how data is being collected, analysed and disseminated, and what their role in the research is expected to be. Participants are also reminded that their participation is voluntary, that they can withdraw from the research at any time without repercussions, how and for how long their data will be stored, as well as their rights and how they can object if they are not upheld. In addition to this information being provided, university ethics committees often require participants to tick boxes confirming that they have understood the different aspects of the research project and their rights. Researchers are expected to collect these documents once the participants have signed them. Hence it is assumed that participants can understand written information and that once they know the basics about the research project, they are freely able to consent or not consent to taking part. As highlighted by Fride Klykken, it is considered good practice to negotiate informed consent throughout the research process, meaning that participants should be asked to confirm their consent to participating in the research before, during, and after they have contributed to the data collection.[20]

From a decolonizing research ethics point of view these standardized procedures are problematic in several ways. As argued by Maria Cascant Sempere, Talatu Aliyu, and Cathy Bollaert, written informed consent forms can be interpreted as unsafe auditing in some countries which can negatively affect the quantity and quality of research participation.[21] Juan Tauri has also contended that in many communities, verbal consent is more culturally appropriate and valid but this is often not acknowledged by universities' ethics committees.[22] Tauri has also warned that these simplified informed consent procedures risk disguising the complexity of the research context and that they focus on the individual and hence do

20. Klykken, "Implementing Continuous Consent in Qualitative Research."
21. Cascant Sempere et al., "Towards Decolonising Research Ethics."
22. Tauri, "Research Ethics."

not consider that in many communities, knowledge is perceived as being collectively constructed.[23] Hence knowledge is owned by the community rather than the individual, and only the community can allow consent for it to be shared. As researchers we will continue to reflexively think about all of these issues while still acknowledging the external constraints placed on us by our universities' ethics committees. This process will include nurturing relationships with the practitioners, which will enable open and honest discussions about all aspects of the research process and the complex context the research is situated in. These discussions will address what information about the research projects practitioners would like to have on paper, whose consent is needed and how it can best be obtained and renegotiated. As an example, if a practitioner thinks that knowledge pertinent to the research project is collectively owned by the organization they are working for, then consent for them to share that knowledge can either be obtained from the other relevant members of that organization, or the research can be designed in a way enabling that knowledge to be collectively shared with the researcher. This would typically mean conducting focus groups as opposed to individual interviews.

The process of ensuring that practitioners' participation in research projects is completely voluntary is another key ethical principle that needs decolonizing. Michelle Brear and Cias Tsotetsi have stressed that the signing of a consent form might prevent some participants from feeling that they can withdraw from the research at any time.[24] In addition, Cascant Sempere, Aliyu, and Bollaert have highlighted that some participants may not have the power or perceived power to say no to participating in a particular research project because of organizational pressures or their cultural norms might make it difficult for them to say no and thereby risk disappointing the researchers.[25] Taking the advice from Ben Gray et al., we as researchers will strive to build trust and interrelatedness with the practitioners, and aim to develop processes and spaces that enable practitioners to make free choices concerning their participation in our research projects.[26]

The final key ethical principle regards confidentiality which concerns keeping the personal data and contributions of participants from

---

23. Tauri, "Research Ethics."
24. Brear and Tsotetsi, "(De)Colonising Outcomes of Community Participation."
25. Cascant Sempere et al., "Towards Decolonising Research Ethics."
26. Gray et al., "Are Research Ethics Guidelines Culturally Competent?"

being exposed outside the research project. This typically includes setting down strict rules for how, if at all, participants can share information about what has been said during the data collection process, and ensuring that any information that can help identify participants is removed during the data analysis process. Decolonizing the way confidentiality is dealt with includes talking with the practitioners about how these processes should be carried out. It also includes appreciating that some participants might want their information kept confidential whereas others want their contributions made public.

CONCLUSION

At the heart of the AWoN researchers' approach to research ethics lies decolonization mainly through reflexive practice and building relationships with the practitioners. Adopting reflexivity in the design and implementation of research projects means critically questioning and examining our own assumptions, beliefs, and actions and how they affect each aspect of the research process. It means continuously setting aside time for reflexive thinking both individually and collectively and approaching the research process with an open and curious mind. Decolonizing research ethics also means building meaningful relationships with the practitioners and continuing to develop new ways in which we can co-create research projects and processes with them. An initial aim is to blur the line between researchers and practitioners with the view to eventually eradicate the line, hoping that one day practitioners will see themselves as equal partners in the research process.

BIBLIOGRAPHY

Armstrong, Andrea, et al. "Trust and Temporality in Participatory Research." *Qualitative Research* 23.4 (2022) 1000–1021. https://doi.org/10.1177/14687941211065163.

Brear, Michelle R., and Clas T. Tsotetsi. "(De)Colonising Outcomes of Community Participation—A South African Ethnography of 'Ethics in Practice.'" *Qualitative Research* 22.6 (2022) 813–30. https://doi.org/10.1177/14687941211004417.

Burke, Kenneth. *Language as Symbolic Action: Essays on Life, Literature, and Method.* Berkeley: University of California Press, 1966.

Cascant Sempere, Maria J., et al. "Towards Decolonising Research Ethics: From One-off Review Boards to Decentralised North–South Partnerships in an International Development Programme." *Education Science* 12 (2022) 236. https://www.mdpi.com/2227-7102/12/4/236.

Cooke, Bill, and Uma Kothari. *Participation: The New Tyranny.* New York: Zed, 2001.

Darroch, Francine, and Audrey Giles. "Decolonizing Health Research: Community-Based Participatory Research and Postcolonial Feminist Theory." *Canadian Journal of Action Research* 15.3 (2014) 22–36.

Datta, Ranjan. "Decolonizing Both Researcher and Research and Its Effectiveness in Indigenous Research." *Research Ethics* 14.2 (2018) 1–24. https://doi.org/10.1177/1747016117733296.

Gaventa, John, and Andrea Cornwall. "Power and Knowledge." In *Handbook of Action Research: Participative Inquiry and Practice*, edited by Hilary Bradbury and Peter Reason, 172–89. Thousands Oaks, CA: Sage, 2001.

Gray, Ben, et al. "Are Research Ethics Guidelines Culturally Competent?" *Research Ethics* 13.1 (2017) 23–41. https://doi.org/10.1177/1747016116650235.

Holmes, Andrew G. D. "Researcher Positionality—A Consideration of Its Influence and Place in Qualitative Research—A New Researcher Guide." *Shanlax International Journal of Education* 8.4 (2020) 1–10. https://doi.org/10.34293/education.v8i4.3232.

Israel, Barbara A., et al. "Challenges and Facilitating Factors in Sustaining Community-Based Participatory Research Partnerships: Lessons Learned from the Detroit, New York City, and Seattle Urban Research Centers." *Journal of Urban Health* 83.6 (2006) 1022–40.

Keane, Moyra. "Research Ethics and Diversity of Worldviews: Integrated Worlds and Ubuntu." *Scholarship of Teaching and Learning in the South* 5.2 (2021) 22–35. https://doi.org/10.36615/sotls.v5i2.194.

Klykken, Fride H. "Implementing Continuous Consent in Qualitative Research." *Qualitative Research* 22.5 (2022) 795–810. https://doi.org/10.1177/14687941211014366.

Msoroka, Mohamed S., and Diana Amundsen. "One Size Fits Not Quite All: Universal Research Ethics with Diversity." *Research Ethics* 14.3 (2018) 1–17. https://doi.org/10.1177/1747016117739939.

Pavia, Catherine M. "Taking Up Faith: Ethical Methods for Studying Writing in Religious Contexts." *Written Communication* 32.4 (2015) 336–67. https://doi.org/10.1177/0741088315601645.

Russell-Mundine, Gabrielle. "Reflexivity in Indigenous Research: Reframing and Decolonising Research?" *Journal of Hospitality and Tourism Management* 19.7 (2012). https://doi:10.1017/jht.2012.8.

Tauri, Juan M. "Research Ethics, Informed Consent and the Disempowerment of First Nation Peoples." *Research Ethics* 14.3 (2018) 1–14. https://doi.org/10.1177/1747016117739935

Thambinathan, Vivetha, and Elizabeth A. Kinsella. "Decolonizing Methodologies in Qualitative Research: Creating Spaces for Transformative Praxis." *International Journal of Qualitative Methods* 20 (2021). https://doi.org/10.1177/16094069211014766.

11

At Calais

A Refugee with a Red Passport

AMLOUD ALAMIR

I HAVE OFTEN ASKED MYSELF: Am I really a German citizen with this red passport? Or is it just a safeguard? After I got this red passport, I searched much more intensively for my identity. Had I finally reached the other side?

I must admit that this red passport had untied some knots. It put me in a position to move between countries, freely, without the fear that the police would come to pick me up, saying: "You have no right to enter the country!" "You don't have the right to stay!" "You don't have the right to ask." So many rights that I had acquired through this red passport. But despite the protection this red passport provides, I still get scared and sweaty when I see the police. I get confused when a security guard approaches me. Even if this fear is unfounded, it is there. By law, I am now treated like a German citizen. But is that enough? Or is there more needed to get to the other side?

I came to Germany more than eight years ago, right at the start of the move of many refugees from Syria. Earlier this year, I received German citizenship. My first trip as a German brought me here . . . to Calais, where there is a Somalian young man named Baher with his stray eyes and a distant dream. The French police had torn down the tents at the border area there. They gathered the belongings of people, stowed them in police cars. In small groups, the young men crossed the road. They had sombre faces. Their eyes nailed to the ground. I could not help but see sadness in their steps. But one of them was walking alone. The young Somali, Baher. He was also sad, but his eyes said nothing. As if he was used to it. He was carrying a small backpack and a smile on his face, but as if he had long forgotten his smile. I walked up to him to say hello in Arabic. His eyes raced searching for my voice. He answered cheerfully, as if the disappointment had disappeared. A stream of questions began to flow between us, as if we had known each other for a long time.

Baher arrived in Calais a few months ago. He tried twice to cross the border to enter Britain. He said to me, "The police have surprised us today in the early hours of the morning. They destroyed our tents and took everything we owned." I quickly asked him if they had beaten him and he replied, "I was not beaten, most of the time there were people from humanitarian organizations near the site. They came soon to witness what was going on. That protected us." At least, that is what Baher thought. He added, "We were forced to return to the refugee relief organization that provided us with water, food, and blankets." This was repeated more than seven times in one month.

Baher's dream was to reach the United Kingdom. He suggests that since its exit from the European Union, the Dublin Agreement no longer works in Britain. Hence, he can get asylum there without fear of being sent back to Italy, where he first landed, like most young men his age. Afterwards, he can work there and pursue his hobby of playing football. He wants to live a normal life without having to take up arms in Darfur, without being used in a war that has mercilessly consumed young people.

I was not in Calais for vacation when I met Bahar. I was with a group of activists. It was my first time. The aim of this visit was to communicate to people on the move there that we feel ashamed of the policies of our European states. These states prevent people in need from entering countries. These people are stuck in limbo. Of course, the states know that it is a coincidence where one is born, inside Europe or outside Europe, so that the value of a human being must not depend on their place of birth. The life of every human being has a value that cannot be taken away at a border. Everyone has the right to seek better chances in life.

But are good intentions enough? Is it enough for us to say that we are ashamed of the policies of our states? Is it enough to have a conversation when you do not have the power to change what happens at the border? Is it enough to say that it is not fair?

My feelings were mixed at first. I was not convinced that showing my emotions would make a difference. It was an experiment to find out what was going on. I discovered a bit of myself.

Baher has arrived in Britain in August 2022. He is staying in a hotel for refugees in Manchester. He and his friends managed to get a small boat that took about four hours across the Channel. The real arrival, however, is still missing. Baher is afraid of being sent to Rwanda. The town from which he fled, where robbery and rape ran through everyday life, is not safe. Baher finds that "flight" will remain the title given to his life. When he fled his village in Darfur, he decided he would never return home because he did not want to be part of an unfair war.

To Baher, Rwanda is not much better off than Darfur. It is one of the smallest countries in Africa, densely populated. It was colonized by Germany in 1884 and occupied by Belgium in 1916. Both European states attempted to establish Christian Tutsi rule. As a result, Rwanda suffered a genocidal civil war that affected its economy, which today is based on so-called subsistence agriculture. So why did the UK decide that it could not accept these refugees? The UK, a country with a strong economy? Instead, it wants to deport them to a country whose people seem to be just scraping by, where people on the move would not have any real opportunities for education or employment. Does Baher not have the right to be like the young men of his generation who dream of a better future?

In his country, there was a problem with the "Janjaweed." The Janjaweed are the men who ride through the neighbourhood while carrying machine guns. As Baher explained: "They raped my neighbours' daughters, so we went to file a complaint with the government. We went out to protest. They burned down our town. They asked for me, but I had fled to Libya before they came. However, they were able to catch some of the sons of the town. They killed them. They are agents of the Sudanese government who launch attacks on black Africans. No young man in Darfur will have a chance for temporary survival if he does not join one of the sides of the conflict. But in the end, he will not survive anyway, as the bullet will kill him wherever he is."

The journey was difficult. When he reached Libya, he slept on the road for fifteen days. He was afraid that someone would arrest him. He was insulted. He was beaten. He tried to work to earn a living, so he went to work on one of the farms. However, after more than a month of work, he did not receive his wages. Together with a friend, he demanded to be paid. The owner of the farm beat them before he drove them away. It was all for nothing.

The cruelties to which Baher was subjected did not stop, but they did not extinguish his smile. Even the tone of his voice was tainted by a note of hope that the next thing to come would be better. With that, as soon as he could collect the required sum for the trip, 2000 Libyan dinars, he decided to flee to Italy. Eventually he managed to get to there by boat.

Recounting the moment he saw the Médecins Sans Frontières ship, Baher said, "I had tears in my eyes. Many on the boat were crying because we were being rescued. We were not dying at sea, eaten by fish. That was on January 19, 2022. The crying rose. I felt that I had reached a country that would respect me as a human being. Nobody would beat me. I would not work for nothing. I would be respected. These countries are countries that respect rights. Nobody hurts anybody." Maybe his name helped him in this escape, because in Arabic his name means the sea. This name could be a spell that protected him in the sea. Because many people drowned trying to reach Europe, risking their lives and the lives of their loved ones.

Before I saw Baher, I was with my friends, fellow activists. I remember our discussion. While we were driving in the car towards the French border, a conversation took place between us, about how would we find the people who are trying to flee, how we would talk to them, and what security measures we would need to take. It was a conversation with European colleagues that gave me nothing but cramps. Despite our very good intentions, the feeling of separation from my friends was strong. How am I supposed to follow security measures when talking to refugees? I am one of them. Just eight years ago, I was with my children at one of the borders, waiting to enter. Was I a danger to anyone then? Is my life more valuable now? Do the needs of Europeans mean more? Are they more in need of care than people like Baher? I felt angry.

What triggered my anger was a dialogue with one of these friends, who wondered about the security measures for when she would get out of the car. She was more interested in her own safety than the safety of others. I knew that this friend had a history of migration herself. She knew what it was like to be a refugee. The long years spent in Europe may have given her this sense of fear, but why? Is there something unconscious that creates this European difference? A difference from those in the tents? A fear of the unknown others? This fear was not a justification for me.

At first, we moved in small groups. I was with this friend. When we arrived, it did not take her long to establish relationships with the people in the tents. She became responsible for translating because she knows many languages. The distance may have been long before she joined the access path to the camp in Calais, but as soon as she had made the first step, she was able to reach the hearts of those who were there. Yes, for a moment, her fear of the unknown had disappeared. She had come closer.

As for myself, I don't know how I managed to evoke smiles and sometimes laughter from the people we were with, without noticing that I did not speak their languages. I felt—I feel—with them. I did not find a difference between me now and me eight years ago. I am still the woman who is looking for security and safety. The woman who wants a better future, despite the fact that I am in Europe with my children now. Nobody must forget that the limits set by human beings can be overcome, but only by those who have faith in a better future.

Back to the present. I remember that my daughter, not too long ago, told me about how the same older woman got on the bus with her several times. The bus my daughter takes to school and back. Every time the woman sees my daughter with Arab features, she looks at her, cursing the immigrants who have taken everything from the Germans. According to her, they looted the Germans, they took their jobs. Once my daughter was even told that immigrants were a pollution for this country. This was repeated several times. Each time, my daughter did not respond because she did not want to cause an uproar. She had the feeling that it would have been useless anyway, since the older woman would win, due to the simple fact that she is German. My daughter did not tell me how these statements made her feel.

She said that anger prevented her from dealing with the woman properly, but she would know better next time. I did not expect this reaction from my 16-year-old daughter. She was a small child when she came to Germany. Most of her memories are probably from Germany. Should she not feel more like a German citizen? I asked her: "Do you expect that life here is not full of people like this woman? You should be able to know how to handle yourself in front of such racist people."

I became convinced that Europe has two faces, one face dealing with people with white skin, and one face dealing with people with brown skin. The Europeans are doing a great job with Ukrainian refugees. It is something that I admire very much, but I just wonder: Why could not all refugees be treated in this way? When Ukrainian refugees escaped the war, many borders were opened for them. They could get employed. They could get educated. They could even enrol in universities. They did not have to have their papers translated. There were no tests to stamp their papers. At the same time, Frontex is involved in human rights violations at the border. People are crying for help, drowning in the Mediterranean. At the border to Turkey, people are stripped of their clothes before they are thrown out. Do these people not deserve dignity like everyone else?

So how can the existing borders be opened? By political decisions? By humanitarian decisions? What can open Europe to the people fleeing the scourge of what is happening in their countries? Perhaps the colour of your skin plays a role. We can see clear differences in the reception of refugees depending on their skin colour, with some getting preferential treatment over the other. Why is there this double standard in dealing with people?

It is important that we are aware that all of us can be exposed to injustice. Injustice could come from a hand with white skin or a hand with brown skin. At the same time, you can only guess which hand will catch you when you fall. Which hand will help you find your way again? My identity may now be more diverse. I have an aspiration to know who I am, who I can be. Where am I in this confrontation? What will I do? Baher reminded me that I may not have been able to get to the other side or far enough to the other side, but I never doubted for a moment on which side I belong. Despite the red passport, I still belong to those who are here, to Baher, to all who seek security and stability.

12

Athliens

À nos corps étrangers[1]

Aude Sathoud

My body in Athens is a mystery.

    I see it in their eyes as I wander around. I remember having been struck by this the first time—the sharp feeling of being looked at. In the big cities of the hegemonic North, where I come from, no one pays attention. Everyone follows their line as in a swimming pool—sanitized and blind. No one cares. I remember that feeling for the first time—being seen, watched, my body taking on a new shape, dimension, substance, through those tenths of gazes. Looked at, screened, identified, assigned, perhaps—*dévisagé*, I paradoxically never experience my body so freely than in those noisy, dirty, lively streets. It is, with each passer-by, given life again, abolished and reinvented—it exists and surrenders.

    I am alive and alive and a lie.

---

    1. This text is made of pieces created-collected between Athens, Paris and The Hague, 2019 and 2023. It (I) was made possible by the past and present love, flesh, and ink bodies of my parents Anne-Sandrine and Hervé, siblings Alix and Andréa, first lover Adèle, *adelphe d'une autre mer* Marleno, inspiration and friend Marina, future-openers Anna and Myrto, all those I crossed eyes and path, and struggled with, stood by, looked up to, became through, in Athens and beyond—and Audre Lorde, Frantz Fanon and Monique Wittig—*inter alia*.

My body is ours.

My name in Athens is an enigma.

I hear *Aoud', Aoudé, Oud, Aouda*. I each time turn around and become, spring up, in a new form, as another person, made out of this unique lip movement and series of sounds. When people ask, "How should I pronounce it?" I have taken the habit to reply, "However it comes out." And in this I am born again, as the co-creation of two subjectivities in friction, as the unexpected product of the collusion of my body against the walls of another's world.

Halfway between Paris and Brazzaville, capital cities of my parents' respective countries, Athens is the city of the in-between, where it seems that all the pieces I am come together to make and unmake sense of my complex rich and beautiful selves. On those ruins, under that sky, up on those hills, above the sea, I feel like I do not have to choose anymore, do not have to name, explain to find, define the wor(l)ds I am.

That is what I will attempt to, here, still. Scattering pieces of poems and essays, memories and doubts, silences, sometimes. Wa/ondering around—me.

For what are we but an endless journey?

HUMAN(ITARIAN) BEINGS—NECROPOLITICS OF THE WORLD-SAVING INDUSTRY[2]

I first got to Athens in June 2018, as a young French undergraduate student flying from *one of the most prestigious*[3] Parisian schools to intern for a month in a small organization supporting asylum-seekers and refugees in the Greek capital—to discover the *real world*, that is, confront myself to the hardships of lives my French identity card and bourgeois upbringing spared me from. I came back six months later to visit, remember. And then again, in September 2020, amidst the COVID-19 pandemic—to stay. I lived there for a total of one and a half year, completing my final Bachelor year online while volunteering, interning, and then working as the Project Coordinator of that same NGO, Zaatar, which I had always kept close ties with.

I am here again, as I start writing this chapter, having come back for the first time since moving away in November 2021. It is now January

---

2. Pieces of this essay were first written as parts of a Political Humanities Bachelor thesis, unpublished, under the title *Of Power's Shiver ou Du Pouvoir qui Tremble*.

3. Hegemon's italics.

2023. I officially am an African Studies Research Master Student in another *prestigious* university—in the Netherlands, this time. I had decided I would not get on any plane before going for fieldwork in Congo, next year. And yet, here I am. Again. Sitting on a balcony, under Athens' sky—as if I had always been. As if I should forever be.

From this experience in, and relationship with Athens, unfolding in time, from those back and forth movements in evolving circumstances and positionalities, I gathered a number of reflections on wandering bodies, the strangers we are made, allowed, or forced to be.

For in a time where a piece of paper, often coinciding with a shade of skin colour, can give or deny one access to the rest of the world, while forcing another to put their life at risk in order to save it, we obviously are not all the same type of migrants. In a time when a piece of paper delivered at birth decides the value of one's life, we obviously are not all the same type of humans.

Some of us were born to become one of the 281 million people identified as international migrants by the United Nations in 2020; one of the 59 million internally displaced people at the end of the year 2021. Some of us were born to be another of those 50, 000 corpses scattered along migratory routes worldwide—50,000 corpses we know of. Some of us were born to travel, expatriate, explore. Others to illegally migrate, escape, attempt to survive.

AN ORANGE HOUSE TURNED HOME—
MEMORIES FROM ZAATAR NGO

Founded in 2015, at the peak of the arrivals of asylum-seekers on the European shores, Zaatar NGO, which operated until 2022, was a little structure dedicated to the support and integration of asylum-seeker and refugee people into the Greek society. From a community centre offering basic services such as hot meals and showers meant to last some six months, Zaatar progressively developed into a well-structured and polyvalent NGO. To a shelter welcoming vulnerable women and children added up psychosocial and legal services as well as language classes and professional trainings at the organization's centre, the Orange House. While a peer-support programme was specifically aimed at LGBTQI+ asylum-seekers and refugees, experiencing a multiple marginalization, a social enterprise was set up in order to both train and employ refugees, thus easing their access to the formal labour market. It is therefore a holistic model of support towards autonomy that was elaborated throughout the years. Like a great number of organizations, Zaatar NGO's founders, when describing their actions, spoke of "empowerment." To the difference of a great number of organizations, however, they had set it as a principle and mission they attempted to achieve every day. Realizing such an ambition revealed to be a matter of gaze, language, and practices, implying a real thinking and choice of paradigm, of politics. Acknowledging one's capacity to take action and responsibility for their choices and lead their own life, actually means nothing less than considering them as a full and capable human being, endowed with intelligence and sensitivity, as responsible and worthy as myself—my equal.

A fundamental closeness and common belonging, that is a shared humanhood, which is precisely destroyed by the "humanitarian ideology."[4]

THE HUMANITARIAN IDEOLOGY

Brilliantly defined by Bernard Hours as "a set of representations leading to the global (multinational, state-controlled, non-governmental) management of victims of conflicts and disasters (natural as political) and of all those excluded from the process of wealth distribution, humanitarian management itself creat[ing] representation,"[5] the humanitarian ideology has invented its own object. The "victim," a moral abstraction suffering from all of the world's evils, apolitical, distant, an un-human body trembling between death and life, must be saved.

As the "main tool of a moral globalization," the humanitarian ideology both proceeds from and contributes to a standardization of values, imposing an hegemonic reading of catastrophic situations taking place in every part of the world, thus decontextualizing them and their *actors-become-victims* to create a general and abstract state of disaster—the "humanitarian crisis," confined to, if not defining, the *Southern* part of the world, the *Northern* part self-assigning the mission of the saviour. The humanitarian ideology, claiming to serve a common humanity, to rise up to the values of some universal humanism, thus ends up recreating

---

4. Hours, *L'idéologie humanitaire*.

5. Freely translated from "c'est l'ensemble des représentations qui provoquent la gestion planétaire (multinationale, étatique, non gouvernementale) des victimes des conflits et des catastrophes (tant naturelles que politiques) et d'une part des exclus des processus de distribution des richesses. Cette gestion humanitaire provoque elle-même des représentations" (Hours, "L'idéologie humanitaire," 1–2).

two humankinds, erecting an ontological and, consequently, impassable frontier between the victim and their saviour, the humanitarian object and the humanitarian actor. It is on that dichotomy, rebranded version of the colonial master-subject couple of Europeans' civilizing mission, that not only the discourse but entire economy of humanitarianism rely, thus raising the question of the ethics of what has become the humanitarian market.

Relying on both public funds and—mainly private donations, NGOs, which aim at producing non-marketable goods or services and at intervening as independent actors in fields which they pretend—and often are experts in, find themselves in a complex and precarious situation, in a constant tension between two imperatives which sometimes oppose each other—the expectations, if not desires, of private funders they need to satisfy in order to carry on their actions and the actual needs of the individuals and populations they work to support.

THE MARKET OF DISINTERESTEDNESS— BODIES FOR SALE TO SAVE

Under a neo-liberal capitalist order, in a world saturated with images and in/de-formation—a society of the spectacle, as Guy Debord insightfully described it,[6] NGOs, which have multiplied in the past decades, do not escape the market's rules anymore. Thanks to the development of their communication services, they have had to constitute themselves as real brands in order to keep on attracting funds.[7] In an economy of donation defined by the distance—geographical turned ontological, between the donors and the beneficiaries, the latter have become more often than not the non-consenting models of the organizations helping them, using their images to advertise their actions and demonstrate their efficiency and necessity to the funders. An activity which now mobilizes entire teams—energy, time, and funds spent speaking about their achievements rather than pursuing them, but without which doing the latter would now be impossible. This dependence on private funds, coming from generous philanthropists often very foreign to the reality on the ground, sometimes leads to absurd situations and the allocation of funds to activities or groups rather than others, not in regards to actual needs but funders' imagination and sensitivity.

6. Debord, *Société du Spectacle*.
7. Cazenave et al., "Vendre de manière désintéressée."

Women, mothers and children are of course the best products on sale, the value growing proportionally to the sufferings and traumas experienced—war, rape, human trafficking...

Some funders moreover do not hesitate to ask for visits of accommodations and encounters with beneficiaries, taking pictures with people and children, in a disturbing though unquestioned reminiscence of human zoos. Others, willing to ensure the good spending of their donations while taking into account the beneficiaries' intimacy, may ask for a picture of the back of a social worker at work when funding their salary, or of a student's hands writing a lesson when offering homework tutoring. What was already a show thus becomes a performance, and what seems to be a simple mark of consideration and respect of people's privacy actually unveils one fundamental *impensé*, an unconscious element of thought, of the humanitarian ideology as a system of signs and, as defined by Hours, a "set of representations."[8] Indeed, if faces are to be blurred, bodies shown from the back, or the picture focused on hands, if people are not to be identified, those very faces, backs and hands could be anyone's. But could they, really? When constituted as signs in such situations, conveying a meaning, presenting the situation we wish to see, we expect as a proof, images obey to and, consequently, act as evidence for, implicit codes and orders.

Those faces may be blurred if they are scarved, those backs bent and those hands black.

TO SEE OR NOT TO SEA?

In the virtual intimacy of an online peer-support group meeting, after exposing the conditions of life and daily challenges people on the move like him have to endure every day in a country where they are fleeing violence and death, seeking asylum in a world claiming to be that of humanism, equality, and freedom, in a gentle sigh, a man asks, "Why?"[9] "Why?" he repeats once or twice. And there is nothing but silence on the other side.

More than access to the labour market and consumption society, integration into a foreign country, economic self-sufficiency, and social stability, what is crucial to work towards and achieve, through a rethinking

---

8. Hours, *L'idéologie humanitaire*.

9. In another but not completely alien context, reflect on "the comity of European peoples went to pieces when, and because, it allowed its weakest member to be excluded and persecuted" (Arendt, "We Refugees," 69–77).

of a set of signs, practices, and beliefs, a choice of gaze and language, is the recognition of individuals and groups, their existence and belonging to the community. Beyond the consideration of the individual as a biological body, social animal, or economic consumer, acknowledging them as a political actor, a human being endowed with fundamental and inalienable rights. If asylum-seeker and refugee both constitute internationally recognized juridical and political statuses allowing rights and protection, the material reality of those conditions and their current necropolitical management in Europe, render the former purely formal.

Confined, for months if not years, by the thousands, in camps initially built to host half their number for a temporary period, going through administrative procedures of asylum-requests lasting years,[10] people on the move are forced into a life of destitution, violence, and uncertainty, wandering in a void and more often than not ending up with a final rejection and obligation to leave the territory. In such a situation, the claiming of one's fundamental rights is made almost impossible. If the daily struggle for physical and existential survival of a great number of them, constant state of anxiety, and unbearable wait for a decision, were not enough to prevent any individual outburst or collective struggle, the fear of being arrested and spectre of imprisonment and deportation finish any politicization impulse. Left with little to no space for expression, nor the voice to tell or denounce, secluded and silenced, asylum-seekers are made invisible, an anonymous and indiscernible mass of disposable bodies. Citizens of a state actively calling for or incapable of preventing their dying, seeking refuge in a state rejecting or making impossible their living on its territory, belonging nowhere, asylum-seekers, soon-to-become undocumented, paradoxically become, as insightfully and painfully put by Hannah Arendt, "nothing but human beings."[11] Nothing but

---

10. In a particular time of global pandemic period, when consequent sanitary restrictions slow down all public services, some asylum-requests' interviews were, at the time of the writing, in 2020, planned for 2023.

11. "If we should start telling the truth that we are nothing but Jews, it would mean that we expose ourselves to the fate of human beings who, unprotected by any specific law or political convention, are nothing but human beings. I can hardly imagine an attitude more dangerous, since we actually live in a world in which human beings as such have ceased to exist for quite a while, since society has discovered discrimination as the great social weapon by which one may kill men without any bloodshed; since passports or birth certificates, and sometimes even income tax receipts, are no longer formal papers but matters of social distinction" (Arendt, "We Refugees," 69–77).

human beings in their weakness and insignificance, in their passing and finiteness—in their fundamental vulnerability.

Nothing but human beings in their sinking into the sea.

CAN THE WHITE SAVIOUR BE BLACK?

My body in Athens is a mystery.
 I see it in their eyes as I wander around.

As I am writing those lines on a new page of my notebook, one morning, sat on the balcony of my friend Marleno's apartment in Athens, they come sit down in the sofa nearby, their cup of coffee in one hand, a magazine in the other. And so we start talking, as we do, always, forgetting time and space, making up words and ways, recalling lost poems.

"You're more Black here than in Paris, I believe," Marleno tells me at some point during our conversation. We have just agreed to say that Whiteness and Blackness were not so much a matter of biology, skin complexion, as of socio-cultural constructions, paradigms, evolving and contextual *praxis* and positionality. They don't exist *per se*—nothing does. Marleno is looking at me, waiting. I am taken aback for a moment.

I do not feel so—Black (black?).

Here.

I—

I never have.

Anywhere.

I believe.

I forget?

That is—people say, remind me. That's when I know, I guess. But *feel*? No. Not really. Neither in Athens nor in Paris. Oh, wait. Now, yes. I do. I have—felt. I am Black, as I write, perhaps. From my student room, in The Hague. I remember arriving there, in early September, I remember getting out of the bus, taking a few steps around, looking and finding the world so—white, indeed. Flat, cold, dull. Finding the world so dead, in fact.

And my body so Black.

"I mean—you stand out as Black, here. Probably more than in Paris. In Athens, in Greece, your Blackness appears more sensational, spectacular, striking, you see?" [*Me, no, I don't, I will never, but them—you all, yes, I guess, I imagine you do, see—me. Black.*] "You are my only Black friend," Marleno adds. "The same way I am the only Albanian friend of most of my Greek friends." I nod. Know. I get it. I take a moment to reflect on that, the fact that most Greeks did not grow up around Black people—or non-Greeks, for that matter, and then deduce—"Black here is migrant." Marleno nods.

Which I am not.

So—to the moment-movement of people looking at me to see, to make, a Black person, body and face, immediately follows a moment of confusion, reconfiguration, at the realization that as Black as it may appear in the first millisecond my body is nothing as that of a migrant's.

My body in Athens is a mystery.

I see it in their eyes as I wander around.

My body in Athens walks fast and confident.

Chin up and head high, eyes straight, shoulders relaxed.

My body in Athens is both alert and calm, curious, and open.

My body in Athens is strong and loud, yet light.

My body in Athens is dressed in good-fabric second-hand clothes wax sustainable shoes my body takes pictures of graffiti on the walls broken cars balconies my body goes in all directions takes naps on benches and whatever street it likes wanders around with no aim in life but to be breathe under the sun in the city.

My body in Athens is not scared but carefree.

My body in Athens is allowed—to be.

My body in Athens is legal.

French-papered.

Heavy-walleted.

My body in Athens is a master's.

—mystery?

My body in Athens is Black and White, all of it and none at the same time

—impossible, that is

and yet.

Here
I
am.

Black as I open the door of the day centre to another black body. And there seems to happen some kind of a revolution—I feel. Suddenly, *the saviour looks like me.*

Black when I tell them my father is Congolese—not your Congo, though, the other, the small one, Brazzaville.

They smile, call me Sister, they say, "You know," they think "You understand."

I don't.

Neither does my father—we will never.

White when I start speaking in my bourgeois French from France to prove to them I am French as well, although one cannot really hear, from my artefacted British accent. Can French speak English, now?

White, when they look at me with a mix of despair and anger in the eyes and ask

why?

White, as I fly to Athens, on this grey Parisian morning of early January, to be(gin). White, as I fly to Athens as a vital escape, an urge to feel and breathe, to recollect the thousand pieces of me. To the hills and the sun and the sea and the sky and the ruins where I lie. White as I fly to Athens to both lose and re-find myself—again.

I seek refuge in that city which denies it to so many. I come to catch my breath in those very same streets where thousands suffocate. I feel the most alive and free right there, where you are trapped.

As you die, I dream

—and call home your coffin.

BIBLIOGRAPHY

Arendt, Hannah. "We Refugees." *Menorah Journal* 31.1 (1943) 69–77.

Cazenave, Bruno, et al. "Vendre de manière désinteressée: le paradoxe de la communication des ONG." In *Dans le management des ONG*, 53–74. Paris: La Découverte, 2020. https://www-cairn-info.acces-distant.sciencespo.fr/le-management-des-ong-9782348059018-page-53.htm.

Debord, Guy. *La Société du Spectacle*. Paris: Buchet/Chastel, 1967.

Hours, Bernard. "L'idéologie humanitaire." *Journal des anthropologues* 77–78 (1999) 277–84. http://journals.openedition.org/jda/3084.

———. *L'idéologie humanitaire ou le spectacle de l'altérité perdue*. Paris: L'Harmattan, 1998.

13

Social Media and Migration

The Polish Case

Karol Wilczyński

It is almost a cliché to say that migration is a polarizing topic. Social media has been crucial in leading to this situation. But how to deal with it? How to make migration an important but not polarizing topic? How to start looking for sustainable solutions that use social media as a tool which will change the debate somehow? These questions could be a starting point for considering the future work in the field of migration in social media as well as for changes needed in the field of NGO and migration activism.

This chapter will briefly present how the migration debate has been shaped in Poland since 2014 (since before the so-called crisis in 2015) by politicians, media influencers, and decision-makers. As a social media specialist working on political campaigns, I witnessed firsthand the effects that the content on these platforms had on public discourse. I will argue that three connections led to the situation in which migration has been used as a tool in political debates. First, a connection was made between migration and national identity. Second a connection was made between migration and values. Third, a connection was made between migration and social polarization. These three factors are crucial in turning migration not only into a polarizing topic in public debate, but also into a "hot potato" on the political scene. Finally, the chapter will offer recommendations by identifying the reasons why migration as a topic in public debate is easy prey for populist politicians and why migration activists usually are not effective in their communication.[1]

THE INTEREST IN IMMIGRATION AND ISLAM IN POLAND

Nowadays it is quite easy to get the data for a general overview of what is happening in public debates. You can check Google Analytics, Meta Statistics or Google Trends to see some basic information regarding what is important. Let us have a look at two terms and the Google search activity regarding those terms, *uchodźcy* (refugees) and *islam* (Islam), between December 1, 2014, and December 31, 2022, in Poland:

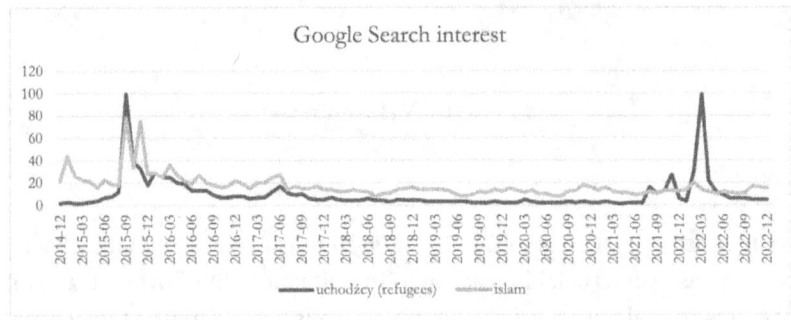

Graph 1: Google Search interest over time (December 1, 2014–December 31, 2022).[2]

Before September 2015 there was basically no interest in refugees and relatively low interest in Islam. High points of interest match the times of election campaigns (EU Election, 2014; Polish Parliamentary Election, 2015), which was observed by many researchers.[3] If we look at

---

1. It is important to note that, although crucial for understanding the dynamics of migration, this chapter will not cover the use of social media by people on the move—for instance how refugees practice transnational politics through social media as they navigate both the subjugation and subversion of power (Marlowe, "Social Media and Forced Migration") or how refugees use information obtained in social media in migration decision-making (Dekker et al., "Smart Refugees"; Alencar "Refugee Integration and Social Media").

2. https://trends.google.com/trends/explore?date=2014-12-01%202022-12-31&geo=PL&q=uchod%C5%BAcy,islam&hl=en-GB.

3. Sobczak-Szelc et al., "Securitisation of Asylum Seekers," 41.

the chronologically first top point in 2014, we observe that it coincides with EU elections. The interest is in Islam. In 2015 the situation is only a little different: "The narrative triggered at that time did not concern as much the influx of asylum seekers to Poland, which was minimal in numbers, but rather the European debate on relocation quotas of asylum applicants among the EU Member States."[4] At the beginning of 2017 an anti-migrant and anti-Muslim campaign was launched by the government in order to distract the public from other important issues:

> The state-funded media outlets seem to carefully select the guests invited to comment on issues related to Islam and its followers, which results in the strengthening of the stereotypical portrayal of a Muslim as "violent," "terrorist," "Jihadist," "sexist," "rapist," "uncivilised," "double-faced," and, in general, a "threat" to European and Christian values.[5]

That is why you can observe a small rise in interest. The fuel would not last for long though. As a consequence, the government moved on, using the topic of LGBT+ to trigger more emotions. And the two last increases in interest in refugees coincide with the humanitarian crisis at the Polish-Belarussian border (since summer 2021), and the full-scale Russian invasion in Ukraine (since February 2022), which resulted in a massive movement of people evacuated from Poland's eastern neighbour. It is the first time since 2014 that immigration and Islam were topics not exploited by politicians, and therefore not artificially "inflated."

However, populist politicians successfully connected the topics of immigration and Islam to national identity and national values, such as security, family, tradition in order to manipulate public opinion by triggering people's emotions.[6] The picture becomes clear when you look at *Centrum Badania Opinii Społecznej* (Public Opinion Research Centre) polls regarding welcoming refugees:

---

4. Sobczak-Szelc et al., "Securitisation of Asylum Seekers," 41.
5. Piela and Łukjanowicz, "Islamophobia in Poland," 466.
6. Bigo, "Security and Immigration."

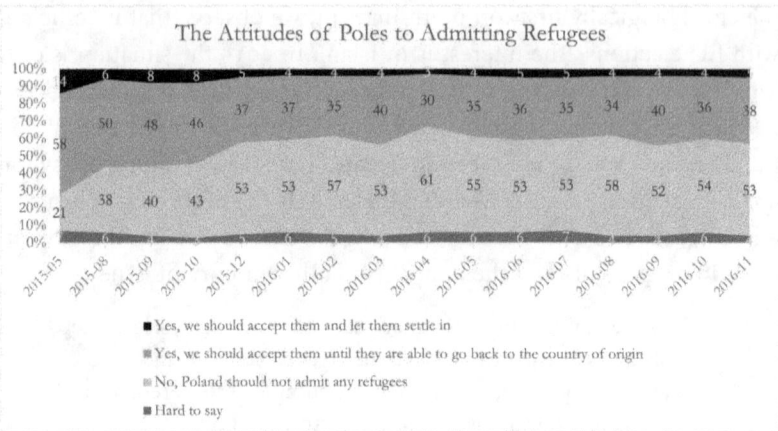

Graph 2: The Attitude of Poles to Admitting Refugees.[7]

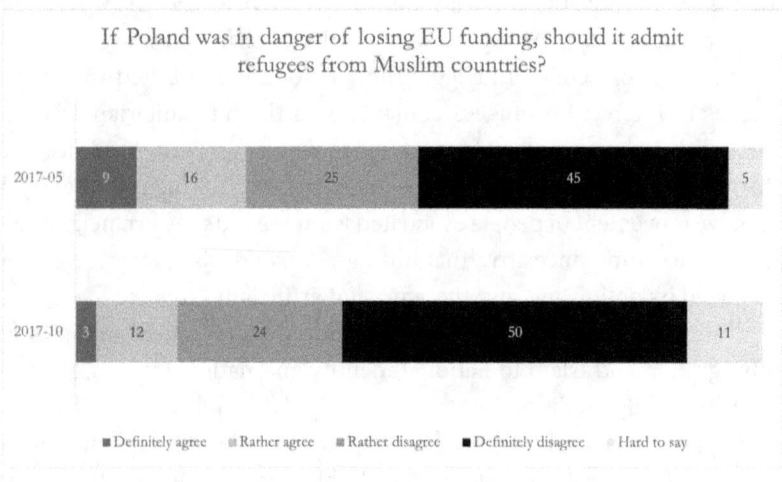

Graph 3: If Poland was in danger of losing EU funding, should it admit refugees from Muslim countries?[8]

Closer analysis of both charts shows that growing opposition to the reception of refugees did not coincide with, for example, terrorist attacks or an increase in the number of people coming to Poland or the EU, but above all with political campaigns. Between May and August 2015, there was the election campaign in which *Prawo i Sprawiedliwość* ("Law and

7. Feliksiak, "Stosunek do przyjmowania uchodźców."
8. Feliksiak, "Stosunek do przyjmowania uchodźców."

Justice") took over power (Graph 2). In April 2016, a campaign by right-wing parties aimed at rejecting the current policy of the European Commission on migration was launched in the V4 countries (the alliance of four Central European countries including the Czech Republic, Hungary, Poland, and Slovakia).

What happened in summer 2017? As in previous periods, there was neither an increase in migration movements in Poland nor new terrorist attacks. However, members of the Polish government played the anti-immigration and anti-Islam card to divert attention from the subject of judicial reform. In July, the Polish parliament, the Sejm, began to process three laws: on common courts, the Supreme Court, and the National Council of the Judiciary. Scaring people with stories about migrants and Muslims did not bring enough results this time though. Protests broke out all over the country. Before the courts, both in large cities and in small towns, people were lighting candles, forming chains of light in support of the rule of law. Unexpectedly, two out of three laws—on the National Council of the Judiciary and on the Supreme Court—were vetoed by President Andrzej Duda. Despite this, at the end of July, the European Commission launched a procedure to investigate a potential infringement of EU rules. In December, it decided to invoke Article 7.1 of the EU Treaty in connection with the violation of the rule of law in Poland, an invocation for which Poland pays a heavy price to this day. However, the fall of 2017 was also the moment when the anti-immigration and anti-Islam fuel burned out, and the government began to focus on abortion and LGBT+.

All in all, then, fearmongering campaigns were not only something which made many people on the move or Muslims suffer from growing xenophobia. From a social and political point of view, it was also crucial that migration was made a "hot potato" on the political scene. The ruling "Law and Justice" party was so successful in its aims mainly because most opposition politicians, members of the elite and the authorities remained silent. They were afraid of losing supporters. Voicing a pro-migrant position in 2015 could mean political suicide. How did this happen? To understand this, let us look closely at three basic connections which were made between migration and national identity, migration and values, and migration and emotions.

MIGRATION AND NATIONAL IDENTITY

Is national identity closely linked to migration? At first glance—not necessarily, and certainly not in the way that populist politicians are gradually building a case. Let us look at two examples:

Picture 1: "This is Poland! Not Brussels! Nobody here is supporting you!"—A very popular meme from 2015, presenting a group of people on the move at the Polish border with a group of men with Polish national symbols facing them. Source: Facebook Group "Nie dla Islamizacji Polski." Author: Unknown.

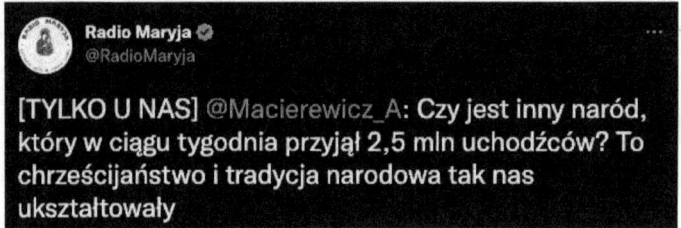

Picture 2: A tweet by Radio Maryja from 2022: "[ONLY HERE] @Macierewicz_A: Is there any other nation which welcomed 2.5 million refugees? This is how Christianity and national tradition have shaped us."[9]

There is no doubt that behind the success of anti-immigration and anti-Islam campaigns was the establishment of a strong link between national identity and migration. Through this link, people on the move were presented as a threat to one specific group—the Polish nation. Populist politicians used the group effect, building quick, easy to understand (even "memic") clichés: Poles are good, migrants are bad.

9. Radio Maryja, "A. Macierewicz."

Moreover, the link allowed them to make the anti-immigration and anti-Islam stance black and white, and therefore very easy to use. Reduced to trivial nationalism,[10] the subject of migration has become an easy tool for manipulation. Instead of being a difficult topic regarding one of the most important challenges of the twenty-first century, migration has become the subject of a simple debate: are you for it or against it? And if you are "for migration," you immediately become an enemy of the nation. The tweet, citing Antoni Macierewicz, one of the leading politicians of the ruling party at the time, shows that the Law and Justice party is using the same link to show the opponents of welcoming Ukrainian citizens as enemies of the nation. What is important here is that this way of presenting the topic also closes any rational discussion on the means and ways to build a migration policy in Poland.[11]

MIGRATION AND VALUES

After connecting migration to national identity and the banalization of the topic, the fear-mongering campaign adopted by Law and Justice was designed to connect the issues of immigration and Islam to the values of security, tradition, and family.

Picture 3: "Immigrants Good Homies. They had a blast with the French."
A very popular meme in 2016, showing Paris after a terrorist attack.
Source: Facebook Group "Nie dla Islamizacji Polski."
Author: Fanpage "Dobre Ziomki Imigranci"

---

10. For more on the banalization of Islamophobia, see Sobczak-Szelc et al., "Securitisation of Asylum Seekers," 63.

11. For more about this context, see Guenther et al., "Strategic Framing and Social Media Engagement."

Why exactly these values? It might not be clear for those who do not know Poland well, but according to most surveys "Family" and "Tradition" are the most important values for most Poles (Family—52 percent, Tradition—45 percent).[12] The biggest fear is then created by this link which presents migration as a threat to these values. That is why Law and Justice did a lot of work to show migrants and Muslims as people who create a danger to family and tradition. This is the way these values can mobilize people. Moreover, feeling secure is one of the most basic, natural needs of human beings. That is why providing a concrete reason to feel insecure might trigger fear and, of course, anger. Insecurity though, as a consequence of the immigration process, is both socially and politically constructed.[13] Another step, for Law and Justice politicians, is to show themselves as "sheriffs" who maintain law and order.

MIGRATION AND SOCIAL POLARIZATION

This is how we get to the clue—emotions. It is through them that the manipulation works. Through them, populists win elections.

Picture 4: "Oktoberfest 2025"
A very popular meme in 2015, presenting a crowd of Muslims at prayer.
Source: Fanpage Jeb z Dzidy. Author: Unknown.[14]

What emotions does the meme above stir up among Poles? Anger towards people who might enforce a ban on alcohol. Fear that Poles will

---

12. ARC, "Wspólne wartości w życiu Polaków."
13. Sobczak-Szelc et al., "Securitisation of Asylum Seekers," 65.
14. https://9gag.com/gag/azq1BgB.

lose their right to celebrate the way they want. And of course, the fear that if Germany is "already lost" to immigrants, then how easily will Poland be "conquered" by them?

Overall, then, manipulating emotions is a powerful way to centre attention around a specific topic. To present yourself as a saviour in a time of uncertainty, a "sheriff" who defends the family that is at the root of the nation. You know whom to vote for in order to save the motherland. Or at the very least you know not to vote for those who—through their political positions or promises—create a substantial danger to us, our lives, our families, our cities, our country.[15]

Crucially, my own experience working with social media shows me that activists and academics who advocate for people on the move are not aware of these connections. Hence, they often create polarizing statements which might help rather than hinder the anti-immigration narratives of populists. They are trapped by the black and white of the memes, thus also presenting migration as a topic that you can only be for or against.[16] So, what can be done?

RECOMMENDATIONS

The lessons I learnt from several years of working in the field of migration and media?[17] Most of all, I would suggest being clear on what is at stake here. It is about people on the move. However, particularly in Poland, it is also about creating the sustainable migration policy that we do not have at the moment. I would say, then, that as decision-makers, stakeholders, activists, and people on the move, we should focus on the purpose—to build a sustainable system of protection of human rights. Consistent adherence to this purpose will allow us to build a coherent communication strategy around it, which populists will not be able to tear down so easily.

1. Remember That Migration Is About Both Refugees and Receivers

We are responsible for welcoming those who seek refuge here. However, there is nothing wrong with also caring about those who have lived here for a long time. As advocates for people on the move, we often react with

15. See also Parrott et al., "Portrayals of Immigrants and Refugees."
16. See also Radojevic et al., "Visual Framing and Migrant Discourses."
17. Ideas below are paraphrased from an article I wrote for the Slovak portal fjuzn.sk in 2022, "How to Break the Vicious Circle of Selective Solidarity?"

indignation when we collide with the xenophobia of fearful people who listen to the populist propaganda that presents migration as a threat. Although this indignation is sometimes justified, we need to develop empathy for people who believe in the populist propaganda of programmes such as TVP, the Polish state television that implements the government's agenda. It is difficult for us to accept the fact that people watching this type of media—of course there are millions of them in Poland—are unable to develop a different image of people on the move. It is difficult for us to see the perspective through the eyes of others.[18] But we cannot only call for empathy for people on the move.

2. Remember That Fear Is Natural

I see a dangerous trend among people who are open to accepting refugees to moralize, rejecting those who embrace populist propaganda. Unfortunately, shutting ourselves in an ivory tower of moral superiority will not help us listen to each other. It will lead to further polarization. We need to look with empathy to understand the sources of fear that fuel populists.

3. Cooperation Is Key

The key to introducing a wise migration policy, stopping the double standard of treating people on the move, dividing between "deserving" and "undeserving" people, is cooperation at various levels: national and international institutions, NGOs of all sizes, governments on local and supra-local levels, and civil society at large. We should use all the ways we can find to ally with each other, even those which might not be obvious, such as working with celebrities. For this, however, mutual trust is needed—and it is born of many years of cooperation. Without cooperation, there is no trust and without trust, there is no cooperation. This could be a vicious or a virtuous cycle. Today is the day we should start turning it around.

BIBLIOGRAPHY

Alencar, Amanda. "Refugee Integration and Social Media: A Local and Experiential Perspective." *Information, Communication & Society* 21.11 (2018) 1588–603.

ARC Rynek i Opinia. "Wspólne wartości w życiu Polaków: rodzina na 1. miejscu." *eGospodarka.pl*, November 11, 2022. https://www.egospodarka.

---

18. See Hochschild, *Strangers in their Own Land*.

pl/178704,Wspolne-wartosci-w-zyciu-Polakow-rodzina-na-1-miejscu,1,39,1.html.

Bigo, Didier. "Security and Immigration: Toward a Critique of the Governmentality of Unease." *Alternatives: Global, Local, Political* 27 (2002) 63–92.

Dekker, Rianne, et al. "Smart Refugees: How Syrian Asylum Migrants Use Social Media Information in Migration Decision-Making." *Social Media + Society* 4.1 (2018). https://doi.org/10.1177/2056305118764439.

Feliksiak, Michał, ed. "Stosunek do przyjmowania uchodźców." In *Komunikat z badań* 163. Warsaw: Centrum Badania Opinii Społecznej (CBOS), 2017. http://www.cbos.pl/spiskom.pol/2017/K_163_17.pdf.

Guenther, Lars, et al. "Strategic Framing and Social Media Engagement: Analyzing Memes Posted by the German Identitarian Movement on Facebook." *Social Media + Society* 6.1 (2020). https://doi.org/10.1177/2056305119898777.

Hochschild, Arlie Russell. *Strangers in their Own Land: Anger and Mourning on the American Right*. New York: New Press, 2016.

Marlowe, Jay. "Social Media and Forced Migration: The Subversion and Subjugation of Political Life." *Media and Communication* 7.2 (2019) 173–83.

Parrott, Scott, et al. "Portrayals of Immigrants and Refugees in US News Media: Visual Framing and its Effect on Emotions and Attitudes." *Journal of Broadcasting & Electronic Media* 63.4 (2019) 677–97.

Piela, Anna, and Anna Łukjanowicz. *Islamophobia in Poland: National Report 2017, European Islamophobia Report 2017*. Edited by Enes Bayraklı and Farid Hafez. Istanbul: SETA, 2018.

Radio Maryja. "A. Macierewicz: Czy jest inny naród, który w ciągu tygodnia przyjął 2,5 mln uchodźców? To chrześcijaństwo i tradycja narodowa tak nas ukształtowały." *Radio Maryja*, April 15, 2022. https://www.radiomaryja.pl/informacje/tylko-u-nas-a-macierewicz-czy-jest-inny-narod-ktory-w-ciagu-tygodnia-przyjal-25-mln-uchodzcow-to-chrzescijanstwo-i-tradycja-narodowa-tak-nas-uksztaltowaly.

Radojevic, Radmila, et al. "Visual Framing and Migrant Discourses in Social Media: The Story of Idomeni on Instagram." In *Understanding Media and Society in the Age of Digitalisation*, edited by Dennis Nguyen et al., 157–82. New York: Palgrave Macmillan, 2020.

Sobczak-Szelc, Karolina, et al. "Securitisation of Asylum Seekers and Refugees in Political and Media Discourses." In *From Reception to Integration of Asylum Seekers and Refugees in Poland*, 41–67. London: Routledge, 2022.

14

From Narrative to Policy and Back

A Glimpse into the Potential of Practitioners

ALESSIA PASSARELLI

ABOUT ONE IN THIRTY people no longer live in the country in which they were born.[1] This includes a vast number of people who moved because of conflicts and civil wars—a number that increases year by year at a frightening pace. And it does not include those who were internally displaced. It only accounts for people who, at the risk of their lives, attempt to cross borders and succeed.

They risk their lives partly because of increasing barriers and security measures introduced by safe countries like those in Europe. Instead of offering protection to those in need, Europe responds by becoming an increasingly "gated community."[2] And yet an alternative is possible, as

---

1. For a helpful statistical overview, see McAuliffe and Triandafyllidou, "World Migration Report 2022."

2. "The typical European policy response to the migration challenge has been to extend border controls, employ military techniques of surveillance, and increase detentions and expulsions. 'Frontex' is the EU intelligence-led agency for coordinating external border security throughout the EU member states. Based in Warsaw, it began operations in May of 2005 and by 2014 had a staff of 317 and an operational budget of €89 million. It is one of several EU agencies attending to the concept of 'Integrated EU Border Management.' In this respect, EU policies are principally focused on security, border control and voluntary repatriation and less focused on developing methods and

different reactions to the challenges of 2015 and 2022 showed. In 2015, in reaction to the so-called "refugee crisis," the national governments pressed for a revision of border controls and more stringent and stricter monitoring of migrant entry. In 2022, however, Europe showed a different face, as it quickly introduced temporary protection mechanisms for Ukrainian refugees and accommodated six million people in the first year of the war.[3]

Faith-based organizations are key actors in advocating at both national and European levels for a more humane approach to people on the move. On the one hand, they underline the need for a shared procedure for requesting asylum; on the other hand, they emphasize the demand for safe passages to Europe and preventing deaths at sea. For example, humanitarian corridors are among the best practices promoted by the Federation of Protestant Churches in Italy and the Community of Sant Egidio, which have enabled several thousand people to arrive safely in Italy.[4] This set a precedent for practices that other European countries later adopted.

This chapter aims to analyse migration and migration discourses from the perspective of practitioners working in or with faith-based organizations. Their lived experiences, including the role of faith in their work, will be contrasted with media narratives and government policies. The chapter will draw on a pilot research project, which investigated practitioners collaborating within A World of Neighbours (AWoN), to show how migration, migration policies, and religion are understood through the experiences of those working on the front lines of accompaniment of people on the move. It will use extracts from some of the interviews conducted in 2022 by the research team and results from a questionnaire directed to practitioners during the first year of AWoN's existence.[5] By

---

programmes to integrate migrants into European societies or on providing legal and welfare provision to those migrants who are seeking asylum in the European member states" (Jackson and Passarelli, *Mapping Migration, Mapping Churches' Responses*, 18).

3. For statistical data on Ukraine that is updated regularly, see UNHCR, "Ukraine Refugee Situation."

4. For the work of Mediterranean Hope, see Mediterranean Hope, "Human Corridors."

5. The aim of the questionnaire was to understand who the practitioners were, what they did, their background, and to understand migration flows and European policies, and ultimately the role of religion in their lives. It was a pilot phase of the project, involving thirty practitioners. Even if the group has changed quite a bit since then, the results of the survey remain. They offer a glimpse into the thoughts of AWoN

that, this chapter offers glimpses into the potential of the practitioners. Their experience puts them in a promising position to counter closed narratives, calling for new policies.

WHY NARRATIVES MATTER

In 2017 the World Association for Christian Communication and the Churches' Commission for Migrants in Europe issued a report: *Changing the Narrative: Media Representation of Refugees and Migrants in Europe*.[6] The London School of Economics published its analysis of the link between media and migration in the same year,[7] while in 2021 UNESCO published a handbook on *Reporting on Migrants and Refugees: Handbook for Journalism Educators*.[8] These reports underlined that the media portrayal of migrants is highly problematic. Migrant voices are lacking. Migrants most often are represented as a voiceless group, with no mentions of their names or their individual stories. When the agency of migrants is accounted for, it is done in a sensationalist way, which contributes to a climate of fear, apprehension, and social instability. On top of that, the facts concerning migration are often distorted.

Three phases concerning a narrative around refugees and migrants could be differentiated: (1) pre-2015; (2) the "refugee crisis" of 2015–2016; and (3) the war in Ukraine in 2022. When in 2007 my colleague Darrell Jackson and I started our work on a report for the Churches' Commission for Migrants in Europe and the World Council of Churches entitled *Mapping Migration, Mapping Churches' Responses in Europe* (with subsequent editions in 2016 and 2021),[9] one of the objectives was to clarify facts and figures, starting from the definition of who is a migrant, to descriptions of why people move. Already at that time, there was the need to explain that there was no "invasion" of Europe. It was important to underline the power of certain passports and the representation of Europeans or Westerners as "expats" vis-à-vis all other people seen as "migrants" with a scale of negative connotations.

---

activists at the time. Together with the interviews, we get a reliable picture.

6. See Pierigh, *Changing the Narrative*.
7. Chouliaraki et al., *European "Migration Crisis" and the Media*.
8. See Fengler et al., *Reporting on Migrants and Refugees*.
9. For the newest edition, see Jackson et al., *Mapping Migration, Mapping Churches' Responses*.

However, the years 2015–2016 represented a narrative change. The European media systematically framed migrants' arrival as a "refugee crisis," and people were identified either as "victimised others" or "dangerous others." More than a million people reached Europe and most of them arrived as a result of the war in Syria in 2016. Arrivals reached unprecedented numbers but, analysing the situation globally, most refugees and displaced people remained outside of Europe, in the countries close to the war territories such as Lebanon (where the Syrian refugees counted as 27 percent of the population).

The practitioners of AWoN also testify to this shift. An interviewee from Germany stressed how the issues related to migration were often presented as a "problem," as migrants were seen as people in need:

> When you talk about migration in public, it's very close to the topic "problem." And so how can this big problem of migration be solved? What way is the best to solve the migration problem? When we talk about migrants, it is very often in a way that they are in need of help and maybe they don't really fit into our society. Yeah, these are the main narratives I would think of. . . . To be honest, I don't hear the phrase "the ship is full" very often, but in the past, it occurred every now and then, especially in the times of the big refugee movement in 2015.

An interviewee from the Netherlands problematized the concept of "refugee crisis," drawing parallels between today and 2015.

> I think there's a lot of talk about streams of refugees and flows . . . as if we are, like, completely overthrown and overwhelmed by refugees. Well, I mean there was maybe more in 2015 when we were told it was really about the refugee crisis. And, I think, when we just started AWoN, somebody said, like, "There is a refugee crisis, but it's not in Europe and there is a crisis in Europe, but it's not a refugee crisis," or something. And I think this is sort of, this saying is completely right, because in the public sphere it's talked about as if it's a big crisis and as if we can't handle it as rich countries. And in our municipality, because I work with undocumented migrants, and, now, when the Ukrainians came, we saw on Twitter and like, "OK, now we're going to have a place for the real refugees."
>
> Yeah, a lot, I mean, I work, like I said, with undocumented migrants, so they were already rejected. They went through the asylum system, one or two or three times, maybe more. They were rejected all the time. I also work with work migrants who

have been here, sometimes more than 30 years, who worked, who even paid taxes in the 90s and they stayed here and then the laws became stricter and stricter. And now they're homeless and all—so taken down by the system or something. And then there's also my work with migrants we see from, for example Indonesia, Philippines. They pretty much work here, like in the informal sector. All those people are in this mostly vulnerable position, because of all those laws and also because of the ideas about refugees.

The issue of "deserving" refugees emerged in comparing Syrian and African refugees with the Ukrainians arriving in 2022 after the outbreak of war. It seems that with the latter group, narratives, perceptions, and policies changed. Suddenly, there was a space for refugees, numbers were not problematic, and getting access to services was less complex. The experience of a Swedish practitioner highlights some of these shifts:

> My answer . . . six weeks ago would have been completely different, right? All of the Ukrainian refugees fleeing Ukraine—prior to that, I experienced the narrative across Europe since 2016 to be a lot about not having space, and that the narrative was a lot about economic migrants and a lot of people questioning why people are fleeing and a lot of people questioning why, why they don't stay in the safest nearest country. So for Syrian refugees, there are several safe countries prior to coming to Sweden or to Germany. Why don't they stay there?
>
> And there was also a narrative on, on crimes and about a lot of male migrants committing crimes. I experienced that narrative, those narratives, to gain ground since 2016. Prior to 2016, since 2015, at least in Sweden, the narrative was quite open-minded. . . . We needed to welcome those people fleeing—but it has changed. So for me it has changed a lot during the fall of 2015, and then gradually changed in 2016, and then it's just gotten worse, basically. There are differences in the narrative depending on if, if we're talking on, like, a European level, our national level or down to local levels. So in my hometown . . . the narrative hasn't been that negative at all.

The interview with the Swedish practitioner took place a few weeks after the beginning of the war when people were still in shock and many countries were opening their borders, letting people in, taking them by car, crossing borders without controls. Highly sensitive gestures that only a few days earlier would have been considered crimes in many European countries—and still were, if they referred to the "other" type of refugees.

To add further elements to the discussion, a British interviewee recalls the intentional migrations of the 1950s and 1960s, pointing out how, although there was a need for labour, fear related to cultural differences and prejudices remained, together with an awareness of the different treatment of migrants related to their origins.

> For the last sort of sixty years or seventy years . . . migration has been enabled and encouraged. Because of, sort of, industrialization and labour shortages. And even at that time, there was unease about it. Uh, but it was generally accepted that it was required. And then more recently, in the last twenty-five years, kind of, under the radar, um, because this was, or this never seemed like an official policy perhaps because it was politically acceptable, but the government had pursued a policy of, um, open migration and to some extent, we didn't have a choice about that because we were part of the European Union. Our economy really benefited and we, you know, increased substantially as a result of migration, mainly from Europe.
>
> And, on the other side, now there is this sense of fear, um, which is emerging in communities, and I think that it's partly related to, sort of, sensitivity and concern about loss of a particular, um, characterization of their country. Um, but, yeah, I, I think fear is the big one and what the Ukraine crisis has really shown is that actually fear is based on, uh, a sense of not being culturally familiar with the migrants that are coming, in other words, feeling, um, feeling they're somehow strange, somehow people are unable that they differ in terms of values, uh, and certainly culture and religion. And, and, and that I think has been really interesting because while the whole sort of narrative about Ukraine, migrants coming to, to UK and to Europe, you know, has been really encouraging, um, but it also underlies the stark difference when that migration was from the Middle East or North Africa. And so, I suppose prejudice is another word that comes in, and fear of, sort of, cultural contamination, if you like, it's not quite the right word.

One argument is that Ukrainians are less "dangerous" because they are more "similar" than other groups due to their skin colour and Christian tradition. They are viewed as, at least in theory, sharing the same values. A German practitioner reports how, in the different phases, refugees were differentiated by creating first- and second-class refugees, and then over time, when media attention waned, the routine brought out the shadow situations or made way for new A-list refugees.

> I feel more that it's all the same again because in 2015 in the beginning . . . it was very good. To help Syrian refugees and to be friendly to them, they were refugees first class. Today, it has changed, of course. Now the Ukrainians, they are the refugees first class. But I don't expect that this will last very long. Maybe it will last a little bit longer because now most of them are women and children. And the Ukrainian culture may be a little bit closer to our culture than the Syrian culture, but I don't expect that in six months, or one year, people in the public will say, oh, we have to give them shelter in our houses. We have to help them. We have to stay together. I don't expect it. OK, I would be very happy if this happens, because I think that everybody in such a situation deserves help from those who are rich and have everything. But I don't expect it.

These short testimonials highlight the importance of media narratives in the lives of people on the move and the work of practitioners. They are not simply a matter of reporting, but they shape consciousness, limiting what seems possible with regards to migration. However, while narratives limit what seems possible, the policies, at least in principle, limit what can be done in practice.

WHY POLICIES MATTER

The constitution of AWoN is not representative of the general population with regards to migration background. Among the practitioners who responded to our questionnaire, 41 percent declared to have migrated themselves. Knowing the realities of migrating, these practitioners remain critical towards their governments' migration policies, and often actively counteract them by providing migrants and refugees with shelter, food, psychological support, language courses, legal advice, and so on.

According to Chart 1, 85 percent of respondents think that people on the move are not treated well. According to Chart 2, around the same percentage think that their work with AWoN has motivated their conviction that migration policies need to change. However, there is disagreement between the practitioners on the exact shape of such regulations. Even though a significant majority of practitioners think that there should not be a distinction between deserving and undeserving migrants, 22 percent think otherwise. Moreover, faced with the statement "Europe should welcome everybody who wants to live here" (Chart 3), opinions differ even more. While 54 percent agree with the statement, 27 percent disagree with the statement, and 19 percent have no clear opinion on the matter.

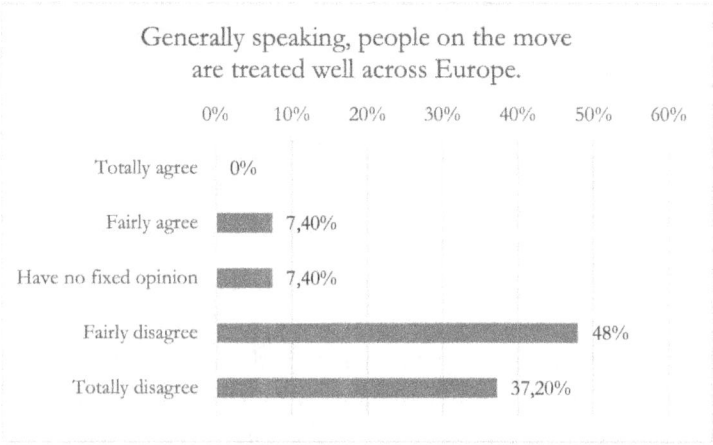

Chart 1: Perceptions of the Situation of People on the Move

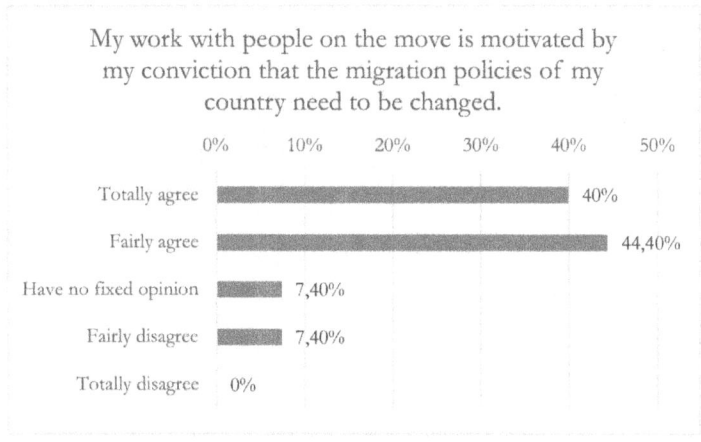

Chart 2: Motivations for Working in AWoN

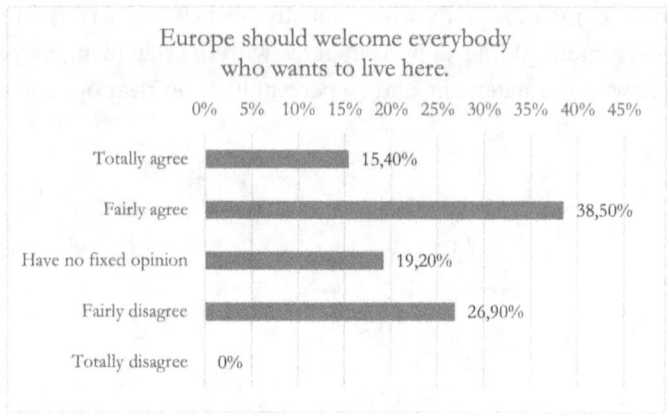

Chart 3: Migration into Europe

But although laws and policies limit the actions of practitioners in principle, that is not always the case in practice. The vast majority of practitioners (86 percent) agrees with the following statement: "I try to respect the law under all circumstances" (Chart 4). However, the picture is blurred if they are asked "If laws are unjust, they must be broken" (Chart 5). In that case 44 percent agree, 30 percent disagree, and 26 percent do not have a clear opinion. Furthermore, similar to previous percentages, 48 percent think that their work with AWoN has made them more critical of the migration policies in their country—while 26 percent do not have an opinion and 26 percent do not agree (Chart 6).

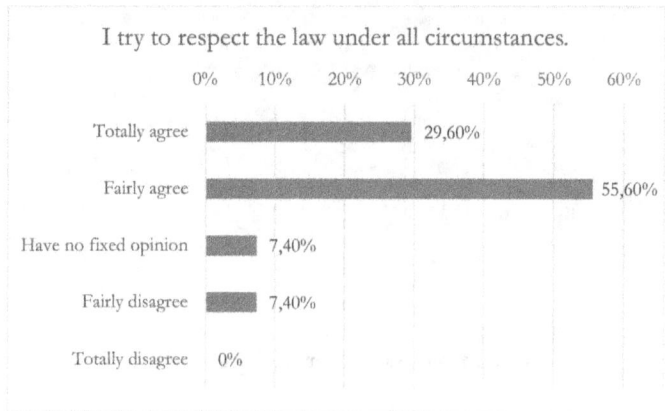

Chart 4: Respect for Laws

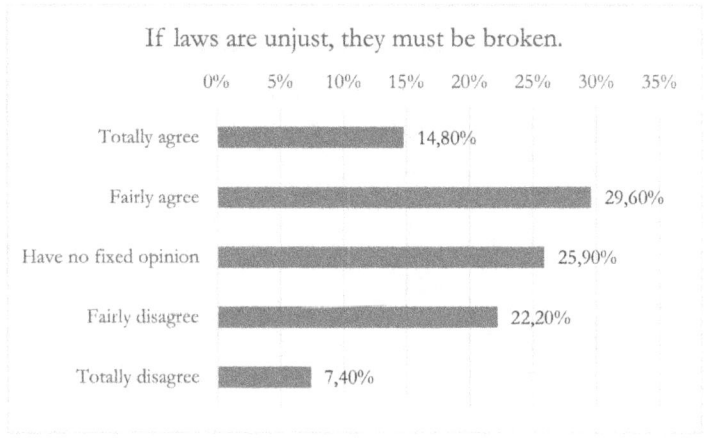

Chart 5: Respect for Unjust Laws

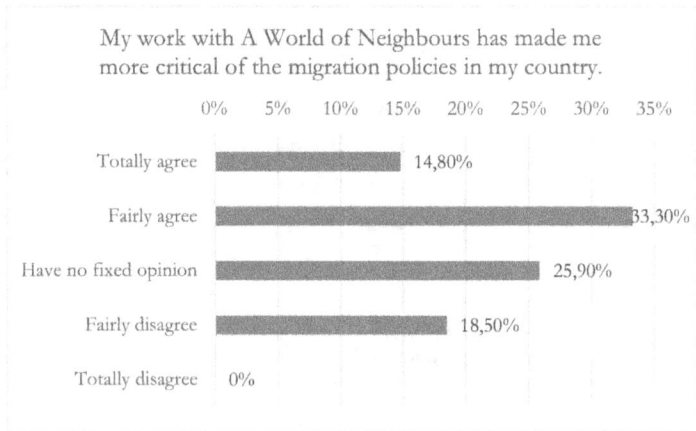

Chart 6: Critique of Migration Policies

In relation to religion, 85 percent of the respondents believe that religion is an important resource for welcoming people on the move. Practitioners come from different backgrounds: 59 percent self-identify as Christian, 18 percent as Muslim and 11 percent as Humanist. Percentages continue to be high in relation to religious practices (prayers, meditation, attending religious services).

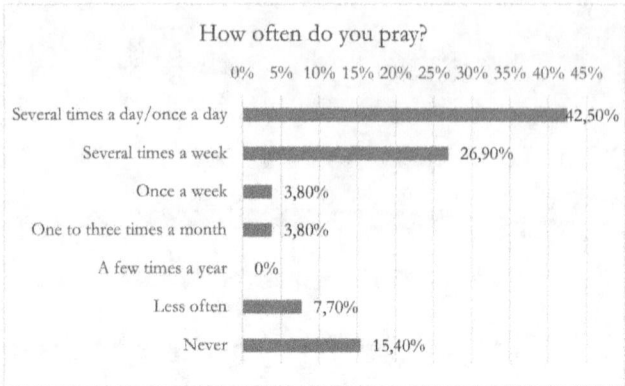

Chart 7: Prayer

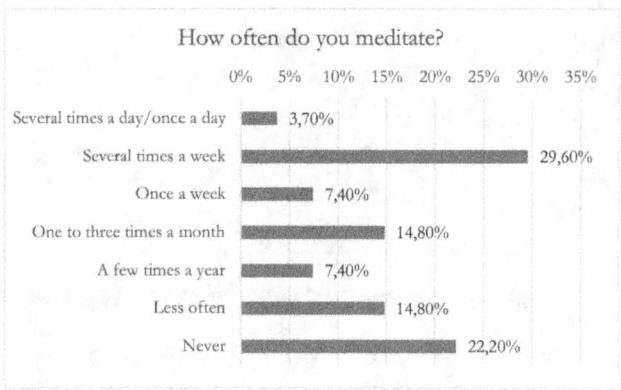

Chart 8: Meditation

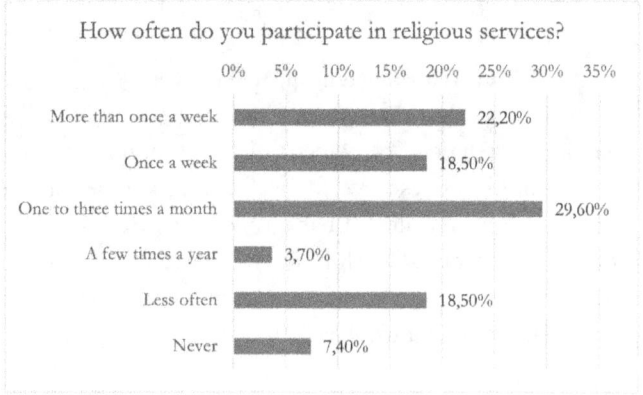

Chart 9: Participation in Services

Around 55 percent agree that working with AWoN has increased their sensitivity towards religious issues. While a similar percentage states that they often read religious books, 63 percent of the sample claims that "every religion has a core of truth." Practitioners also consider encountering people from different religions as an enrichment (more than 90 percent). Religious diversity is seen as a resource rather than a problem or a threat (with respect to media representation). When asked whether "it is easier to work with people of the same religious or non-religious background," 66 percent of the respondents disagreed, 22 percent had no definite opinion and only almost 15 percent agreed.

These charts show that practitioners in AWoN are aware of the situation of migrants. Although religiosity is not a requirement for AWoN practitioners, religion plays an important role for them. The multi-faith set-up helps them to learn more about other faiths and their own faiths. This seems to break down prejudice, which in turn can lead to new narratives about migration.

WHAT AWON CAN DO

This chapter has attempted to interweave the debate on migration policies and the media portrayal of migrants and refugees with practitioners' experiences related to AWoN. We can draw several conclusions from the responses of practitioners.

First of all, there is a clear correspondence between reports about the influence of the media on how migrants and refugees are perceived and consequently treated in European countries, and what practitioners, in different countries, have experienced and lived.

Second, different treatment is given to refugees and migrants according to the country of origin, reasons to migrate, and way of arrival. These factors are used to stratify people on the move. Such a stratification was seen with the outbreak of the war in Syria and then the beginning of the war in Ukraine in 2022.

Third, being a part of the A World of Neighbours project and working closely with migrants and refugees—and in some cases being migrants or refugees themselves—increases awareness of migration routes and national and European migration policies. Awareness often leads to awareness-raising in society and involvement in network advocacy.

Fourth and finally, although being a believer is not a requirement to work within AWoN, religion plays an important role for practitioners.

The interfaith component helps them to learn more about their own religion and to interface with and approach religions. Meeting people of different cultures and faiths also helps to recognize and break down prejudices, contributing to a more inclusive and respectful society. Practitioners, then, are in a promising position to counter the closed narratives that restrict the welcoming of people on the move in Europe. Of course, networks like AWoN are not the solution to all problems or to all perceived problems that have to do with migration, but they offer a pertinent point of departure.

BIBLIOGRAPHY

Chouliaraki, Lilie, et al. *The European "Migration Crisis" and the Media: A Cross-European Press Content Analysis.* London: LSE, 2017.

Fengler, Susanne, et al., eds. *Reporting on Migrants and Refugees: Handbook for Journalism Educators.* Paris: UNESCO, 2021.

Jackson, Darrell, and Alessia Passarelli. *Mapping Migration, Mapping Churches' Responses: Being Church Together.* Brussels: CCME and WCC, 2020.

Mediterranean Hope. "Human Corridors." *Mediterranean Hope,* n.d. https://www.mediterraneanhope.com/en/humanitarian-corridors.

McAuliffe, Marie, and Anna Triandafyllidou, eds. *World Migration Report 2022.* Geneva: International Organization for Migration, 2021.

Pierigh, Francesca. *Changing the Narrative: Media Presentation of Refugees and Migrants in Europe. A Project of the World Association for Christian Communication—Europe Region and the Churches' Commission for Migrants in Europe.* Brussels: CCME and WACC, 2018.

United Nations High Commissioner for Refugees (UNHCR). "Ukraine Refugee Situation." *Operational Data Portal* (ODP), n.d. https://data.unhcr.org/en/situations/ukraine.

Part III

The Change

15

The Evolving Torah of Human Migration

Notes on a Jewish Theology of Migration

Rebecca Lillian

In 2021, at an online version of the customary late-night text study ritual known as *Tikkun Leyl Shavuot*,[1] I offered a lesson on the Jewish ethical imperative to welcome foreigners with compassion, protect refugees and other vulnerable migrants, and not to stand idly by in the face of xenophobia. My session was titled "You Know the Soul of the Stranger: The Evolving Torah of Human Migration" and was based on a selection of traditional Jewish texts from biblical and rabbinic sources, and medieval and modern commentaries on them.

Although my rabbinate is devoted to *Torah lishma*—the Jewish concept that studying our sacred texts for the love of learning is an integral aspect of Jewish religious practice—I had not intended this lesson to be only that. It was inspired by five years of working directly with newly arrived refugees from Syria and Afghanistan with my colleagues at an interfaith social cohesion project in Malmö, Sweden, between 2015 and 2020. There were days when at least one thousand people per day were

---

1. *Tikkun Leyl Shavuot*, the custom of creating study circles that discuss Jewish texts through the night of Shavuot, was likely developed in the sixteenth century. The concept has its main roots in the *Zohar*, the primary source of Jewish mysticism, but more recently the practice has expanded far beyond the mystics.

arriving at Malmö Central Train Station. Our primary role was to create a space where newcomers could meet one another and locals of all backgrounds; there were informal classes in Swedish and English on how to navigate the Swedish infrastructure; there were opportunities for all of us to share music, food, handwork, and stories. I became part of a regional network of other activists and people on the move. In the process, I began to create educational resources to share with other activists who were either Jewish or interested in a Jewish text-based perspective on the ethical imperative to welcome newcomers and protect refugees. This chapter is a continuation of that project.

Following the session, a friend—the scholar and activist Zachary Gallant—asked whether I would be interested in working with him on a project about Jewish migration theology. I replied that I rarely read theology; my teaching is modelled on the traditional text-based *shiur*.[2] But then Zachary pointed out that he had done some research into the work of Christian theologians who are working on migration theology, finding out that a vast majority of their biblical citations were from the Torah (Pentateuch). And yet, to his knowledge, no comprehensive study of post-Torah Jewish texts on migration theology had been undertaken to the extent that it has been done in Christianity. Zachary's early research into this led him to a question he posed to me: Perhaps no "theology of migration" within Judaism has been identified because Judaism, in addition to being a theology of repairing brokenness, and a theology of relationship, *is* migration theology.[3] And so we began to work together, and my reflections on a Jewish theology of migration are indebted to Zachary. My intention in this chapter is to open a conversation sparked by Zachary's question: To what extent can Judaism be described as a "theology of migration"?

It is no wonder that most biblical citations in Christian theologies of migration come from the Torah. The five books of Moses contain story after story of people forced (or, in the case of Abraham, commanded) to leave their homes and seek refuge in a foreign land. There are also the tales of wayfarers, refugees, and other people on the move being welcomed with warm and generous hospitality. We meet the first Jew[4] when

---

2. A *shiur* is a study-session on a portion of Judaic text, combining a brief lecture by a teacher followed by a small group study and discussion.

3. Zachary Gallant discusses this in depth in an unpublished paper, "Judaism as Migration Theology."

4. Or so Abraham is often called by today's Jews. Actually, he was the first

then Avram and Sarai heed the divine directive of *Lech lecha:* "Leave your native land, leave your ancestral home, leave all that is familiar to you ... and you shall become a blessing" (Gen 12:12).

One of these blessings is that Abraham and Sarah become the exemplars of hospitality. According to a rabbinic midrash, Abraham and Sarah always kept their tent flaps open on all four sides so that they could watch in every direction for wayfarers who might need some shade, some water, and some sustenance in the harsh desert climate. Another midrash states that wherever this nomadic family found themselves, they would always put up their tents in the middle of a crossroads—not the most comfortable spot to reside, but one that gave travellers greatest access to these generous hosts.

In one of the oft-recounted stories about Abraham, God appears to him through the trees where Abraham is camped. But at the very moment that God calls out to him, Abraham notices three men approaching. He does not wait for them to come to the door, but runs out to greet them, offering rest and refreshment. Abraham's bold decision became the basis for an abiding principle in Judaism: "Greater is hospitality than receiving the Divine presence."[5] Faced with a choice between communing with God and choosing human hospitality, Abraham took the latter. He understood that the truest way to understand the Holy One is to see the Divine image in the face of another human being. He knew that to serve God and to offer hospitality to strangers are *not* two distinct concepts. They are in fact one and the same.

Genesis also portrays our ancestors—from Abraham and Sarah through Jacob and his enormous family—as climate refugees, fleeing to Egypt to escape a famine in the land. Indeed, that is precisely how the children of Israel ended up in *Mitsrayim*.[6] Although Joseph's high position allowed the Israelites to live well for generations, when a new Pharoah who did not remember why these were supposed to be "the good immigrants," came to power, the Israelites were enslaved for centuries.

This seemingly interminable period of oppression is why the Jewish people "know the soul of the stranger" (Exod 23:9). The Torah unceasingly reminds us that because of this, we are required to welcome every

Hebrew—the Jewish people did not exist prior to receiving the Torah at Sinai.

5. Babylonian Talmud, Shabbat 127a among many other places.

6. The Hebrew name for Egypt is *Mitsrayim*. Although it is close to the Arabic place name *Misr*, the name is also equated with the word for "straights" or "narrow places," because the Israelites suffered under slavery there for 400 years.

stranger and treat them with compassion. Indeed, the injunction that is repeated the most often in the entire Torah concerns the treatment of the *ger* (רג), the stranger or foreigner. From the initial revelation at Sinai and throughout the forty-year-long trek through the wilderness towards the Promised Land, the Holy One cautions the nascent Jewish people against oppressing the stranger no fewer than thirty-six times. According to the Babylonian Talmud (Kiddushin 27b), it may be as many as forty-six.

The commandment to safeguard the stranger first appears in the Torah portion known as *Mishpatim* (Laws), part of a long, multifaceted list of complex decrees. Many of them pertain to other aspects of social justice, such as protecting widows and orphans, ensuring that the poor have food to eat, and treating itinerant labourers fairly. Other laws discuss damages and reparations; important rules for governing a wholly new society of formerly enslaved people. The injunction not to harm the stranger fits well with these other laws, but it stands out because of its repetition (it appears twice in this Torah portion alone), and because the historical-psychological reasoning that lies behind the commandment is unique to the discussion of how to treat the foreigner.

None of the other laws promulgated in *Mishpatim* make mention of the reasoning behind them. Biblical scholar Nechama Leibowitz points this out, highlighting that we are not merely commanded to treat the foreigner well, we are also required to develop empathy as an outgrowth of our own negative experience as a persecuted minority.[7] Whenever we meet a foreigner, we are bidden to put ourselves in their position by remembering how we felt when we ourselves were strangers in another land. In other words, this commandment has a two-fold impact: it ensures that the strangers in our midst will be treated well, and that members of the new covenantal community will deepen their sense of compassion. Eventually, this compassion develops into love; we are taught to love the stranger in the same way that we are to love our neighbour—as we love ourselves.

> When strangers reside with you in your land, you shall not wrong them. The strangers who reside with you shall be to you as your citizens; you shall love each one as yourself, for you were strangers in the land of Egypt: I יהוה am your God. (Lev 19:33–34)

---

7. Leibowitz, *World Zionist Organization*.

By concluding this decree with "I am your God," the Torah implies that to love the foreigner as we love ourselves is Godly behaviour. Later Moses affirms this message as he explicates several Divine attributes. Interestingly, though, the only specific Godly behaviour that Moses enjoins the Israelites to emulate is to love foreigners, reminding the community once again, "for you yourselves were foreigners in Egypt" (Deut 10:17–19). The exodus from *Mitzrayim* serves as the archetypal locus of Jewish historical reference[8] and is the prooftext for welcoming, protecting, and loving the stranger, based upon having been enslaved in Egypt.

A treasure-trove of commentaries on the Exodus story is the *Passover Haggadah* (meaning narrative) which, written and edited over centuries, is unique within the vast Jewish library. It is used, not in the synagogue or *bet midrash* (house of study), but at home, around the dining table, and is designed to appeal both to children and adults. Like countless other Jewish books, it contains an array of rabbinic texts, biblical quotes, and medieval commentaries, but is not meant to be an anthology to study. It contains exquisite liturgical pieces, but it is not prayed as liturgy. It includes beloved songs, from the *Hallel* section of Psalms to juvenile story-songs, but it is not sung as a choral piece. It contains dramatic stories meant to be recited aloud, but it is not the script for a play to be watched passively. Instead, the *Haggadah* is used at the most significant event of the Passover festival, the ritual meal called a *seder* (order), which celebrates liberation from slavery, entering a covenantal relationship with the Holy One at Sinai, and the possibility of ultimate redemption. Each individual *seder* is as unique as the people who gather, and versions of the *Haggadah* are as varied as the Jewish people. The book serves as a combination of script, background story, stage directions, and guidelines for the seder and its ritual foods, storytelling, blessings, and songs, so that during a festive meal around the family table, ritual, liturgy, and even culinary elements are orchestrated to transmit a vital past from one generation to the next.[9]

The traditional *Haggadah* discusses at length two distinct aspects of liberation and redemption found in the Passover story: freedom from the actual physical and political enslavement, as well as the long evolution of spiritual liberation that begins with Abraham emerging from idolatry and continues with the newly liberated Israelites forming a relationship

---

8. Yerushalmi, *Zachor*, 40–43.
9. Yerushalmi, *Zachor*, 40–43.

with the Holy One. Then the *Haggadah* brings a section of biblical history that seems unrelated to the Exodus story. The narrative begins: "My father was a wandering Aramean. He went down to Egypt with meagre numbers and sojourned there; but there he became a great and very populous nation . . ." (Deut 26:5).

For centuries there has been a *makhloket*, a hermeneutical dispute among sages, regarding why this passage appears in the *Haggadah*. But to read "my father was a wandering Aramean" in the context of migration theology, this section of the *Haggadah* encourages us to envision the continuation of our journey towards the promised land, by reminding us that once we evolve into a free people living in the promised land, we will nonetheless never be permitted to forget our collective history as a people on the move. Perhaps this is why the *seder* includes a reminder of the "first fruits" ritual that will ultimately be enacted annually on the festival of *Shavuot*. Not only are we commanded to remember that the land and all its produce belong to the Creator, but we must also recall that we as a people are the children of a wandering Aramean, who was at once a person on the move, and the exemplar of how to welcome and protect other migrants.

Following the destruction of the Second Temple, the *Shavuot* offering and accompanying statement about the wandering Aramean continued only in our texts. The festival of *Shavuot* evolved into a commemoration of the revelation at Sinai, and the counting of the *Omer* ritual that connects *Pesach* to *Shavuot* became a mystical spiritual practice. And the connection of the festival to our migrant history was reified when the rabbis instituting the reading of the Book of Ruth on Shavuot. It is a brief book that begins as the migration story of a Jewish family who became climate refugees, fleeing to Moab when a famine plagues their home in Judah. Tragically, following the death of her husband and sons, the only remaining member of this family was Naomi. As she prepares to return home alone once the famine has ended, Naomi's Moabite daughter-in-law, Ruth, insists on coming with her. In a migration as radical as Abraham's in *Lech Lecha*, Ruth leaves her home for an unknown foreign land, not because God tells her to go, but because of her unmitigated *hesed* towards Naomi.[10]

Ruth's migration narrative is unique in the *Tanakh*. She faces significant risks as a single woman of child-bearing age. She is offered

10. Pardes, *Ruth*.

protective hospitality upon her arrival in Judah, eventually not only marrying an Israelite but joining the people of Israel. The Talmudic sages consider Ruth to be the first Jewish proselyte, and her behaviour serves as a model for how converts should be treated. Eventually, this immigrant woman becomes a foremother to King David, thereby becoming a founding figure in the Davidic line that will, in the end of days, bring forth the individual who will usher in the messianic age. Most understandings of Jewish theology view the ultimate redemption as flowing from King David and by extension Ruth. By centring a migrant woman and a newcomer to Judaism in this way, Jewish theology must indeed be understood as a theology of migration. This becomes even clearer when we examine the interwoven cycles of the Jewish calendar.

Two types of cycles serve as the foundation of the Jewish year. The lunar-solar calendar ensures that we celebrate the festivals in their proper season, reminding us of their biblical agricultural roots. *Pesach*, the spring festival of liberation is celebrated in the first month of the cycle. *Shavuot*, the first harvest festival at which we commemorate the revelation at Sinai, is celebrated 49 days later. *Sukkot*, the joyous week-long harvest festival during which we take all our meals in small huts (and those in warm climates actually sleep in them) in memory of our history as migrants, must take place in the autumn. Taken together, they are named after the physical pilgrimages by which they were celebrated in ancient times; this is another aspect of Judaism as migration theology.

The other cycle is the Torah reading cycle. The *chumash* is divided into portions and one is read and studied and expounded upon each week, with special sections added for festivals and other holy days. And so, the migration narratives of Genesis and the journey out of Egypt and towards the Promised Land remain a never-ending trek; the archetypical spiritual trope that it is the journey, not the destination, that is our focus. Along the way we are reminded that after we are liberated from the narrow straits, we are inspired to contemplate the spacious spiritual questions regarding redemption, liberation, and salvation. And we learn that the only way to truly experience these is by embodying Divine attributes such as compassion, empathy, grace, benevolence, and generosity—and by greeting both the foreigner and the native-born with an equal measure of these. And so it is, that to view ourselves at once as both the stranger, and the one who is obligated to welcome and safeguard the stranger is, to paraphrase Jonathan Sacks, very near the core of the mystery of Jewish existence itself.[11]

BIBLIOGRAPHY

Gallant, Zachary. "Judaism as Migration Theology." Unpublished paper, n.d.
Leibowitz, Nehama. *World Zionist Organization*. Jerusalem: Department for Torah Education and Culture in the Diaspora, 1976.
Pardes, Ilana. *Ruth: A Migration Tale*. New Haven: Yale University Press, 2023.
Sacks, Jonathan. "Healing the Heart of Darkness (Mishpatim)." *Covenant and Conversation*, 2015. https://rabbisacks.org/covenant-conversation/mishpatim/healing-heart-darkness.
Yerushalmi, Yosef Hayim. *Zachor: Jewish History and Jewish Memory*. Seattle: University of Washington, 2011.

---

11. Sacks, *"Mishpatim."*

16

At the Table of Jesus

The Theology of the Open Supper

Mártha Bolba[1]

Weekly communal dinners have been a part of the social landscape for seven years at the Józsefvárosi Evangelical Community Centre in Budapest. This open table community meets in the churchyard at the table of Jesus. Everyone is invited to cook, drink, pray, sing, and talk together. We sing grace: "You have invited us to feast, for this fellowship we thank you, for you loved us so much that you became human, gave us bread, and ate with us. Come, Jesus, be our guest, bless this, that which you have given us. Amen." As part of the opening ritual, the pastor asks: "Who did the cooking?" As a thank you we give the chef a round of applause. What have they cooked? The chef introduces the recipe and the food's history. (It is particularly exciting when someone shares a family recipe, cooked their favourite dish, or, in some cases, when someone from another country shows us the flavours of their home). Afterwards, the pastor reads from scripture and shares reflections. The guests are quite hungry at this point. The dinner guest (invited speaker, facilitator, or a professional community) is introduced, and then the pastor wishes everyone a nice meal. Dinner is followed by a twenty-minute presentation,

---

1. Translated from the Hungarian by Stephen Dolan.

followed by an hour-long discussion. Dinner is made from local ingredients. Everything is environmentally conscious. We do not use plastic utensils, and we compost the rubbish. We always cook two kinds of food, including a meat-free option. We are open to a wide range of NGOs and their clients. The dinners tend to be more garden-party style in the summer, and in the winter, they are held in the church and usually include a smaller crowd.

The dinners are inspired by Jesus' Galilean table fellowships. The goal is to make Jesus' table accessible to all. We are conscious of gender, class, and race differences, and seek a format that is as inclusive as possible because we would like to invite everyone into the presence of God. This is necessary because congregational worship does not fit everyone. The communal form of liturgical communion is very formal and more suitable for an educated audience. Classical music accompanied by the organ, the heightened language of the liturgy, the frontal form, the symbolic meal—they all make it difficult for people of non-church social groups to participate.

In this chapter, I present the experiences from these seven years of communal dining. I describe the context in which I found myself as a new pastor to a struggling congregation. I discuss the efforts at trying to revive it and make it more open to the disenfranchised. I show how the idea for the dinners arose in organic steps, which theology laid their foundations, and how being able to find a role during the dinners empowered those on the margins of the church, giving them a renewed sense of belonging.

THE CHURCH

Ten years ago, I came to the congregation of the local Evangelical-Lutheran Church in Hungary in the eighth district of downtown Budapest, as a young assistant pastor tasked with the mission of building a community. This district, Józsefváros, is home to 80,000 people. It is one of the developing areas of Budapest, with newly built apartments side by side with poor municipal tenement houses, which have not been renovated for 70 years. There are 130 of these run-down tenement houses within a 5-minute walking radius of the church, with 20,000 poor tenants, a large proportion of whom belong to the Roma ethnic minority.

The primary school nearest to the church is attended by children of sixteen different immigrant ethnicities. There are also ten major homeless

AT THE TABLE OF JESUS 191

shelters in the neighbourhood. Desperation and poverty are associated with drug use and prostitution. An estimated 3,000 intravenous drug users live in the neighbourhood of the church. Over the past 20 years, several social work organizations have started their operations here as part of the European Union Urban Renewal projects. Due to limited project funding, and projects lasting only a few months, these initiatives were not really suited to be a means of community development.

THE COMMUNITY

In 2012, the congregation had no connection with its surroundings and neighbourhood. The congregation was not socially embedded, owing to prejudice and fear, with a dominating desire for self-defence. One of the members of the congregation used to warn people entering the churchyard to close the door quickly to prevent "the gypsies" from coming in.

The attic of the one-storey building was a university dormitory, and on the ground floor, twenty small apartments surrounded the 600 sqm park-like churchyard. The building was in poor condition, with one fifth of the apartments uninhabited. The rest were occupied by elderly couples belonging to the congregation. The building did not meet the infrastructural requirements of a state-run home for the elderly, so it did not receive any state subsidies. The congregation became financially unsustainable and bankrupt.

The congregation's worship was attended mainly by the elderly residents of the house. The congregation had not had a baptism in a long time, practicing their faith life as an isolated institution. The community described themselves with words like "ageing," "poor," "powerless," and "run-down." One elderly resident spoke of the church's fate like this when we were being introduced: "They are just waiting for us to die."

In 2012, during the first week of my pastoral mission, I organized a dinner concert. I invited everyone. I made flyers and put them in the letterboxes down the street. I invited the plumbers who came to the house, relatives of the elderly residents, and the university students. I asked for help from other congregations to prepare the venue. On that day, we wrote prayers, sang together, and ate together in the garden by candlelight with an international community. The Dutch Continental Singers were our guests. Seventy people came together. The Dean, who wanted to demolish the building, came to the event and left us a watermelon as a gift, hoping that the church would be revived. It was a scorching summer evening.

THE CONTEXT

I got to know the neighbourhood, its municipal institutions, local pastors, social service providers, and NGOs. I asked everyone how I could help, what I could do for them. To my surprise, these organizations told me how we could work together. Everyone had some sort of good idea; we can complement each other and get each other's activities operational.

At the time, professional civil society organizations were experiencing a devastating drain of resources, with social services in the area, such as low-threshold addiction services and the youth club, shrinking by a tenth. The housing crisis then spread to Budapest, with rents skyrocketing compared to incomes. In the municipal elections, the winner's political campaign talked of cleaning up and the fight against drugs, which in practice meant cutting off resources to professional organizations and depriving them of their preferential use of municipal premises. The organizations were left without shelter. Several services moved out of the neighbourhood, leaving people without support. Quite unsuspectingly, I approached the organizers of a housing activist movement with the opening sentence, "What can I do to help?" They responded not long after by saying that it would be good if I could participate in the movement as the pastor. I then went on to speak at three demonstrations, where I told them of Jesus' stories about human dignity. Each demonstration was organized around a disenfranchising constitutional amendment. One was in support of the dignity of homeless people, the other was against a constitutional amendment allowing for a segregated education system preventing equal educational opportunities for Roma children.

THE TABLE

In the meantime, I was called to the holistic missionary trend, according to which God is on a mission towards humanity, calling the whole of the person to God. I have been very inspired by the ideas of liberation theology, the practice of civil disobedience, and nonviolent resistance that founded the Black civil rights movement in the United States as a means of promoting social change. I also read the stories about Jesus, how Jesus touched people, and how God came to us in Christ. The idea of accessibility spoke to me. How accessible is Jesus' message to the people around us? How do we see the world around us? Who has a place at Jesus' table, in our Eucharistic communities? How many million are represented by this format, which the Gospels have transmitted to us, calling us to share. I quickly experienced that it was hard to invite people to the Sunday morning liturgical services accompanied by organ music.

The Gospels, the biblical books about the life of Jesus, record many instances of Jesus participating in dinners. Jesus often told a parable in which a dinner was the setting for the story. One could say that the hallmark of Jesus' movement was the communal dinner. Even on the last night of his life, he dined with his friends and taught us to remember him in this way. At Jesus' table there were tax collectors, fishermen, and sectarians. Among his followers we find women, children, Samaritans, and Gentiles. On Jesus' last night, he washed his disciples' feet, so that he, the master of the house, the host, was the one who did the slaves' work and served his disciples. Jesus opened the table community for every nation. He was very close to his ethical foundation when he encouraged his followers to practice as hosts without expecting anything in return.

I was looking for a form that reflected these table communities of Galilee. A format that reflected the generosity of God when he invites us to his table. I wanted to create an event that would fit the way God shares himself with us. This is the nourishing, joyful table fellowship of Jesus. We needed to find a format where there is room for children to move and be noisy. We need a space that is more relaxed than the classic Bible study conversations, which overwhelmingly look like sitting in a circle to talk about texts. At the table, everyone can speak up, this is a more relaxed speaking situation. Freedom is also given at this dinner, because if one is not moved by a particular topic, one can move freely out of the situation, one can start a small group conversation, and so relationships are made between people, from different cultures, social backgrounds, educational backgrounds, or stages of life.

THE FELLOWSHIP

Part of the story of the open dinners is that we started by contacting clients of a social service provider who work with those on the threshold of addiction within the district. We organized a summer camp for the children of drug-addicted sex workers at the community centre. On one of the last days of the daytime summer camp, one of the mothers sat down on the bench next to us and started telling us about the fact that she had no stove or oven in her apartment. They use an electric hot plate for heating and cooking. If only we knew how well she could bake buns!

One of the camp leaders came up with the idea to open the church kitchen every Friday to the women working in the area and cook together. That is how the shared Friday lunches started. Everyone brought a small part of the ingredients, and we cooked. Later, when many refugees from Syria arrived in 2015, we also held cooking clubs on other days. Mums with young children from the neighbourhood started to come. It was fun to clean and cook vegetables together. Later it evolved so that in the mornings the mum and baby group members did the kitchen preparation, and this is how we could serve dinner at 6 p.m. on Wednesdays. Dinner was moved from Fridays to Wednesdays so that the students from the countryside could also take part in the dinner. The exhibition opening dinner of homeless artists from a psychosocial support art project was attended by a community of active citizens interested in civic life in the area. The art gallery, art therapy for psychiatric patients in homeless care, exhibited their artworks in the church hall. The artwork had a trauma-relieving effect and provided a healing experience for both the creators and the recipients.

The Roma extended families of the area joined in the open dinner occasions, and because we equipped our kitchen with sufficient tableware and tables for our dinners, we were able to host Roma families for their family mourning ceremonies. An extended Roma mourning family of 80–100 people could hold their wake service in our church. This means that from the day of the death until the burial, the extended family spends every night together at the wake, around a common table, comforting and strengthening each other.

THE INVITATION

We have been able to call those on the margins of the Church and invite them into this more relaxed and welcoming format. People who were not religious or who called themselves nonbelievers or atheists came to the dinners in good spirit and participated in the conversation. We also tried to respect the dietary requirements of people of other faiths. There was no problem when Muslim halal food was prepared for us and everyone ate it. It was then that I first experienced what a taboo-breaking and revolutionary step the practice of Jesus' table fellowships was. Jesus invites everyone to his table.

A homeless housing activist from our congregation was a constant volunteer in preparing the dinners, setting the table, and clearing away afterwards. Nicholas's original trade was also in waiting tables, so he was able to use his professional role to be a useful member of the community again. He was not there as a homeless person queuing for food, but he was there in his role as host. This gave him dignity and respect within the community. A homeless woman, who lived in a tent, cooked regularly at the open dinners, and her chicken soup was the best.

The open dinners are attended by people of different political views. The right-conservative leaning church clerk often cooked her favourite family recipe for the colourful group—a multigrain soup.

THE GROWTH

Compared to liturgical communion, which we also practice in church, these dinner garden parties have a much more relaxed feel. This style allows people to move away from the front lines and have deep personal conversations with each other, while the rest of the community may be discussing the dinner topic at hand. In this way, group cohesion can be strengthened as everyone has the opportunity to engage periodically in deep personal conversations. Children also have space at these occasions, being able to play in a safe environment with the large, moving outdoor toys.

Our dinner themes are also diverse. Social service organizations are introduced, or a group of activists present the social cause they are currently fighting for. For example, we hosted the association From Street to Home, which has dreamed up a "Housing First" type of social housing agency, and is helping an increasing number of clients who have experienced homelessness to find a safe home again after an undignified life on the streets. Or the Secure Start Children's Home, which offers free early development for families from disadvantaged neighbourhoods. Or the Rosa Parks Foundation's Invisible School for Roma Children, which works for equal educational opportunities for Roma children. Moreover, theologians, professors, playwrights, and poets have all sent or brought us topics. Alongside the bodily nourishment, we take care to provide spiritual nourishment as well.

The communal dinners also have an organic character. We do not advertise our dinners anywhere, we do not hang up posters, we do not get much social media coverage. We want this community to grow organically from person to person, and not become a spectacle or attraction. Therefore, we do not practice a particular public relations activity. We do not allow it to be promoted as a food distribution event, where crowds of poor people stand in long queues and very pitiful but, regarding the homeless, quite humiliating images can be taken—or for the churches sponsoring the food distributions, the whole event looks good as a publicity stunt to show the goodness of the poor. We have decided not to host a food distribution event, here the poor are not objects of charity but part of the community, they are at eye level, we cook and eat with them. The homeless people here are the hosts. It's not charity, it's community. We speak about societal problems and because of the presence of activists, many words are said about social justice and ways to move societal change forward.

Throughout the seven years of organizing these dinners, their situation changed quite significantly. We started the dinners without any money. Initially, the congregations' donations ensured we could get ingredients. But as the interest grew, we were able to secure more funding. Today, we are no longer the only community to organize such dinners. Our church supports twenty-four other small community service projects with similar values through the Andorka Esther programme. In this way, we work to ensure that everyone has a place at the table of Jesus.

17

The Significance of Ethnic and Religious Identity for Refugee Support
The Case of Muslim Communities

ATALLAH FITZGIBBON

AS A RESULT OF Islamic Relief's increasing participation in domestic programmes focussing on poverty amongst marginalized groups by our European offices, I have had the opportunity to travel across the continent. Liaising with our staff, I have explored the experience of Muslim communities in their interaction with migrants. What I have to say here is based on my observations as a practitioner, my personal interaction with people—rather than from structured research. As such, it is a personal interpretation of the situation.

It has been fascinating being part of and witnessing a very young community in constant change over the last forty years, with the second and now third generation descendants of migrants growing up and negotiating their identity within Europe. This has led in some places to the formation of new suburban and second-generation communities that are based on an evolving understanding of their role and identity in society and an integration with European values and culture. In many cities in Europe, the Muslim community is very visible both because of their ethnic identity and dress, but also through their impact on culture, from architecture to food, clothing, and the introduction of very tangible contributions to a modern multi-cultural and diverse society. The role of religion within migrant groups, at least in some countries, has also contributed to far more culturally and religiously literate attitudes to spirituality and multi-culturalism, although mainly in the larger towns and cities. What is less understood is how all these factors affect the motivation, experience, and reception of migrants in Europe.

Islam has a strong heritage of forced migrant protection, stemming from the original teachings of the Qur'an, as well as from historical examples taken from the lives of great Prophets—from Abraham, to Moses, to the Prophet Muhammad. This heritage includes strong—even stern—commands on the importance of seeking refuge if one is facing persecution, as well as on the duty of providing asylum to those who need it. It is a tradition which provides a robust and generous framework for the protection of and provision for forced migrants, enshrining rights such as the rights to dignity, non-refoulement, equal treatment, shelter, healthcare, family reunification, and protection of property.

In my experience of interacting with Islamic institutions, however, I have often been struck by the low level of community organizing around supporting migrants. Over the last seven years, an increasing number of Muslim humanitarian institutions, such as Islamic Relief, Muslim Aid, and the As Suffa Institute, are leading a trend towards targeting support to migrants, but the mosque communities are not generally mobilizing to the same extent. What might be the reasons for this?

In my experience, in so far as religion as a motivating factor in supporting migrants is important, it lies secondary to the traditional role of chain migration and support by the ethnic diaspora, which remains dominant in enabling migrants to effectively navigate the difficult and challenging journey to their intended destination. Talking to host communities in Italy, for example, they noted the speed with which certain ethnic groups, such as Syrians and Somalis, were able to quickly find support and move to northern Europe. Mosques and related meeting facilities often act as a location for congregating and sometimes shelter, but mosque governance committees have not tended to provide structured support to migrants.

The first reason for this, in many parts of Europe, is fear of censure and retaliation by local authorities and local host communities. In many parts of Europe, particularly in the South and East, Muslim communities are conscious that they live a precarious and thinly tolerated existence on the fringes of societies, that are at best antipathetic to their existence and at worst violently opposed to their presence. Very often mosques may not have official permission to act as places of worship, particularly in countries which still refuse to include Islam as an officially state-recognized religion. Mosques are often subject to acts of vandalism and attack, such as in Budapest, where the Imam told me in 2018 of firebomb attacks. An attempt by the local Muslim community, who were themselves recent migrants to Hungary, to visit refugees in the transit zone with Serbia was denied, with the excuse from the authorities that they might proselytize, whilst Hungarian Christian agencies were allowed access and, in at least one case, were allowed to distribute Bibles and baptize. Even in Britain, which is considered a safe and secure country for Muslims to live, mosques are regularly the target of hate attacks and vandalism. There is a tangible fear that any overt support for migrants would bring this hostility into the open and fan the flames of racist and Islamophobic fear.

The second reason is capacity. Many mosque governance groups in Europe are drawn from first generation migrants with limited education and experience of national law, particularly in areas of civil rights, and imams are often narrowly educated in their countries of origin, usually just in religious studies. Many mosques do not have paid staff and those responsible see their obligation in fairly narrow terms in relation to the provision of collective prayer space solely. Mosque organisers usually have little understanding of the rights of asylum seekers within the immigration system, having come predominantly through legal and formal migration channels. Again, fear of retaliation and breaking the law, or at least attracting condemnation, for supporting illegal immigrants is a factor in closing down formal support. This reflects the political disempowerment of many Muslim communities who feel that they are at the margins of society.

Associated with this is, thirdly, the narrow understanding around support services for migrants. Many believe the care of migrants is the responsibility of the state and that they need not extend services to them. This is obviously not the case in relation to migrants without official status, or where asylum seekers receive insufficient support for their basic needs.

The fourth reason relates to the nature of first-generation migration to Europe. Communities came with a priority of community formation amongst their ethnic grouping first and foremost. My experience in Birmingham in the UK showed me that nearly all mosques reflected patronage and support from very specific ethnic and linguistic communities.

These communities would settle in close proximity to one another almost in an exact recreation of village communities from the countries of origin. First generation migrants have in some cases a sense in which they are competing for space within that society with other migrant groups for limited resources. There may also be racism and prejudice based on pre-conceptions, but also animosities, rooted in conflict in countries of origin, as has been witnessed by conflict and violence within refugee groups in transit. There has not yet formed a mature sense of belonging or social responsibility to the wider community and a more fully formed sense of citizenship. Inevitably many established Muslim communities see themselves as migrants, and for many, their needs, fears, and concerns, consciously or unconsciously, are different only in scale to those of the newcomers. They are struggling to establish themselves and, in some cases, be accepted, and this, although no excuse, perhaps leads to a reduced perception of their responsibilities, as well as in many cases their understandable lack of material and organizational capacity to respond. Their perception of the state's capability or willingness to support migrants is often hopelessly exaggerated, as well as the more complex needs that they could fulfil. In most traditional societies, family and clan are the principal source of humanitarian and social support and there may be a perception that most migrants will have these linkages within their diaspora, which in many cases is patently not the case.

Fifth, this state of affairs has often not been helped by the seeming "invisibility" of the Muslim community to local government and institutions, including churches and others responding at ground level. They often have no idea how to navigate the diverse groups and identify representation and support from the Muslim community, however fragmented it might be. In some cases, there is an unwillingness to do this, fed sometimes by prejudice and fear, but sometimes, particularly in Southern and Eastern Europe, the Muslim community and its institutions have been driven underground and into informality. For this reason, the potential power of inter-faith organizing for migrant support can be so therapeutic and impactful for all concerned. Sometimes Muslim refugees, particularly when they have been persecuted by Muslims in their countries of origin, have no desire to seek support from the Muslim community, but in others, the need for spiritual support and identification with their faith community will be a visceral need. This all points towards the need for far more sensitisation of all groups concerned to migrant needs, not least local Muslim communities.

Protection of their religious identity clearly influences migrants' decisions around identifying a final destination for their journey. Particularly once families are reunited or in formation, thoughts turn to fears of assimilation for their children as well as of facing endemic racism, Islamophobia, and discrimination presenting barriers to their progress. This is one of the principal reasons cited by Somali refugees who often became secondary migrants to Britain from mainland Europe. Britain and more accurately the large multi-cultural cities where large migrant communities from Pakistan and Bangladesh had established thriving Muslim communities, presented attractive opportunities to protect their Muslim identity, as well as the economic opportunities provided within these thriving communities. The relative lack of institutional hostility to Islam and Muslims within Britain, coupled with the establishment of mature and politically empowered Muslim communities, often with British Commonwealth linkages, remains a substantial pull factor with migrants, who will take enormous risks to reach there.

Along with the sense of impermanence which usually accompanies first-generation migrants, there is also the complications of forging their own sense of identity, especially amongst their descendants. Second and third generations often feel less affiliation with ethnic identity than they might with either religious or national identity. The profound conscious and unconscious introspection that occurs amongst migrants around identity, meaning, and values is a complex process with diverse outcomes. For those many young descendants of migrants who start to identify as Muslims primarily, the significance of the faith of new migrants, in addition to the rights of refugees more generally, is a factor in empathizing over and above purely ethnic considerations. It has taken time for this group to mature and become institutionally active, and it is happening in the form of humanitarian organizations and initiatives which still remain fairly peripheral.

However, a change is discernible throughout the continent—a change which might signal new concerns for migrants among Muslim communities. The growing congregation of educated, empowered, and religiously active people has led to a new generation of mosque formation, which has been termed the "suburban" mosque, formed by wealthier and more educated migrants having the social confidence to move out to the suburbs or away from the ethnic enclave, who start to form social circles based on religious rather than ethnic affiliation. Sociologically, this indicates maturing identities within the Muslim community where complex internal searches for the meaning and purpose of faith engage with national ethics, religion, and culture, and in most cases a successful emergence of a confident and non-conflictual identity. Much of the active humanitarian support to migrant groups is increasingly being organized by this more confident segment of the Muslim community, with an enormous growth in charitable institutions in northern Europe.

I have not come across any significant research into religiosity amongst migrant communities and outcomes around assimilation, integration, conversion, and alienation, although I have seen evidence of all these happening. What is very interesting for me, is historically the gradual emergence of a European Muslim community that transcends ethnic identity and culture. However, this will probably take many decades to significantly alter and influence Europe's attitude and prejudices around migration. It is nonetheless an important step in the right direction.

18

Making Space for the Other

Jakob Wirén

Is this seat available? I scooch over to make space for a new passenger on the seat next to mine. Somewhat reluctantly, perhaps, because my own comfort decreases, but also without hesitation since it is a public space where we ought to share the available seats on the bus. Had the question regarded my own seat, I might have considered whether that person was likely to need the seat more than I do. There are many passengers on the bus. Some of them have luggage and occupy more than one seat. Some stand up in order to leave room for others. One person spreads his legs widely, seemingly unaware of the fact that the person next to him thereby has little room at her disposal.

As human beings, there is a common public space that we must share. Sometimes concretely, as on a bus, sometimes metaphorically speaking. Sometimes we share this common room willingly, sometimes grudgingly. In some cases, we are those who take space at the expense of others.

To make space for another person in a spirit of hospitality and generosity is an ideal in all the major faith traditions. Yet, there are occasions when we must stand up for ourselves and protect our space and integrity. Rosa Parks is remembered and celebrated for her decision *not to leave* her seat on the bus.

Admittedly, there are some differences between bus rides and interreligious encounters. Nevertheless, both concern place, space, and the opportunity to show and receive generosity.

In this chapter, I reflect on making space from different perspectives. I mainly focus on Christians' responsibility to make space for the religious other. This is not because making space is more of a concern and duty for Christians than for others. On the contrary, it could rightly be seen as an obligation for all people, regardless of faith or no faith. Christians are certainly not alone in taking space at the expense of others. However, some aspects of "making space" must be done from within each faith tradition. In some cases, one has to speak from one's own perspective—in my case, as a Christian theologian—and not on behalf of someone else's. In other words, the question of making space is a mutual process. Hospitality is not unidirectional.

INTERFAITH RELATIONS

At the heart of this book lies a particular form of interfaith relations, namely the praxis within the interreligious network A World of Neighbours (AWoN). It is an innovative and unique network that is dedicated to making space for the religious other. In theory, but most of all through praxis, that network is focused on "keeping our humanity" by making space for each other.[1] Other chapters of this book deal with AWoN more explicitly, whereas my contribution explores political and theological aspects of interreligious work in a way that, I hope, provides a broader context for people of all faiths who, in different ways, seek to make space for the religious other.

On the one hand, AWoN is unique, yet it is also an example of something obvious and inevitable that has always existed. After all, interfaith relations are not something new. The major faith traditions have all developed in milieus more or less multiethnic and multireligious. It could be argued that the interfaith reality presents itself in a new way when digitalization, globalization, and migration bring us together more frequently, but interreligious encounters and dialogues are actually as old as the phenomenon we call religion.

People have different opinions about interfaith activities. There are critical voices within the different traditions as well as outside of them. To

---

1. "Keeping Our Humanity" was an interreligious summit organized by A World of Neighbours in February 2022.

a certain extent, one can understand that interfaith work challenges well-known patterns and traditions, and raises issues of identity that may be sensitive, but at the end of the day interfaith encounters happen whether we want them to or not. In that sense, the most important thing is not how we feel about it. Interfaith relations are facts that we must cope with, relate to, and reflect on.

So, what do interfaith relations and dialogue look like? When speaking of interfaith dialogue, one is likely to think of high religious representatives meeting each other in formal settings. This is certainly an important part of interfaith dialogue, but not the only one. We could distinguish between a few different kinds of interfaith dialogue: *dialogue between religious representatives; dialogue on theological matters; the everyday encounter; the dialogue of mysticism; practical collaboration; cooperation in times of crisis*. These six forms of dialogue overlap to some extent and further variants could be added. Nonetheless, I mention these different forms to underscore that we should not interpret notions such as interfaith dialogue and interfaith relations too narrowly. It is something theoretical *and* practical; something for cerebral occasions *and* for everyday life; something organized *and* spontaneous; something for scholars *and* lay persons; something that goes on all the time *and* something that is intensified in certain times; something that concerns everyone *and* something for the few, something that happens between close friends *and* something that happens when strangers meet.

In Sweden, where I live, the most established form of interreligious dialogue is local interfaith councils, which exist in several cities all over the country. They consist of representatives from the different faith communities and congregations located in the area. Some of the representatives are religious leaders, priests, rabbis, and imams, others are lay persons.

As we have seen already, there are many ways to arrange interfaith dialogue and cooperation, but the local interfaith council is an institution that can be found not only in Sweden but across the world. I will take the interfaith council as an example and point of departure when continuing the discussion on making space for the religious other.

LOCAL INTERFAITH COUNCILS

On the agenda in the local interfaith councils in Sweden, one typically finds practical and political issues that have to do with social cohesion and religious freedom: How can we contribute to the wellbeing of our neighbourhood or our society?[2] How can we challenge stereotypes and prejudices against religion and people of faith? It has to do with the role of religion in society, finding places to pray, different faith communities' possibility to live and practice their faith in society. In other words, the "dialogue" is often a form of cooperation, rather than a theological conversation. It is about getting to know each other, developing mutual trust, and to help each other in times of crisis. This kind of practical support is about making space for the religious other in very concrete ways.

In my interviews with members of these councils—representatives from different faith traditions—they speak of friendship. In fact, that is the most common response I get when asking what they see as the primary purpose of the council.

The participants experience that religion gets a lot of negative media attention; that the general image is that people of faith are intolerant and incapable of getting along with people of other faiths; that religious differences cause conflicts and violence. It is in this perspective, that the alleged importance of visible friendship should be seen. One aim is simply to present a different picture, to show that interreligious friendship exists, and that religion can be a positive asset in society. At the same time, it is obvious that the councils have a hard time getting publicity for this message. Needless to say, negative news make more intriguing headlines than positive ones. But the issue of friendship is not primarily a media concern. In many cases actual friendship develops. When the interfaith councils have developed a certain level of friendship and trust, there are many occasions when the representatives make actual space for the religious other. When there are incidents of an antisemitic, Christophobic or Islamophobic nature, members from the council stand up for each other. An imam in Sweden describes it the following way:

> It becomes a safety net for me as a Muslim in society. When people talk about the extreme Muslims and there comes a priest and a rabbi and they say: "I know the Muslims, we have been together with them. This picture is not right," then there is someone who raises his voice and is on my side. When I talk positively about Islam, since I am a Muslim, they think that I am proselytizing.[3]

---

2. The descriptions of local interfaith councils below are based on Wirén, *Att ge plats får den Andre?*

3. Interview, quoted in Wirén, *Att ge plats för den Andre?*, 138.

Other representatives mention crises of different kinds, such as when a mosque was burned down, or a synagogue vandalized. On these occasions, already established relationships proved valuable and were occasions when they made space for each other in concrete ways.

Relationships take time and have their challenges. This is certainly true also for interfaith relations. For instance, the premises for different faith communities are not equal. In the case of Sweden, one faith community—the Lutheran Church of Sweden—is seven times the size of all other faith communities, Christians and non-Christians, together. Such a situation impacts numbers, resources, network connections and naturally affects the conditions for the different faith communities and thus also the relationships between the representatives. It does not make friendship impossible, but these asymmetries are real and something that the representatives must deal with. Apart from the already mentioned asymmetry, there are political, historical, and ideological aspects that challenge the relationships. One representative comments on this fact:

> There is great suspicion between orthodox Christians and Muslims and extreme groups are formed on both sides. . . . At the same time, great things are done. I mean, people who really try and want to work for peace and do not acknowledge these borders.[4]

Interfaith relations are not always easy. The experience from local councils in Sweden testify to this fact. But when they work, they play an important role for the persons involved and for the society in which they take place.

As a matter of fact, the practical and political aspects of making space for the religious other do not seem theologically controversial in any of the great traditions. Rather, defending the religious other's right to live and exercise their belief in society proves to be a sacred obligation in most traditions. In other words, when representatives from different faiths engage interreligiously, they do so for a variety of reasons (among them: creating good opportunities for one's own community, building social cohesion, making space for the religious other, or simply because it is fun and enriching), but these reasons are not necessarily formulated from a common interreligious perspective. On the contrary, they are often rooted in the particular traditions. By way of example, the Jewish representatives may argue based on God's covenant with the Jewish people and the calling of being a light for the nations. As a rabbi says in

4. Interview, quoted in Wirén, *Att ge plats för den Andre?*, 135.

my interviews: "A Jew should take part in the society where she lives. Engage in the maintenance of the city, associate with everyone who lives there... to take part and to interact with others, that is part of the essence of Jewish life."[5]

One Jewish representative refers to the Bible story where Abraham receives three strangers only to discover that they were angels (Gen 18). In other words, theological notions such as covenant and the duty of hospitality form a basis for Jewish interfaith commitment.

Muslim representatives argue that God calls them to be good neighbours. One imam states:

> The definition that we have in Islam, irrespective of where you are, is that we are responsible both for Muslims and for non-Muslims. All humans must interact and coexist. To understand each other and live in peace together. God has created us different. There is a purpose with that. We complement each other, we must live together on earth, in peace, just as God wants.[6]

The imam continues his way of reasoning by quoting the Qur'an and states that these are arguments from religious freedom and interreligious cooperation:

> If Allah had willed, He would have made you one community, but His Will is to test you with what He has given each of you. So compete with one another in doing good. To Allah you will all return, then He will inform you of the truth regarding your differences. (Q 5:48)

The imam's views on other theological issues are rather traditional, and he does not hesitate to name Islam superior to other religions. Nonetheless, the theological foundation for making space for the religious other in society runs deep in the tradition, as he understands it.

Christian representatives refer to God's omnipresence through the Holy Spirit and to God's love for all of creation. Christians are not allowed to care for their own only, but are called to love and care for all human beings.

As we have seen, the theological rationale differs and is particular to the respective faith traditions. Nevertheless, these different rationales provide legitimacy for an interfaith praxis that makes space for the religious other.

5. Interview, quoted in Wirén, *Att ge plats för den Andre?*, 183.
6. Interview, quoted in Wirén, *Att ge plats för den Andre?*, 145.

In my interviews with representatives from different faith communities, I do not find any romanticizing of interreligious dialogue. Experienced participants know that this kind of work takes a long time to build but is easy to destroy. I meet experienced practitioners with a profound understanding of religious difference and for the challenge of interreligious dialogue. But I also meet the conviction that there is really no alternative but to meet, talk, and collaborate, for the sake of the world.

MAKING THEOLOGICAL SPACE

So far, I have discussed the issue of making space on the level of making political space, defending one's role in society. But as I have hinted at, the issue of making space for the religious other is also a theological question. Admittedly, it is not often discussed in the ordinary work of local interfaith councils. These gatherings are more hands-on, and the level of theological education varies substantially between the representatives. Nevertheless, the fact that the issue of theological space is not explicitly on the agenda of interfaith councils does not make it unimportant. Rather, it is something that effects relationships and conditions interfaith cooperation in a more subtle way. Returning to the analogy of travelling on the bus, theological views and religious sermons can work as a too strong perfume or a too loud mobile phone that occupy space in a different sense and make the journey uncomfortable for the religious other. This becomes clear in the interfaith councils. One rabbi explains his feelings when Muslim representatives joke about Noah drinking wine as a misunderstanding in the Hebrew scriptures: "When we finally have got to know each other so well . . . we can explain that we do not see this as funny . . . the idea that one has altered/revised the Holy Scriptures. For us it is shameful to assert such things."[7] This is not necessarily the most obvious example of lack of theological space, but what is at stake in this and other situations is an experience of non-recognition, of not being respected in one's faith. When the preaching and theological convictions of my own tradition are articulated in a certain way, there is no room for other faiths. The relationship to Judaism is arguably the most significant example of what it means (not) to make theological space for the religious other. The issue of theological space is not about denying differences or claiming that all religions are the same. It is about leaving a

---

7. Interview, quoted in Wirén, *Att ge plats för den Andre?*, 189.

little room in one's own faith to the recognition of the other's. To explain more properly, I shall start in a different way.

A LACK OF THEOLOGICAL SPACE

In many Scandinavian churches we find beautiful paintings on the walls and ceilings. Among the more famous ones are Albertus Pictor's works. They are detailed images from the Bible and from church history. One popular motive is Cain and Abel—the first brothers who also killed each other. In Härkeberga Church, in the Diocese of Uppsala, this motive has a prominent position in the church ceiling. In that painting, we find the story's bad guy, Cain, with typical anti-Jewish features: a pointed straw hat, a goatee beard, a big, crooked nose, and yellow clothes. The good guy, the victim and brother Abel, is portrayed in a pious and slender way, with no sign of the mentioned features. It is overexplicit that the bad guy is a Jew according to the negative stereotypes of the time, whereas the younger one looks completely different, even though they are brothers. There are plenty of theologically motivated anti-Jewish images. In the same church alone, one also finds a man with a pointed hat and crooked nose ridiculing a group of Christians celebrating the Eucharist.

A few things can be noted from these and similar paintings: first, it is a Christian sacred house. That fact says something about the close connection between Christian prayer life and anti-Jewish notions. Second, the stereotyping is explicit and brutal. Third, it rests on a highly selective way of reading the Bible, where the question of who a Jew is, is asked and answered ideologically rather than historically or biblically.

The notion that the Jewish tradition once was a true religion, but no longer is, is called supersessionism. According to this view, Judaism was a *prologue* to Christianity. Something that once was important but no longer has any proper meaning. Or: Judaism is the *contrast* to Christianity—the dark background against which the bright Christian story appears even brighter. Or: Judaism is the *scapegoat* of Christianity, the reason for all sorts of evil things, including the murder of the Son of God. In this narrative, Judaism is Cain, but not Abel; Judas but not Peter; the greedy tax collectors, not the good disciples.

In what way are medieval mural paintings relevant for the question of theological space today? If the examples of Christian strategies of making Judaism invisible, irrelevant, or ridiculed were confined to sixteenth-century art, it would perhaps not be of any great significance.

But unfortunately, throughout the Christian tradition, there has always been a stream of supersessionism towards Judaism. This is true also of today. Elsewhere, I have analysed hymns in the Church of Sweden from the perspective of supersessionist theology. The reason for choosing this material was not that the hymnbook in the Church of Sweden distinguished itself in a negative way, but rather because supersessionism in different forms is so common that it can be found almost anywhere. From these analyses we can see that well-known notions such as Zion, Israel, and People of God are used in the hymns in such a way that the Christian church tends to replace the Jewish people. Similar mechanisms can be found in the New Testament and in other early Christian texts too. Sometimes the supersessionist mechanism is subtle and limited to one of many interpretations. Sometimes it is more brutal and explicit. How can Christians handle this part of their own heritage? I do not think that the solution is to remove all hymns and texts that can potentially be interpreted in this way. But it is important to develop an awareness of how different notions and trains of thought have served to make the Jewish people invisible in the history of salvation. When a congregation in the Church of Sweden sings about how "God's saved Israel" worships the Triune God, it is a common expression of Christian eschatology.[8] But it also raises questions of the other Israel: What about the Jewish people in this hymn? Do they represent an "unsaved Israel"? Or, if we apply a more generous interpretation, are the Jewish people included when congregations sing about "God's saved Israel"? Does "Israel" refer to the Jewish people *and* the Christian church? In the latter case, we still have an eschatological vision few Jews would be comfortable with: the praising of the Triune God and pledging loyalty to the covenant of Jesus Christ.

Supersessionism and triumphalism come in different forms, some of which are more violent than others. It is a challenging task to remove all sorts of triumphalism, but for a theology that seeks to make space for the religious other, it should be a priority to foster an awareness of how the question of space play out theologically. This is a theological question with concrete and practical implications, to which many interfaith councils could testify. The Jewish scholar Jacob Neusner articulates the challenge:

---

8. Eschatology is a theological term referring to "the last things." Traditionally, it deals with death, judgment, and the final destiny of the soul and of humankind.

> How can I form a theory of the other in such a way that within my own belief I can respect the other and accord to the outsider legitimacy within the structure of my own faith?[9]

As already mentioned, the question of theological space is not limited to a Christian view of Judaism but concerns all faith traditions and how they relate to each other. In all these relationships, there is a question of respecting and recognizing the other and giving her legitimacy within the structure of one's own faith. How can this be achieved? I would like to conclude by suggesting four guiding principles.

First, Resisting Theologies of Contempt

In this chapter, I have exemplified theologies of contempt with Christian supersessionism towards the Jewish tradition, but there are examples of toxic theologies in most religious traditions. In Christianity, the teaching on prophet Muhammed poses another example of theologically motivated derogatory teaching. Among these descriptions, Muhammed is portrayed as a false prophet, a paedophile, someone possessed by demons. The Islamic scholar William Montgomery Watt is probably right when he states that

> None of the great figures of history is so poorly appreciated in the West as Muhammad. Western writers have mostly been prone to believe the worst of Muhammad, and, wherever an objectionable interpretation of an act seemed plausible, have tended to accept it as a fact.[10]

Examples in various traditions could be multiplied. Theologians can only take responsibility for their own tradition. One cannot revise someone else's. In fact, one cannot undo one's own tradition either. Rather than deleting or denying parts of one's own tradition, making theological space is about engaging with it critically and self-critically in order to move beyond theologies of contempt.

Second, Doing Theology in the Presence of the Other

More common than theologies of contempt are theologies of invisibility: the praxis of doing theology as if the religious other did not exist at all. Ignoring or making someone invisible is also a way of not making space

---

9. Neusner, *Jews and Christians*, 110.
10. Watt, *Mohammad at Mecca*, 52.

for the religious other. It may not be necessary to have a religious other perspective on every theological discourse, but too often this perspective is lacking altogether. When the religious other is not present in one's theology, he or she is not recognised as religious other. Such failed recognition impacts relationships in several ways.

When theology is performed in the presence of the religious other, something changes. Good advice for priests is that they should prepare their sermon as if their Jewish or Muslim friend was present in church. That advice works for theological thinking in general. It does not require compromising the particularity of one's own tradition, nor its truth claims. Still, it does something with the tone and the perspective that may further the legitimacy that Neusner asks for. To do theology in the presence of the other entails reflecting theologically about the other's faith.

In the 1960s, the Christian theologian Wilfred Cantwell Smith claimed that Christian theology had resources to explain the existence of the Milky Way and all the galaxies, but not the existence of the Bhagavad-Gita.[11] Doing theology in the presence of the religious other is to respond to Cantwell Smith's challenge. To acknowledge the existence of the religious other theologically, resisting the temptation to reduce her into a "not yet member of my own faith."

Third, Minding the Eschatological Horizon

If the language of creation is universal and the language of revelation particular, the language of eschatology is provisional. It seeks to articulate a hope that "no eye has seen, no ear heard, no human heart conceived" (1 Cor 2:9). Ultimately, God is a mystery that cannot be comprehended. Therefore, God's consummation of creation also remains a mystery that we cannot foresee or comprehend. Hence, a certain level of agnostic caution is reasonable when talking about the ultimate. As a matter of fact, it is not only reasonable, but also theologically necessary, given that God is the ultimate mystery. From this follows that there are certain kinds of questions, such as comparisons between truth claims of different faiths or certain superlatives that cannot be definitively answered in the here and now. They have to be postponed in light of the eschatological horizon. Most Christians and many people of other faiths would agree that we do not know what the ultimate eschatological hope looks like, nor how

---

11. Smith, *Faith of Other Men*, 133.

different religious traditions belong together. This agnostic awareness should be included in one's theology of religions.

Sometimes, eschatology is associated with competing salvific claims, mutual condemnation, and religious terror. It is true that post-mortem expectations can be an arena for conflict and violence. But in the end, I see the eschatological horizon as fundamental to theology of religions. It opens up and gives fresh air to interfaith encounters. It focuses on what all people have in common, regardless of faith: the future. It provides a basis for agnostic caution and doctrinal humility.

Fourth and Finally, Being Rooted in One's Own Tradition in Order to Be Open to the Other

Sometimes people think that interreligious dialogue is about minimizing religious differences and finding the lowest common denominator. My experience differs from that view. Rather, Christians, Jews, and Muslims motivate their work theologically based on their own tradition. How sophisticated this motivation is, depends on the level of theological interest and education, but it is clear that the foundation for religious freedom and human dignity is strong in each religious tradition, but also that it takes different shapes.

Making space is not equal to leaving one's space. Rather, it is on the basis of one's own space, that one can provide space for the religious other. In other words, to make space for the religious other, in praxis as well as in theology, is never about betraying one's own tradition. On the contrary, it is the rootedness in one's own tradition that gives the motivation for interfaith cooperation and it is within the structures of one's own faith that one is able to make theological space for the religious other. The praxis of openness, and the theology of openness can be found deep down in one's own tradition.

BIBLIOGRAPHY

Neusner, Jacob. *Jews and Christians: The Myth of a Common Tradition*. London: SCM, 2003.
Smith, Wilfred Cantwell. *Faith of Other Men*. New York: New American Library, 1965.
Watt, William Montgomery. *Mohammad at Mecca*. Oxford: Clarendon, 1953.
Wirén, Jakob. *Att ge plats för den Andre? Religionsdialog, ersättnginsteologi och Muhammed som profet*. Stockholm: Verbum, 2021.

19

Collaboration Beyond Borders

When Felix Unogwu and Anne Kjaer Bathel Met

CECILIA SAHLSTRÖM

IT IS IN MEETINGS between people that development takes place, and Anne Kjaer Bathel and Felix Unogwu are a shining example of this. It may seem like a coincidence that they met, but it was their shared interest in creating a society where people are given the opportunity to flourish and develop, that brought them together. Both were invited to A World of Neighbours, whose mission is to empower practitioners through networking, both interfaith and intersectional, with the aim of creating social cohesion and development. During the three months of these meetings, discussions included leadership, refugees and integration.

During a workshop, Anne and Felix ended up in the same group. It didn't take long before they realized that both of them had an extra strong commitment to helping people with a forced migration background to work. In different ways, they had both experienced society's lack of ability and infrastructure to make use of refugees' skills. What Anne and Felix had in common was that they both believed that every person has the right to a dignified and meaningful life, which is one of the pillars of a functioning society. People who live in exclusion year after year lose initiative, they lose hope and confidence. Felix, who worked for the city of Malmö on issues related to extremism, and Anne, who had set up the ReDI School of Digital Integration in Berlin, Hamburg, and Munich, among other places, realized that they shared many of the same backgrounds.

ALL PEOPLE HAVE A HISTORY THAT HAS SHAPED THEM

Anne Kjaer Bathel and the Journey Towards ReDiSchool

Anne's great grandfather Paul Riechert lived and worked in Schleswig Holstein, Germany. He was a book printer and owned a print shop. After his experiences as a soldier in World War I, he became an active pacifist. His son, Martin Riechert, Anne's grandfather, was born in 1913 before the outbreak of the War. He eventually followed in his father's footsteps as a publisher and pacifist. When Adolf Hitler came to power in 1933, they were both harassed by the German Storm Troopers (SA). Among other things, their clothes were torn off and they were thrown onto a cart that was pulled through the city. Around their necks, the SA had hung signs reading "I am a traitor and my family is the same." On several occasions, both father and son were thrown into prison for no other reason than to be intimidated. They were kept there for one or a few days before being released. Eventually they realized their lives were at risk, and fled to Kolding, Denmark in 1933.

For Anne, their story has formed a childhood where pacifism and social commitment were the driving forces.

As a young adult, Anne first chose to study for three years as a *Kaospilot* in Aarhus, Denmark. Then, possibly as a consequence of her upbringing, she went on to a Master of Peace Studies in Japan. After obtaining her degree, it was time to decide what to do next. She was faced with the choice of staying in Japan or getting back to Europe. She finally chose Germany in 2012, which she saw as the heart of Europe, settled in Berlin, and started the Berlin Peace Innovation Lab in collaboration with Stanford University.

In 2015, when millions of refugees were coming to Europe due to the war in Syria, the Berlin Peace Innovation Lab organized a workshop at the Berlin City Hall, with the aim to come up with new ideas to help newly arrived people get a good start in Germany. Given her own history and choice of studies, it was natural for Anne to think about what she and society as a whole could do for refugees in camps in and around Berlin.

After a while, she realized a vitally important voice was missing in the brainstorming: the new arrivals. Anne therefore decided on the working principle "Stop talking about refugees. Start talking *with* refugees." It was the refugees themselves who knew what they could do, what they needed, and what dreams for the future they had. Anne went to one of Berlin's refugee camps to find out what the refugees wanted, needed and desired. In the camp, she discovered that people had a few possessions and that their lives consisted of paperwork and waiting.

By chance, she met Muhammad Asir, a computer engineer. Muhammad was distressed that he did not have a computer, which in turn created fears of losing his skills while in the camp. The processing rate of each person's application for asylum was slow. The fact that the processing was also an obstacle for the refugees to get out of the camp, did not help either.

Anne reacted to how poor the infrastructure was, how the bureaucracy seemed to pacify people on the move. No one had shown the slightest interest in all the skills they possessed, and the risk of losing them was very high.

She had to start somewhere, she thought, and wrote a post on Facebook asking people to help start a tech-school for refugees. She was surprised at how many people responded. She ended up having her entire apartment full of laptops and over thirty people who offered to help. Weston Hankins, a computer engineer and CTO of a start-up company offered to teach the people in the camp who were interested in learning to code. At that moment, the idea of a school to spread IT knowledge was born.

Anne and friends set up a website, made a logo, and a month later started a pilot project. Many questions required many answers. What should be taught, what was needed to make it work? For Anne, it was already obvious that the target group was refugees.

One problem was that the refugee camp had poor internet access. Another was that all the donated computers were of different types: Apple, Microsoft, German keyboards, English keyboards, adequate battery, no battery, and so on. It was complex, to say the least. The lessons were five minutes long instead of the intended two hours. The second class was better. She knew that new problems would arise and mistakes would be made along the way. But the important thing was to learn from them and develop. And so they have.

Initially, they relied entirely on volunteers to run classes, but soon the workload became too much to do on the side of busy work schedules. An official organisation and full-time staff was needed to coordinate volunteers, students and infrastructure. Here, the experienced business consultant Ferdi van Heerden stepped in to help structure the organisation and two of Germany's most seasoned social innovators, Stephan and Joana Breidenbach, helped Anne and the team set up ReDI School as a legal entity, which could receive donations and hire staff. It was no longer a hobby—it was a job.

The first company to provide support was the steel industry company Klöckner & Co. The partnership made it possible to hire a small team to coordinate the community. On Valentine's Day 2016, the first IT course started at the ReDI School.

More donations and new partnership started coming in. Facebook donated as much as €100,000 after Mark and Priscilla Zuckerberg visited the school in Berlin. And Klöckner & Co returned matching the funding from Facebook. ReDI was not a one-off project—but a real school.

Today, ReDI School operates in Germany, Denmark, Sweden and in Cyberspace.

Since meeting Felix Unogwu through A World of Neighbours, ReDI School has opened in Malmö.

Felix Unogwu's Escape from Nigeria Led to Interest in Helping Other Refugees

Felix grew up in Nigeria in a wealthy family, where his father was a doctor and his mother a businesswoman. He was the child of a wealthy man with good prospects for a good life. But that would drastically change because his father was also an activist and political opponent of the Nigerian government. His father openly criticized the military government for corruption and was therefore considered a threat to the regime. He was murdered, but no one knows who carried out the murder or why, other than to conclude that it had to do with his father's criticism of the regime. In Nigeria, there is something called "unknown soldiers," which means that the killer was connected to the military regime, but never identified. Felix was forced to flee Nigeria because of the risk of being murdered himself. He ended up in Stockholm.

Felix was dressed far too thinly when he arrived in central Stockholm on that September night in 1995. He was seventeen years old and all he had with him was a bag, 100 dollars, trauma and frozen grief.

He was cold, hungry and had nowhere to go. A man showed him a nearby hotel. He stayed there for one night and had breakfast in the morning. Then he ran out of money.

After checking out, he sat down on a bench without knowing what to do or where to go. Then, for the first time, he allowed himself to mourn his father, the flight and everything he had lost. He was sitting there crying when an African man came up to him and asked what was wrong. Felix told him his story and that he had no money or shelter. To Felix's surprise, the man invited him to his home in Tumba, which is a municipality just south of Stockholm. Felix was grateful that the man took pity on him. After three days, the kind host told Felix that he had to go to the police for help.

Since Felix's experience was that the police and authorities could mean death, he hesitated, but his host told him he had to. After a great deal of hesitation, Felix walked with trembling legs into the police station.

Felix had to tell his story to a police officer who would then drive him to a refugee camp outside Tumba. Felix felt very hesitant to even get into the police car, but the officer assured him that it was safe and that no one would hurt him. Finally, Felix got into the car.

Once in the refugee camp, he was given a bed and food. At the time, the camp was full of refugees from the former Yugoslavia, where the war was still going on. However, they had brought the conflicts with them and fights broke out all the time. The fights and the constant conflicts scared Felix and he would crawl into bed, pull the blanket over his head and cover his ears. When he complained to a woman in the camp, she told him he could go to Malmö instead. He did so, ending up in a small refugee centre on Celsiusgatan in Malmö. Today, he looks from his workplace in Malmö City, straight into the room he had at that time.

Eventually, Felix ended up in a refugee centre on the outskirts of Lund. Every day he would go out and admire the silhouette of the city. Felix decided that one day he would live there.

Eventually, he started walking the four kilometres to the Lund City Library every day. His toes ached; his shoes were not suitable for walking such distances.

On one of these days, a woman came up to him outside the library and expressed her admiration for his African clothes. He told her about himself and the woman, who was a teacher at a nearby school, eventually invited him to come and talk about his experiences and life in Nigeria to her class. He did so and felt happy and empowered.

A while later, the woman came to him at the centre and asked if he wanted to give a lecture to the whole school. He would even be paid. That moment and that day would be the turning point for Felix.

Another turning point was when he and Anne Kjaer Barthel met. And today he leads the ReDI School in Malmö.

MEETINGS THAT MAKE A DIFFERENCE

When people meet, anything can happen. Historically, we find many encounters that have created change. Some have involved conflict, others have created opportunities for development, others have meant that people all over the world have had significantly improved living conditions. Some have even ended with the Nobel Peace Prize.

When people meet, bonds are strengthened, tolerance and respect increase and, not least, we are seen as individuals. To be reflected in others is to be made visible and to make visible.

Those who are on the run have lost everything and perhaps even their identity. In the refugee camps, they are reflected by other people in the same situation and the risk of frustration and anger are great. Moreover, the fact that refugees are perceived and treated as a homogenous group reduces their chances of entering society and joining a community.

In Sweden, as in many countries, integration is lacking and asylum seekers are relegated to a life of waiting. The bureaucracy that surrounds refugees and our societies' lack of infrastructure for refugees, play a major role in this passivity. These shortcomings threaten people's inherent dignity and right to a fruitful and successful life. They are also a threat to equality and equity and have the negative impact of creating a segregated society of outsiders that never gets the opportunities for social mobility that others do.

By giving Felix and Anne an opportunity to meet, the chances for these excluded people to create a future for themselves, get a job and opportunities to take a place in society have increased greatly. The meeting between Anne and Felix has already made a difference for many through the ReDI School, which is now active in Malmö. The two shared the same activist DNA and were able to draw on it to create synergy. Anne and Felix are proof that meetings play a crucial role in development.

A prerequisite for starting a school like ReDI is a collaboration with the municipality concerned. Without the municipality as a collaborating party, it is financially difficult to try to build a sustainable and scalable organization if you want it to reach out on a broad scale.

In Germany, it takes about five years on average for refugees to get a job. For most women, it takes even longer. In Sweden, the average is eight to nine years. For women with post-secondary education, it takes seven years before 50 percent are in employment. For the students who have attended ReDI School, however, it takes one year to get a job after their training. According to Ramböll Consulting, this corresponds to a saving for the municipality of around EUR 75,000 per student in reduced social benefits and including tax revenues. Not to mention the gain in reduced social exclusion and suffering that ReDI School's efforts contribute to. From all perspectives, the initiative is a genuine win-win situation. The cities of Malmö, Munich, and Hamburg have understood this and have therefore contributed funds to support ReDI School in its work against passivity and segregation.

When Anne and Felix met through A World of Neighbours, Anne realized that Felix was the way into Malmö. He worked within the city of Malmö on extremism issues and thus had the necessary entry point. Felix was excited about the possibilities of the ReDI School. His own experiences made him particularly interested in the situation of other refugees. He was well aware of the isolating effect that being a refugee has on people and how difficult it is to overcome the trauma they often carry with them. The additional trauma of being in a refugee camp increases the risk of abandonment and paralysis.

Anne Kjaer Bathel's ReDI School's mission is to build something that is both sustainable and scalable. ReDI School is about improving the lives of as many people as possible, rather than making a monetary return. And to a large extent it is about collaborating creatively. But just because something works in Berlin doesn't mean it will work elsewhere. After developing the ReDI School, and building up operations in Berlin, Munich, Hamburg, and other cities, the ReDI School also started in Denmark, where they have schools in four different locations.

For Malmö, it all started in the spring/summer of 2022. Felix Unogwu is the leader of the school and also works half-time at Malmö City. It is important for the school and its purpose that Felix is based in Malmö City's administration, because he understands and knows how to get through the bureaucratic twists and turns. Without that input, ReDI

School would have had a much more difficult time building the organization. The involvement of a municipality is a guarantee that the school will succeed in its goal of utilizing and developing people's skills, that no matter where you come from, you should be given a chance to move forward and not get stuck in passivity.

In Germany and Denmark, ReDI School is aimed at both women and men, while in Malmö it is mainly aimed at women who are excluded. The aim is to be able to reach out to anyone who needs to enter the workforce. IT is a way in, especially as there is a major shortage of such skills in many European countries. This is a chance to break through barriers of resistance. Moreover, most IT companies are international, so speaking the national language is not required.

Felix's experience from the autumn school in Malmö is that the women—and a few men—who have participated so far, have developed and now feel more confident. Several women have dared to show more of themselves than ever before. They also become ambassadors for the ReDI School for future refugees.

"When you work together, it has a ripple effect. One becomes two, two becomes four, four becomes eight and so on. It is in meetings with others that development occurs. It is when you talk to each other and not about each other that you really learn something," Anne explains.

For the future, both Anne and Felix see the ReDI School becoming large and forming an infrastructure that works for all countries' refugee reception.

Anne Kjaer Bathel's greatest dream, albeit with a certain degree of humility, is that ReDI School receives the Nobel Peace Prize for its extensive work to create structure and opportunities for everyone to live in dignity. And not least that the countries receiving refugees also highlight and use all the skills that are currently being lost due to a lack of infrastructure. This is what she wants the ReDI School to contribute to. The fact that it will take time and that it is a delicate task is something that neither Felix nor Anne hesitates to admit.

The important thing is that each country takes responsibility and does something to prevent negative spirals. The ReDI School is a symbol of a changed and new direction!

20

Fighting Now, Dreaming Ahead

A Conversation with Anna Stamou

AUDE SATHOUD

ANNA STAMOU, SPOKESPERSON FOR the Muslim Association of Greece, wanted to quit multiple times.[1] But as the next day rises, she decides to continue: "I try to grab a chance to meet and have good people around me. I find little light rays and catch them for a while. And that's why AWoN is important, that's why it is needed."

I met with Anna in Athens to talk about growing up in an open-minded family during a time of dictatorship, her conversion to Islam, and her fight for justice for every human being. The following interview is a glimpse into her profile as a practitioner and her collaboration with AWoN.

A FLEETING MOMENT

What a book chapter will never completely render is the beauty of a fleeting moment as you are welcomed with your favourite Greek biscuits and a cup of green tea, as you sit down in the warmth of someone's home and listen to their story. Anna and I cherished this peaceful space, as we got to discuss much more troubled and dark realities. Anna may have

---

1. A version of this chapter has been published at https://aworldofneighbours.org.

inherited that capacity to nurture hope and kindness in the face of hardships and adversity from her childhood. As the child of an "average Greek middle-class family of non-practicing Orthodox" growing up under the Colonels' dictatorship (1967–1974), Anna remembers both the censorship of music and arts and the struggle of her family, most notably her grandfather, against social injustice. At home, they said Muslims and not Mohammedans, the derogatory term a number of Greeks were using at the time. At home, the family owned a copy of the Qur'an.

Growing up in this open-minded, socially-oriented environment, Anna asked herself a lot of questions, and introduced herself to numerous life philosophies, religious, and spiritual schools and traditions. On her journey, she discovered Islam.

"I have to study this," she remembers telling herself, "that is what I am looking for." To her Egyptian husband-to-be, whom she has met in the meantime, she one day shares her wish to convert. "Take your time, study some more, I'll give you books," is his reply. So, Anna does, and starts taking Arabic lessons, looking for some more resources about Islam in Greek—only to realize almost none exist.

Despite the historical presence of Muslim populations dating back from the Ottoman Empire in the North of the country and the increasing number of Muslim immigrants settling in the country since the twentieth century, only a few books exist for Greek-speaking people to learn about Islam. So Anna, encouraged by her Arabic teacher, decided to undertake the translation of accessible works about her new faith. "Nothing extreme nor too sophisticated, nothing academic—only the basics, so that anyone willing to learn can get an introduction to Islam."

A DISTINCT CLASS

And that is how it all started. For the absence of Islamic knowledge and representation is not limited to Greek libraries—it concerns the entire society, within which Muslims often face ignorance, stereotypes, and discrimination.

"There are so many things which make Muslims a distinct class within Greek society," Anna explains, pointing at the obstacles to enter the Greek administration, become a teacher, a lawyer, for people of Muslim origins or faith.

> If you want to clean the streets, for sure you can. Those discriminations are in total contradiction with the social diversity

of Muslim populations spread throughout the country, which, from workers to ship owners or doctors, is no different from that of the Greek population in its whole—so why is there such a situation?

It is not for herself that Anna decided to turn her feeling of injustice into action. "We have to restore things for the next generation."

As the strong civil and human rights advocate she has become since joining the Muslim Association of Greece, Anna has been going from one conference to another, hailing national and international policy-makers, civil societies, and religious bodies on topics as diverse as Islamophobia, racism, civil rights of minorities and migrants each time she gets the occasion. It was this, her energy and determination, that caught the attention of late Dirk Ficca in his quest for passionate practitioners working to build a more humane Europe all over the continent.

> I met [AWoN] and it was genuine—that's when I knew. That's when I wanted to be a part of it. When I received Dirk's first email, I got excited but wanted to remain cautious as well. I have been doing this for over twenty years now, so I have some good experience with political promises and fantasies—but Dirk and the first members of AWoN were so determined, they kept reaching out. We can recognize when something is real and when it is not, you know? So I said, why not? and I first joined them for a working group in 2020 in Malmö.

GENUINE PEOPLE

That's when Anna knew for sure she had made the right choice:

> I saw them, all those people from different religions, sitting together, it was so nice and simple. I could see it in their eyes—their seriousness. That's really important for me, that they saw what they wanted to undertake with a humane look. They did not have some random agenda and funds to cover it. I met those people, and they were genuine—that's when I knew. That's when I wanted to be part.

Anna joined AWoN "with only complaints," she laughs.

> I shared Greek issues, our never-ending problems of corruption, the terrible treatment of people on the move, how the situation, since the Syrian war, has gone out of hand, inhumane and uncontrollable.

Anna came with complaints—and she was listened to:

> That's what I appreciated from the beginning with AWoN, there was no wishful thinking nor empty words about some promised land. We know we are talking about high degrees of rejection and not definitive success. But only with such an honest understanding can we build a relation of trust and then share good feelings with each other. That is what AWoN is for me: good, positive feelings.

Good feelings which are more than needed in the support of people on the move in Greece. One of the first receiving countries of asylum-seekers and so-called "hotspot" on the continent for the past few years, Greece has seen the burgeoning of a number of NGOs and governmental programs providing first-aid and emergency support to newcomers—who, once the people they work with are not newcomers anymore, find themselves with no perspective for the future. For Anna, the necessity is to strategize for the future, although it does not come without challenges:

> But how can you plan for the ten years to come when you ignore the open wounds of the present? That notion of "people on the move" takes all its meaning here, in Greece, where people do not want to stay, where no one can tell where they will end up. When they arrive here, people obviously do not think of integrating—they just try to survive! And how can they integrate, when they want to stay, when they have to live in containers or in the streets?

In Anna's opinion, those mistreatments are nothing but a deliberate political choice from the Greek and the leadership more broadly, which works at discouraging people from coming. Showing me some pictures of the Greek President proudly posing along border guards, Anna goes on.

> As early as yesterday, our Minister of the Police was once again repeating how important it is for Greece to secure European funds in order to build walls in Evros (in the north) to protect the country. But protect it from whom? From people who have no shoes? Who have nothing to eat?

CREATING AN ACTION PLAN

In such a context, where far-right discourses and policies have reached the highest levels of power in a number of European democracies—some ministers of the current Greek government indeed make no secret of their fascist sympathies—documenting and condemning the situation is not enough anymore.

> We need an action plan. Do we focus on first-aid needs or create a strategy? We do both. We keep the emergency support services running but need to start long-term planning now—it has been way too long already.

Anna however does not ignore the depths and complexity of the issues we all have to struggle against, such as the historical roots and ongoing geopolitical dynamics of the conflicts forcing people out of their homeland.

> Our countries are there, so of course those people think it is reasonable to come find a safe place here. We have Greek soldiers in Mali! You are in my country, why can't I be in yours? I don't come to conquer but give me a chance to live. That's as simple as that. We need to let people live. We need to stop creating refugees.

AWON: "A SPACE TO DREAM AHEAD"

To Afghan practitioners whom she met through AWoN, Anna recalls, she had nothing to say but sorry—and that she would keep on fighting by their side, against all odds. When I ask where she finds her energy, she takes a few seconds to think before sighing:

> I don't know, actually. I started all this being so optimistic. But it's been over twenty years now, and that is a long time with temporary smiles. I will be honest, I am very pessimistic about the situation. I often want to quit. And I don't know anyone working in that field who has not gone down in burnout at least once. So yes, I think of quitting often. I say "I will do this and then I quit." I actually wanted to quit, already, a few years ago.
>
> And then I saw Dirk. I saw Dirk and the founding members of AWoN, all older than me, and I thought to myself "Look. Look at those people, they still have hope. They really believe in it." So, I went along and, if you ask me, that's probably how I keep on going. I try to grab a chance to meet and have good people around me. I find little light rays and catch them for a while. And that's why AWoN is important, that's why it is needed.
>
> We have this platform, aimed at supporting people on the move—that is what is happening now, that is the crisis of the

present. There won't be fewer wars in the years to come—there'll be more. So, we need to nurture and share that mindset we have here so that it can be replicated in more and more contexts and places around the world. In the beginning, no one knew about us. Now, I see more and more people recognizing and appreciating our work, our values, our vision. So, we have to create those spaces, those small cracks in the wall. For in those pockets of kindness we may not solve all the problems, but we may find the space to dream ahead.

21

Just Care

Ethics in A World of Neighbours

ULRICH SCHMIEDEL

"AND I JUST FELT LIKE, no, I don't want to be in a setting where we're just continuing the programme. That's not why I'm in A World of Neighbours. I'm in enough efficient organizations, you know, where everything is about the programme.... The purpose for me here is... about meeting all of you as human beings."[1]

We are sitting in Brussels. The summit of the multi-faith refugee relief network A World of Neighbours (AWoN) has brought together activists who work with people on the move across Europe. In our conversation, Ruth—the name is a pseudonym—makes her statement. What she says points to something that AWoN can create but cannot control: encounters. The practice of encounters—"meeting all of you as human beings"—is embodied in AWoN. But it is a precious and precarious practice, at risk of getting lost in the day-to-day demands for the efficiency of programmes and the efficacy of policies that confront any network engaging with people on the move. In our conversation, the activists agree with Ruth. In some ways, it is a staggering statement. Brussels is the centre of Fortress Europe, a continent with one of the most dangerous and

---

1. Ruth, in conversation at a summit of A World of Neighbours, Brussels, 2022.

deadly borders in the world.² We have discussed the news of pushbacks by Frontex, the European border forces.³ Yet we nod in agreement when Ruth calls for encounters.

In this chapter, I take Ruth's call as a point of departure to discuss the ethics of migration. While I have worked with AWoN for about five years, collecting qualitative- and quantitative-empirical data in a team of scholars from sociology, anthropology, and theology, I would like to concentrate on Ruth's statement about encounters here. I suggest that AWoN's practice of encounters promotes an ethics of care. This ethics of care revolves around the insight that life is sustained by relationships. Acting on this insight, AWoN cuts across the categories of "migrant" and "non-migrant." In a way, the activists prefigure a postmigrant society in which there are neither migrants nor non-migrants. Of course, the activists know that, according to the United Nations High Commissioner for Refugees, about one hundred million people have been forced to flee across the globe,⁴ so living as if there were neither migrants nor non-migrants is strange. Yet while it appears eccentric or escapist, AWoN's prefiguration of a society in which the categories of "migrant" and "non-migrant" have lost significance actually allows the activists to challenge how the conversation about the ethics of migration in Europe is conducted. If the ethics of migration—by ethics, I mean reflection on how people act and ought to act—is characterized by the categories of "migrant" and "non-migrant," then a concentration on encounters requires this ethics to be re-thought. AWoN's practice is a promising point of departure for such a postmigrant re-thinking.

ETHICS OF MIGRATION IN PRINCIPLE

Overall, ethicists approach migration through the articulation and application of principles. Two approaches have characterized the debate for decades: communitarianism and cosmopolitanism.⁵ Without simplifying too much, these approaches can be set up as opposites. I suggest that they offer competing answers to one question: "Who is my neighbour?"

---

2. Jones refers to the border around the European Union as "the world's deadliest border" (*Violent Borders*, 12).
3. See Fallon, "Revealed."
4. See UNHCR, "Figures at a Glance."
5. For a helpful overview, see Wilde et al., *Struggle Over Borders*.

The principles of communitarianism prioritize the political self-determination of a community like a country over the individual right to freedom of movement. As a consequence, communitarians argue that borders ought to exist. In the communitarian ethics of migration, I am called to protect my community or country, even if that comes at the cost of the migrant. My ethical duty revolves first and foremost around the non-migrants rather than the migrants. *They* are "my neighbour." The principles of cosmopolitanism, however, prioritize the individual right to freedom of movement over the political self-determination of a community like a country. As a consequence, cosmopolitans argue that borders ought not to exist. In the cosmopolitanism ethics of migration, I am called to protect the migrant, even if it comes at the cost of my community or country. My ethical duty revolves first and foremost around the migrants rather than the non-migrants. *They* are "my neighbour."

Although their answers to the question of who is my neighbour are competing, the two approaches correspond in their assumption that the categories of "migrant" and "non-migrant" are central to the ethics of migration. This assumption lurks behind the attitude that it is "us" who decide about how we engage with "them." As Donatella Di Cesare argues in *Resident Foreigners: A Philosophy of Migration*, communitarianism and cosmopolitanism are both built on the attitude of a detached "we" that decides about who ought or ought not to be admitted into Europe.[6] It is a "we" watching from the safe distance of the shore as dinghies with people on the move arrive or attempt to arrive. It is a "we" that is *not* on the dinghy.

What lurks behind the controversy between communitarianism and cosmopolitanism is a core characteristic of democracy.[7] All democracies are characterized by a tension. Peoples' rights to self-determination as a political community clash with the human rights that are independent of membership in any community. The human rights that are independent of membership in any community clash with peoples' rights to self-determination as a political community. Mindful of this tension, political philosopher Seyla Benhabib has come up with a mediating position.[8] Arguing against both a communitarianism that sides with peoples' rights to self-determination at the expense of human rights, and against a

6. Di Cesare, *Resident Foreigners*, 20–22.

7. For the significance of this tension for people on the move, see the classic Arendt, "We Refugees."

8. She presents the position in Benhabib, *Another Cosmopolitanism*.

cosmopolitanism that sides with human rights at the expense of people's rights to self-determination, she calls attention to the negotiation and re-negotiation of all rights.

In *The Rights of Others*, Benhabib explains how people claim rights.[9] One example are the protests through which people on the move have called for citizenship. With the slogan "We're here because you were there"—coined by the activist and author Ambalavaner Sivanandan, who directed the anti-racist think tank Institute of Race Relations in London—people who had come to the UK have pointed to colonialism as a cause for migration. Through persistent protests, they were able to secure some of the rights they had been denied, rights that were created for non-migrants rather than migrants.[10] Benhabib argues that protests like these can initiate a "jurisgenerative politics," a politics that generates laws in a way that prompts a community to conceive of membership ever more expansively, thus turning outsiders into insiders, at least in the long run.[11] Through jurisgenerative politics, "my neighbour" emerges as fluid rather than fixed, expanding from non-migrants to migrants. Benhabib's mediating position, then, shows that the categories of "migrant" and "non-migrant" that communitarianism and cosmopolitanism take for granted are not as stable as they seem to be.

Nonetheless, the approaches of communitarianism and cosmopolitanism have been adopted in theology.[12] The Bible is claimed by both communitarian and cosmopolitan theologians. These claims are possible because the Bible contains a variety of stories and statements on how to respond to people who have had to flee their homes. There are biblical passages that call for inclusion. There are biblical passages that call for exclusion. "This is of course not a new problem when it comes to using the Bible for constructing ethical responses," theologian Susanna Snyder contends.[13] "Scripture is . . . frustratingly varied in terms of its stances on a whole range of issues. Each book was addressed to a particular people at a particular point in history . . . and it is thus impossible simply to apply biblical teaching to a complex contemporary phenomenon like migration

---

9. See Benhabib, *Rights of Others*.

10. Of course, the struggle continues. See Patel, *We're Here Because You Were There*.

11. Benhabib, *Rights of Others*, 169. For a theological account, see Meyer, *Fremde Bürger*.

12. See Heyer, "Migrants as Feared and Forsaken."

13. Snyder, "Encountering Asylum Seekers."

to come up with 'dos' and 'don'ts.'"[14] Snyder's contrast between a biblical "ecology of fear" and a biblical "ecology of faith" makes clear that the crucial question for theology is not what the Bible says, but how to read what the Bible says.[15] The Parable of the Good Samaritan is a striking example.

The Parable[16] is well known: Jesus is asked what one must do to inherit "eternal life." He answers with the double-commandment of love, a commandment that is central to all three Abrahamic[17] faiths: love God as you love your neighbour, love your neighbour as you love God. "And who is my neighbour?" Jesus is asked. In response, he tells the story of the Good Samaritan. A Jewish man is lying on the street. He has been injured by robbers. Two men pass by without helping him. The third man, a Samaritan—from a people in long-standing conflict with the Jews—stops. "Moved with pity," the Samaritan assists the injured man without asking for reimbursement or reward. "Which of these three, do you think, was a neighbour to the man who fell into the hands of the robbers?" Jesus asks.

Although the parable seems straightforward, it has stirred up controversy among theologians.[18] In the ethics of migration, there are at least two answers to Jesus' question: one more communitarian and one more cosmopolitan. (No surprises here.) For the communitarians, the neighbour is a close neighbour. Those who follow the commandment to love your neighbour in its communitarian interpretation are not called to love everyone, but they are called to love the people who are close to them in particular. For the cosmopolitans, however, the neighbour is not a close neighbour. Those who follow the commandment to love your neighbour in its cosmopolitan interpretation are not called to love people who are close to them in particular, but they are called to love everyone.

In public debate and political discourse, closeness is often associated with culture, leading to an ethics of migration that prioritizes people who are considered culturally similar over people who are considered culturally dissimilar. Religion is a central category in the construction of culture. In Europe, Islam is singled out increasingly. Elena Fiddian-Qasmiyeh, a political scientist who specializes in migration studies, has

14. Snyder, "Encountering Asylum Seekers," 357.
15. See Snyder, *Asylum-Seeking, Migration and Church*, 129–96.
16. Luke 10:25–37 NRSV.
17. Connecting Judaism, Christianity, and Islam under the figure of Abraham is tricky. See Hughes, *Abrahamic Religions*.
18. For the variety of interpretations, see Strømmen and Schmiedel, *Claim to Christianity*, 135–37.

analysed the reporting on migration in the European media. She emphasizes two ideal types that appear in the news.[19] On the one hand, the image of the "good migrant" is frequently invoked, seen as female, in need of help, and passive, waiting for European support. This is the sort of person that is presented as deserving of "our" help. On the other hand, the image of the "bad Muslim" is also frequently invoked, seen as male, not in need of help, and active, not waiting for European support. This is the sort of person that is presented as not deserving of "our" help. Of course, empirically, these ideal types do not exist. Yet, according to Fiddian-Qasmiyeh, the images impact jurisdiction on asylum in European countries because they are so pervasive.

The concentration on Islam that Fiddian-Qasmiyeh identified is crucial to the rejection of people on the move. Across Europe, migrants are often read as Muslims and Muslims are often read as migrants, even if they are not. Since the Russian attack on Ukraine, organisations like AWoN have pointed out that migrants who are not identified as Muslims receive more support than migrants who are identified as Muslims.[20] Their point is *not* that the support for Ukrainians should be stopped. On the contrary, their point is that the support for Ukrainians shows a distinction drawn between "deserving" and "un-deserving" people on the move that is anchored in their religion or their perceived religion. This is Islamophobia, a racism that targets Muslimness or perceived Muslimness.[21] Islamophobia stabilises or re-stabilises the categories of "migrant" and "non-migrant," even after they have been exposed as unstable.

To summarize, the debate in the ethics of migration in Europe is characterized by two approaches that offer competing answers to one question: "Who is my neighbour?" For communitarians, the neighbour is first and foremost the non-migrant. For cosmopolitans, the neighbour is first and foremost the migrant. These approaches mark the conversation about the ethics of migration in a variety of disciplines, including theology. Despite their competing answers, both approaches assume that "migrant" and "non-migrant" are crucial categories in the ethics of migration. In presuming these categories, principles can be articulated and applied. In AWoN, however, ethics is more a matter of practice than a matter of principles. AWoN revolves around the practice of encounters.

19. See Fiddian-Qasmiyeh, "Faith-Gender-Asylum Nexus."
20. See Wilczyński, "Three Things to Learn."
21. See the contributions in Malik, *Anti-Muslim Prejudice*.

ETHICS OF MIGRATION IN PRACTICE

During our conversation in Brussels, Ruth points to the practice of encounters. Her statement presents a contrast between programmes and practices. I suggest that AWoN's practice also asks the question "Who is my neighbour?" Yet the answer is neither "migrant" nor "non-migrant," but "all of you as human beings."

Carol Gilligan is commonly credited with the conceptualization of the ethics of care. As a psychologist at Harvard University, she studied how people make decisions. She criticized the fact that psychological studies on decision-making were all too often based on male rather than female participants.[22] She contrasted two ways of making decisions. The one concentrates on abstract rights and is often associated with a male perspective on ethics. The other concentrates on actual relationships and is often associated with a female perspective on ethics. These ways of making decisions "display different modes of moral understanding, different ways of thinking about conflict and choice."[23] Gilligan stresses that she is not interested in essentializing these perspectives, as if a focus on abstract rights was "essentially" male and a focus on actual relationships was "essentially" female.[24] On the contrary, Gilligan insists that the concentration on relationships is central to all human beings.[25] Yet psychologists have ignored this concentration by listening to male rather than female participants. *In a Different Voice*—the study that laid the foundations for her ethics of care in the 1980s—Gilligan amplified the voices of those who have not been heard. The ethics of care that these voices articulate revolves around the insight that "life . . . can only be sustained by care in relationships."[26]

Ruth's statement resonates with the distinction that Gilligan draws. There is a voice of calculation, on the one hand, calling for efficiency. This is what Ruth presents as programmatic. There is a voice of care, on the other hand, calling for encounter. This is what Ruth presents as practical. "The purpose for me here is . . . about meeting all of you as human beings," she insists. Ruth challenges the conversation about ethics. One could put

---

22. Gilligan, *In a Different Voice*.
23. Gilligan, *In a Different Voice*, 32.
24. Gilligan, *Joining the Resistance*, 17–18.
25. As a consequence, she is critical of the debate that pitted justice against care and care against justice. See Gilligan, *Joining the Resistance*, 11–12.
26. Gilligan, *In a Different Voice*, 127.

Gilligan's words into her mouth. She "calls for a new way of speaking, a change in the very terms of the conversation about ourselves."[27] In *Joining the Resistance*, Gilligan summarizes this new way of speaking succinctly: "Care is a relational ethic grounded in the premise of interdependence."[28] The "we" that is at stake here, then, is anything but detached. It tries to put itself into the shoes of the people on the move who arrive or attempt to arrive in Europe, presenting "us" as a part of "them" and "them" as a part of "us."

Interdependence is central to the ethics of care. AWoN stresses the significance of interdependence between those who are and those who are not on the move.[29] In the presentation of the network, interdependence—the fact that the self is vulnerable to the other and the other is vulnerable to the self—is not interpreted as something negative but as something positive: the ability to relate to each other, to be affected and to affect.[30] According to Gilligan, such vulnerability is a root for resistance against the status quo.[31] Stressing the significance of vulnerability for how the world is seen, she is not asking how to apply ethical principles to practice, but how to apply ethical practice to principles so that ethics can be re-thought from the bottom up. Debates about distributive or redistributive justice—who owes what to whom—are re-oriented by putting relationality at the centre. "This resistance makes trouble in the sense of challenging . . . the value of losses that have come to be taken as in the very nature of things."[32] Ruth's statement offers such a challenge.

According to Ruth, the efficiency of programmes and the efficacy of policies are values that come with losses. Of course, organizations that work with people on the move must be efficient and effective. Ruth is not so naïve as to suggest that AWoN could do without programmes and policies. In fact, she is involved in the discussions and the drafting of them. But she stresses that programmes and policies run the risk of a loss. "I'm in enough efficient organizations. . . . My purpose here is to meet all of you as human beings." The contrast between programmes and practices that she proposes, then, points to a new way of seeing the world.

27. Gilligan, *Joining the Resistance*, 14–15, 22, 24.
28. Gilligan, *Joining the Resistance*, 23.
29. AWoN, *Keeping Our Humanity*, 36.
30. AWoN, *Keeping Our Humanity*, 36.
31. Gilligan, *Joining the Resistance*, 85.
32. Gilligan, *Joining the Resistance*, 106.

In accordance with the ethics of care, her question is not about how to apply ethical principles to practice, but how to apply ethical practice to principles, so that these principles can be based on relationships. Following Ruth, refusing the loss of relationships is a point of departure for political work that draws on an ethics of care, "work to bring a new order of living into the world."[33]

Arguably, then, the new order of living that AWoN works towards is one where the categories of "migrant" and "non-migrant" lose significance, because these categories run the risk of preventing rather than promoting relationships. AWoN presents relationality as its normative anchor. As it is put in the presentation of the network: "When accompaniment is rooted in the recognition that both the 'received' and 'receiving' are vulnerable, in deeply human ways, then mutual transformation is possible. And it is in mutual transformation that lies the basis for any authentic friendship."[34]

Crucially, the concentration on relationality is not meant as an escape from politics. The activists know that privilege and power prevent conditions under which such friendships can be built on equal footing. Vulnerability is shared by everyone, but it is shared *unequally*. Some are more dependent than others. It would be foolish to think that friendships—no matter how "authentic"—can erase the inequality that is ingrained in migration regimes inside and outside Europe. Yet the call for friendships between people who are and people who are not on the move—note how AWoN avoids the categories of "migrant" and "non-migrant"!—has consequences for politics.

The activists argue that people on the move ought to "have 'a seat at the table' when ... leaders are making decisions about their lives."[35] This call rests neither on a communitarian ethics of migration with its focus on non-migrants nor on a cosmopolitan ethics of migration with its focus on migrants, but on a central concept of democracies: people who are affected by a policy should articulate it and people who articulate a policy should be affected by it.[36] In the case of migration, this means that "the receiving" as well as "the received" ought to come together to think through what a just politics of migration might look like.

33. Gilligan, *Joining the Resistance*, 163.
34. AWoN, *Keeping Our Humanity*, 36.
35. AWoN, *Keeping Our Humanity*, 4.
36. See Schmiedel, "Theopolitics of the Migrant."

This call promotes the "jurisgenerative politics" that Benhabib presented. AWoN is not waiting for such politics to play out in public and political conversations about migration in Europe. As the increasing and intensifying restrictions in the migration regime of the European Union indicate, it is not likely that membership will be defined in expansive rather than exclusive ways anytime soon. Policy concerning migration is made by non-migrants rather than migrants. Countering these constrictions, AWoN calls for the deliberate and decisive blurring of the boundaries between migrants and non-migrants in the making of policy, pushing for a jurisgenerative politics.

The activists aim to live accordingly, prefiguring relationships that would characterize a postmigrant society in which the categories of "migrant" and "non-migrant" have lost significance. Countering the inequalities in privilege and power as far as possible, they life *as if* the society they work towards already existed. Hence, AWoN cuts across both the principles of communitarianism, with their concentration on the non-migrant as neighbour, and the principles of cosmopolitanism, with their focus on the migrant as neighbour. In AWoN, "my neighbour" is "all of you as human beings."

Theologically, AWoN's practice of encounters is crucial because it calls for a reversal of roles that characterises the Parable of the Good Samaritan.[37] What is striking about the Parable is that Jesus answers the question "Who is my neighbour?" with a question. Referring to the three men who encountered the person in need of help, he asks: "Which of these three, do you think, was a neighbour to the man who fell into the hands of the robbers?" Jesus turns the question back onto the one who posed it in the first place. Hence, the parable can be read in accordance with the core concern of the ethics of care—neighbourliness is about actual relationships rather than abstract rights. Such a reading points to interdependence. In the encounter, the "I" is dependent on "the neighbour" and "the neighbour" is dependent on the "I." Both can affect and be affected. Both are "vulnerable, in deeply human ways," because a liveable life can only be sustained by care in relationships.[38] These relationships

---

37. See Jeanrond, *Theology of Love*, 35.

38. Butler's account of vulnerability is inspired by the ethics of care. See Butler, *Force of Nonviolence*, esp. 185–204, the postscript where Butler warns of any simplistic politics of care. For a striking theological study of vulnerability, see Stålsett, *Political Theology of Vulnerability*.

are the point of departure for tackling the differential distribution of vulnerability that marks Europe's migration regimes.

Here, then, lies the central characteristic of the ethics of care. In an ethics that is concerned with abstract rights, the subject is envisioned as independent. Its decisions about what ought to be done—who is my neighbour, what is or is not owed to my neighbour—is made autonomously, in a detached way. Both cosmopolitanism and communitarianism rest on the assumption of a self-enclosed autonomy. In an ethics that is concerned with actual relationships, however, the subject is envisioned as dependent. Its decisions about what ought to be done—who is my neighbour, what is or is not owed to my neighbour—is not made autonomously, not in a detached way. On the contrary, the subject is not self-enclosed, but vulnerable, with the ability to affect and to be affected. It is committed to care. Justice becomes more a question of practice than a question of principles. This is not a critique of the articulation and application of principles in the ethics of migration. It is a call for principles to come out of practices of encounter, so that the ethics of migration is not rooted in the calculation of limited resources but in the creation of unlimited resources: relationships of care.[39]

To summarize, the ethics of care stresses that care in relationships sustains a liveable life. AWoN embodies the ethics of care through its concentration on encounters. Through encounters, the migrant is recognized as dependent on the non-migrant and the non-migrant is recognized as dependent on the migrant, which blurs the very boundaries between migrant and non-migrant. Care means "meeting all of you, as human beings." Behind the critique of the principles of cosmopolitanism and communitarianism that the ethics of care voices is the normative question of the subject that makes ethical decisions. AWoN is not oriented around a subject who is independent but around a subject who is dependent. From this interdependency follows the political demand for participation.

POSTMIGRANT NEIGHBOURHOODS

To sum up so far, I have contextualized and characterized AWoN's ethics as an ethics of care. Exploring Ruth's critique of the collaboration in AWoN, I have suggested that this ethics of care cuts across the categories through which the conversation about the ethics of migration in Europe

---

39. For a convincing conceptualization of care as "praxis," see Conradi, *Take Care*.

is commonly conducted. This conversation is dominated by two competing approaches: communitarianism, with its assumption of the non-migrant as neighbour, and cosmopolitanism, with its assumption of the migrant as neighbour. AWoN resists both the communitarian and the cosmopolitan assumption through its concentration on care. Encounters between "the receiving" and "the received" demonstrate that both are vulnerable.[40] Of course, there is a differential distribution of vulnerability between "the receiving" and "the received"—any passport signifies privilege and power—yet both affect and are affected by each other. The ethics of care puts relationships at the centre, thus calling for a resistance against a way of seeing the world that accepts this differential distribution. In AWoN, this resistance is rooted in relationships of care between people who are and people who are not on the move. The mutual transformation that follows and flows from such relationships calls a fundamental assumption about migration into question. For AWoN, there is no clear-cut distinction between the categories of "the migrant" and "the non-migrant." Since both affect and are affected by migration, they ought to think through migration together. The "we" that makes decisions consists of people who are and people who are not on the move.

By way of conclusion, I would like to point to the significance of religion for AWoN's ethics of care. Countering a conceptualization of religion that takes faith as a marker to distinguish between people who are culturally close and people who are culturally not so close, AWoN's ethics of care calls on religion as a marker of relationality. Given AWoN's make-up—there are non-religious and religious activists in AWoN—the concentration on relationships implies friendships across religions, such as, say, Christians working with Muslims and Muslims working with Christians. Since the categories of "migrant" and "non-migrant" are often conceptualized through religion—as the Islamophobia in Europe's response to people on the move affirms—friendship across religions is crucial for the resistance against Fortress Europe. It drives AWoN's critique of the inequalities in the treatment of European and non-European refugees, which the war against Ukraine has highlighted. AWoN is living proof that religion ought not to be reduced to a marker of identity in a clash of cultures that justifies inequality in the treatment of Muslims and

---

40. See the classic account of the encounter at the core of ethics, Løgstrup, *Ethical Demand*, 8–28.

non-Muslims.[41] On the contrary, for AWoN, religion is not building but blurring the boundaries between "the receiving" and "the received."

Altogether, then, AWoN's ethics of care could be characterized as a postmigrant ethics. The concept of postmigration originates in theatre. Scholars such as Naika Foroutan have adopted and adapted it for the study of migration. Foroutan, a social scientist who specializes in immigration and integration research, speaks of "the postmigrant society" as a "promise of plural democracy."[42] She stresses that European societies are postmigrant rather than migrant societies. In these societies, migration is the new normal. This new normal does not depend on whether the members of the postmigrant society like it or dislike it. It is a fact. And if it is a fact that migration is the new normal, then the binary between "migrant" and "non-migrant" becomes blurred. The postmigrant society is about the "negotiation and recognition of equality as a central promise of modern democracies, which refer to plurality and parity as principles," regardless of whether a person does or does not have a history of migration.[43] According to Foroutan, the postmigrant society "poses the fundamental question of how we can get beyond the social dividing line of migration, if we want to live together in societies that are becoming more and more plural."[44] The situation of the postmigrant society, then, calls the way justice has been conceptualized into question. Neither the communitarian nor the cosmopolitan approach actually answers Foroutan's fundamental question of how to get beyond the social dividing line of migration. But AWoN has a simple but significant answer to this question: "through authentic friendships" that allow for "meeting all of you as human beings." This answer is not the end of the ethics of migration. Encounters remain precious and precarious, between control and uncontrollability.[45] Yet this answer is a promising point of departure for figuring out a postmigrant ethics of just care for Europe.

---

41. For a consideration and critique of impact of the clash of cultures on conversations about migration, see Strømmen and Schmiedel, *Claim to Christianity*, 15–36.

42. Foroutan, *Postmigrantische Gesellschaft* (my translation).

43. Foroutan, *Postmigrantische Gesellschaft*, 13–14 (my translation).

44. Foroutan, *Postmigrantische Gesellschaft*, 18–19 (my translation).

45. For a helpful conceptualisation of encounter between control and uncontrollability, see Bobrowicz, "Keeping Religion in the Closet?"

BIBLIOGRAPHY

Arendt, Hannah. "We Refugees." In *The Jewish Writings*, edited by Jerome Kohn and Ron H. Feldman, 264–74. New York: Schocken, 2007.

Benhabib, Seyla. *Another Cosmopolitanism*. Oxford: Oxford University Press, 2006.

———. *The Rights of Others: Aliens, Residents, and Citizens*. The John Robert Seeley Lectures 5. Cambridge: Cambridge University Press, 2004.

Bobrowicz, Ryszard "Keeping Religion in the Closet? How Legible Religion Shapes Multi-Faith Spaces." PhD diss., University of Lund, 2022.

Butler, Judith. *The Force of Nonviolence: An Ethico-Political Bind*. London: Verso, 2020.

Conradi, Elisabeth. *Take Care: Grundlagen einer Ethik der Achtsamkeit*. Frankfurt: Campus, 2001.

Di Cesare, Donatella. *Resident Foreigners: A Philosophy of Migration*. Translated by David Broder. Cambridge: Polity, 2020.

Fallon, Katy. "Revealed: EU Border Agency Involved in Hundreds of Refugee Pushbacks." *Guardian*, April 28, 2022. https://www.theguardian.com/global-development/ 2022/apr/28/revealed-eu-border-agency-involved-in-hundreds-of-refugee-pushbacks.

Fiddian-Qasmiyeh, Elena. "The Faith-Gender-Asylum Nexus: An Intersectionalist Analysis of Representations of the 'Refugee Crisis.'" In *The Refugee Crisis and Religion: Secularism, Security and Hospitality in Question*, edited by Luca Mavelli and Erin Wilson, 207–20. London: Rowman & Littlefield, 2016.

Foroutan, Naika. *Die postmigrantische Gesellschaft: Ein Versprechen der pluralen Demokratie*. Bielefeld: Transcript, 2019.

Gilligan, Carol. *In A Different Voice: Psychological Theory and Women's Development*. Cambridge: Harvard University Press, 2003.

———. *Joining the Resistance*. Cambridge: Polity, 2011.

Heyer, Kristin. "Migrants as Feared and Forsaken: A Catholic Ethic of Social Responsibility." *Interdisciplinary Journal for Religion and Transformation in Contemporary Society* 6 (2020) 158–70.

Hughes, Aaron W. *Abrahamic Religions: On the Uses and Abuses of History*. Oxford: Oxford University Press, 2012.

Jeanrond, Werner G. *A Theology of Love*. London: Bloomsbury, 2010.

Jones, Reece. *Violent Borders: Refugees and the Right to Move*. London: Verso, 2016.

Løgstrup, Knud Ejler. *The Ethical Demand*. Edited by Hans Fink and Alasdair MacIntyre. Notre Dame: University of Notre Dame Press, 1997.

Malik, Maleiha, ed. *Anti-Muslim Prejudice: Past and Present*. Abingdon: Routledge, 2010.

Meyer, Lukas. *Fremde Bürger: Ethische Überlegungen zu Migration, Flucht und Asyl*. Zurich: TVZ, 2017.

Patel, Ian Sanjay. *We're Here Because You Were There: Immigration and the End of Empire*. London: Verso, 2021.

Schmiedel, Ulrich. "The Theopolitics of the Migrant: Toward a Coalitional and Comparative Political Theology." In *Christianity and the Law of Migration*, edited by Silas Allard et al., 212–29. London: Routledge, 2021.

Snyder, Susanna. *Asylum-Seeking, Migration and Church*. London: Routledge, 2016.

———. "Encountering Asylum Seekers: An Ethic of Fear or Faith?" *Studies in Christian Ethics* 24.3 (2011) 350–66.

Strømmen, Hannah, and Ulrich Schmiedel. *The Claim to Christianity: Responding to the Far Right*. London: SCM, 2020.
Stålsett, Sturla J. *A Political Theology of Vulnerability*. Leiden: Brill Academic, 2023.
United Nations High Commissioner for Refugees (UNHCR). "Figures at a Glance." UNHCR, n.d. https://www.unhcr.org/uk/figures-at-a-glance.html.
Wilczyński, Karol. "Three Things to Learn from One of the Biggest Activist Networks." AWoN, n.d. https://aworldofneighbours.org/3-things-to-learn-from-one-of-the-biggest-activist-networks.
Wilde, Pieter de, et al., eds. *The Struggle Over Borders: Cosmopolitanism and Communitarianism*. Cambridge: Cambridge University Press, 2019.
A World of Neighbours (AWoN). *Keeping Our Humanity*. Stockholm: Church of Sweden, n.d.

Conclusion

"You Have A World of Neighbours"

Antje Jackelén

"You Have a World of Neighbours"—that is what it says on Petra Hall's embroidery that made her win the competition in the Backbone project.[1] The idea behind this embroidered theology is as simple as it is ingenious. It is about "you." That is, you are seen and spoken to, you are addressed, you are called upon. It is a way of making clear that you are part of something bigger than your own "I." After all, you are a member of the human family! The embroidery shows a door that is open. Did you turn the silver knob, flinging the door open in a sudden desire to get to know the world beyond your own doorstep? A quite natural curiosity for us humans, isn't it? It is from inside your "home, sweet home" that you look at the world out there. The opening may be small, and yet, you catch a glimpse of the whole globe. The whole world is there, at your doorstep, and it is a world of neighbours. This is a "glocal" vision at its best. The local intertwined with the global, the global present in the local.

---

1. See Kjellsdotter Rydinger's chapter in this book, "Embroidering Theology."

"You Have a World of Neighbours."
Embroidery: Petra Hall. Photo: Magnus Aronson.

The winning embroidery gives the impression of a peaceful image. It catches the moment where you are not yet asked to do anything. Just enjoy the beauty of the moment. The world of neighbours is not yours to produce; it is already there. It is a gift. Take that in before you turn to the tasks and the challenges. Only after contemplating the beauty of the gift is it time to think about what needs to be done and get to work. It is ours to sustain this world of neighbours, to rebuild faith in it when thwarted, to mend it when violated, to find it again wherever it is lost.

LIVING IN(TO) A WORLD OF NEIGHBOURS

"A world of neighbours" represents a hopeful worldview, without succumbing to romanticism. Neighbours do not always live in harmony with each other. They don't always agree, their interests can clash, they can quarrel, they can be friends and stop being friends. However, there is a baseline of solidarity. If the roof of my house is on fire without me knowing it and my neighbour sees it, I trust that they will rush to save me and call the fire brigade—not just because they want to save their own house, but because they actually care.

We are each other's neighbours. When it comes to migration, I find this sentence a more powerful, dignified, and realistic starting point than "we need to integrate them" or "they need to integrate." Successful integration is in fact a fruit of cultivating neighbourliness and building good neighbourhoods.

Migration is as old as humanity. It happens all the time, both voluntarily and involuntarily. And not in all cases is it clear whether migration is forced or by free will. There are many mixed cases. Decisions about whether political crises or climate emergencies should motivate migration to give children a future can be extremely difficult. When is it too early to leave? When is it too late? Where should one go? When visiting Northern Iraq in January 2017, with the war against ISIS (Daesh) still going on in Mosul, I met with a group of young adults, members of Christian congregations. They were struggling hard with the question of whether to leave or not to leave. Would they be safe in the years to come? Would they dare to build families under current conditions? While the young men seemed to be more inclined to leave and build a new life somewhere else, the women tended to argue for staying. This country needs us—you don't leave an ailing relative, do you? The existential qualms that often precede migration deserve understanding and respect.

Envisioning a world without migration and without the necessity to receive migrants is as unrealistic as it can be. It is obvious, but still needs to be said: there is no stereotypical migrant. Migrants are as different from each other as any humans are. Migrants are as perfect and as imperfect as humans are.

Having lived in four different countries, I am a migrant myself, although I was never subject to forced displacement. After finishing school in Germany as an eighteen-year-old, I spent fifteen months in Switzerland working in the hotel sector. With the authorities, I was registered with a "Fremdenpass" a stranger's passport. Twenty-two years old, I came to Sweden as a guest student with a scholarship from Germany. For young Europeans of my generation, it didn't seem like a big deal to move between countries. These were the years when border controls gradually disappeared, and it was easy to move between countries in Western Europe. What was to become the European Union was understood as a peace project that would make sure that "Never again war in Europe!" would not just be words but shape a new reality. Nevertheless, for staying in Sweden, I was required to have financial guarantees from my parents in Germany that clearly exceeded what I needed to live my rather frugal student life. A privileged migrant I was.

When my husband and I decided to settle in Sweden, I needed a permanent residence permit. Overall, the application process was straightforward, even though some of the interview questions seemed funny and others an infringement on our integrity. We felt somewhat uneasy, though, when we realized that the unit for foreigners was located in the police department for criminal offenses.

Moving between countries, languages, and cultures, even if it is by soft and gentle migration, brings challenges as well as assets. Even after decades in a new country, the immigrant may still feel a sense of never fully belonging. At the same time, embodying several cultures and perspectives simultaneously also comes with a blessing, regardless of the level of appreciation by the surrounding community. There are experiences that people who have immigrant backgrounds can share or recognize in each other, no matter how different the circumstances that led to migration in the first place.

In the early 1990s, the so-called "Lasermannen" shot eleven people in the Stockholm area. One person died and several others were severely injured. All victims had dark hair and/or dark skin. In response, immigrants in Sweden decided to go on strike for some hours an afternoon in the middle of the week. The idea was to create an awareness of the significant contribution by immigrants to the workforce.[2] At the time, I served a rural congregation in Southern Sweden. On that afternoon, I decided that I would answer phonecalls and explain about the strike and that I was part of it. People on the other end of the line would fall silent for a few seconds and then say: "But you are not one of those!" The hurt felt double: the Swedish racism against those members of the human family that are not Northern or Western European, and the denial of my identity as a person with a migrant background.

In 2001, two weeks before the attacks of September 11, my husband, one daughter, and I relocated to the USA. I was on a visa that allowed me to work as a professor at the Lutheran School of Theology at Chicago (LSTC). However, if I for some reason would lose my job, I had eleven days to leave the country with my family and our belongings. Family members had no access to a Social Security Number, hence no chance to get a cell phone, to name just one example. Technically, we were "non-resident aliens," except for tax purposes, where we were "resident aliens." A high level of non-belonging, as it were. Nevertheless, socially, we

---

2. See Hansen's chapter in this book, "Reality Checking the Economics of Migration," particularly the figures regarding foreign-born contributors to the work force. Hansen notes that since 2008 the entire net addition of working age people in Sweden has consisted of the foreign born.

experienced the highest level of belonging that we have ever had in our lives. We became part of a diverse and vibrant community of neighbours. We were graced with an intellectual and a spiritual home.

A Christian faculty member at LSTC was married to a Muslim woman; the way they both lived their faith with mutual love and respect was an inspiration. One day, Muslim students moved in as neighbours—they had come to study Christian theology, because they wanted to build excellent skills in interfaith dialogue. The faculty wondered—not without some nervousness—how it would be to teach the Bible, the Trinity, or Creation and Evolution with Muslim students in the room. Finally, a colleague said: "Let us remember that we love to quote the Bible on how good hospitality is; now is the time to put those words into practice." We embarked on an exercise of doing theology in the presence of the other.[3]

To us, the Muslim students were very good and friendly neighbours. Living with them in the diverse and special neighbourhood that is Chicago's Hyde Park gave me experiences and skills that were extremely helpful in relating to the growing diversity in Sweden. It prepared me well for the partnership with Dirk Ficca that would facilitate the development of both Open Skåne and A World of Neighbours (AWoN). Without that lived experience, I would hardly have had the courage to spearhead the initiative and to motivate others to join. Ultimately, it was the ideas, and the energy invested by Ficca, and by all those who eventually joined the work and provided the resources for it, which made it happen. When I look back, I feel a profound sense of gratitude. We did not know on day one what we would be doing on day 365 or what we would have achieved after 24 months. The initiative required a listening and responsive leadership—always ready to make changes and try new ways in pursuing the vision.

The pre-summit of AWoN in Malmö, Sweden, in January 2020 was a milestone. The way towards the envisioned summit appeared to be well-prepared, and yet new insights and the pandemic changed the whole concept. The digital event "A Week of Neighbours" in February 2022, culminating on the very day of Russia's attack on Ukraine, built motivation and capacity, and touched hearts and minds. No one could doubt the relevance of the theme "Keeping our humanity." Looking back at the period between 2009 and 2022, the triad of "Challenge," "Call," and

---

3. See Wirén's chapter in this book, "Making Space for the Other."

"Change" that structures this book is well chosen—even though in reality there were many challenges, many calls, and many changes.

AN ASSET-BASED APPROACH

When I lived in the USA, every now and then I would meet people who proudly told me "I am Swedish, you know!" And I would ask "Oh, then you speak Swedish?" "Not a single word," used to be the response, "but my great-grandfather was from Småland, you see." I was struck by the fact that in the US, you are first- or second-generation American. In Sweden, you are first- or second-generation immigrant. It sure makes a difference if you see hybrid identities as a problem or even a threat, or if you see them as an asset.

It is the asset-based approach that Dirk Ficca was so conscious about. We first met during preparations for the meeting of the Parliament of the World's Religions in Barcelona 2004 and subsequently in Melbourne 2009. At the time, he was the Executive Director of the Parliament. After Melbourne, where I had participated with an interfaith group from the Lund and Malmö area, Dirk came to Lund, where I had become a bishop, to explore possibilities for a social cohesion project in Malmö and Scania.

The project took off—not without challenges, yet it became the predecessor to "Open Skåne" and provided inspiration for other initiatives, most notably AWoN. Apart from financing, engaging stakeholders and creating a sustainable organization proved challenging. Much to our surprise, the business community were the first to grasp the idea and to support it. Their rationale: unless we have a social cohesive society where families can flourish, we will not be able to recruit the workforce we need in this economically expansive area. While the business sector was not the first interest of the church and other religious actors involved, the concern for social cohesion created enough overlapping consensus to join forces. The politicians of the municipality and the region were rather slow in their engagement with the project. Their support came late since they felt a bit uneasy with the involvement of religion. This was not too surprising, since "religion is private" is a Swedish dogma, which in turn contributes to religious illiteracy on all levels. Consequently, relating to religious communities creates insecurity and sometimes clumsiness. It happens that municipalities are unwilling to participate unless all religions are represented.

For the Church of Sweden and the Diocesan Board in Lund, the organization as a network felt difficult. If we don't "own" it or know exactly who is in control, we cannot support it financially, was the initial response. Bearing in mind that this occurred about ten years after the Church of Sweden was disestablished as a state church, the attitude is certainly understandable. Nevertheless, network organizations are part of the present and the future. They will become more of a reality for the church as well, not only for economic reasons but also because they can be the best way of achieving things. Given this background, I see it as a great success that AWoN managed to move from a project initiated and supported by the Church of Sweden into a structure of its own.

The method that eventually led to A World of Neighbours was based on the following elements, as developed by Dirk Ficca:

- Use a community asset-based approach.
- Mobilize mainstream religious communities as agents of change.
- Establish trust between mainstream and immigrant religious communities.
- Encourage mainstream religious communities to serve as a bridge between immigrant religious communities and the broader society.
- Tap into the cultural values that promote respect for diversity.
- Foster a shared vision for social cohesion.
- Create a rationale and infrastructure for cultivating social cohesion that involves all sectors of society.

In a letter dated May 31, 2010, addressed to me after a visit in Sweden, Dirk wrote:

> It was meaningful to speak together about the difficult situation facing minority immigrant communities across Europe, especially Muslims. Over the course of the rest of my trip—including visits to Germany, Switzerland, and Belgium—I became more and more aware of the depth of this challenge, and its potential for future social unrest. If there was ever a time for the interreligious movement to make a difference, this is it.

If political awareness at that time had taken note of this diagnosis—would the attitude towards religious and migrant communities have developed in other ways? Would we be in a different social and political situation now?

In 2015 and 2016, Europe experienced the so-called refugee crisis—in fact a crisis in European cooperation rather than in migration. Focus of the initiative moved from creating social cohesion in already diverse cities to the situation of migrants before, during, and after the move. Church organizations and their partners tried to accompany people on the move, when they arrived, and during the legal and social processes in the countries of arrival. They provided services and spread knowledge about the conditions from which migrants were suffering. They drew attention to the vulnerability of people on the move, especially children and women, as well as to their resilience.

The photo of little Alan Kurdi on the beach of Bodrum, Turkey, drowned as his family tried to make their way to Europe in September 2015, released a wave of compassion. Many people volunteered at train stations and other places to help arriving refugees. Europe saw an outpouring of solidarity that was truly heartwarming. "It is a humanitarian honeymoon," Ficca said, "it will not last." And it didn't.

And yet, volunteers have persevered, they have coped with frustrations, secondary trauma as well as compassion fatigue, and some became skilled practitioners. Support structures were created. According to the report *A Time of Encounters*, in 2015, more than 80 percent of the parishes in the Church of Sweden were engaged in refugee work. One of two parishes started some kind of new work.[4] However, it was not only a case of parishes helping the new arrivals. The newly arrived also contributed to church life. The Church's worshipping community is one of the far too few places in society where a newly arrived person can contribute from day one. The work, encounters, and relationships that emerged have affected parishes profoundly. As a vicar in the report says: "Theologically, many parishioners and co-workers have found the meaning of life: to love one's neighbour by helping the vulnerable. The identity and mission of the parish in society has [sic] become clearer."[5] The work was neither simple nor frictionless, and yet its necessity was hard to dispute. In the long run, no one can preserve their dignity as a human being while the dignity of their neighbours is trampled upon. Whoever wants to follow Jesus can do no other than to show humanity: "I was a stranger and you welcomed me" (Matt 25:35).

---

4. See Hellqvist and Sandberg, *Time of Encounters*.
5. Hellqvist and Sandberg, *Time of Encounters*, 8.

CALL AND CHALLENGE

In a way, the call was very clear. The biblical love commandment and the emphasis on care for the stranger provide direction and strength. The Lutheran World Federation (LWF) never failed in its support. Since its inception in Lund in 1947, in a post-war Europe in ruins, care for people on the move and work in refugee camps has been at the centre of its engagement. "Refugees lose many things but never their human rights," was one of the messages from the LWF leadership to the member churches.[6] In June 2022, the LWF together with interfaith partners Islamic Relief Worldwide (IRW) and the Hebrew Immigrant Aid Service (HIAS), and in collaboration with AWoN, Finn Church Aid, Faith to Action Network, and the Network for Religious and Traditional Peacemakers, hosted the two-day conference "Welcoming the Stranger, Shaping the Future." Some fifty faith actors from almost forty countries across Africa, Asia, Latin America, Europe, the Middle East, and North America gathered to highlight and strengthen their work at both local and national levels. Bringing together religious leaders, UN officials and grassroots responders was meant to facilitate increased cooperation for better protection and a stronger welcome for displaced people around the world.[7]

In September 2018, the World Council of Churches, together with the Dicastery for Promoting Integral Human Development and the (then) Pontifical Council for Promoting Christian Unity held a world conference in Rome. It brought together governmental, intergovernmental, civil society, academic, religious, and ecumenical leaders and actors from around the globe to reflect and together seek cohesive and realistic responses to the phenomenon of increasing xenophobia, racism, and populist nationalism in political and social responses to migrants and refugees. Populist nationalism was defined as "the deliberate manipulation and exacerbation of people's fears, concerns and insecurities about the negative impact of migration on their families, communities and cultural identities, for the purposes of political self-interest and electoral advantage."[8]

The conference message declared that "to refuse to receive and help those in need is contrary to the example and calling of Jesus Christ. Claiming to protect Christian values or communities by shutting out those who

6. LWF, "Refugees Lose Many Things."
7. LWF, "Welcoming the Stranger."
8. WCC, "Global Conference on Xenophobia."

seek safe refuge from violence and suffering is unacceptable, undermines Christian witness in the world, and raises up national boundaries as idols."[9] The idea of national borders as idols was thought-provoking. It does not preclude the necessity of a country defending its own borders against an aggressor. However, most importantly, a country must protect its soul.[10] For otherwise, what are the borders worth?

The conference also stated that the churches are "called to live out, on a daily basis, the welcome of the stranger but also the protection and the mutual encouragement to all—each in the diversity of their origins and history—to participate according to their own talents in the building of a society that seeks peaceful well-being in equality and rejecting all discrimination."[11] They should seek to raise a narrative of love and of hope, against the populist narrative of hate and of fear.[12] The fear underlying much of the hostile attitudes and actions needs to be acknowledged and dealt with constructively. If ignored, conference participants reasoned, the fears will permeate public discourse and influence opinions and policies. This will threaten the human and moral values of society and undermine respect for human rights and humanitarian law.[13] Six years later, it stands clear that the participants were more on point than they would have liked to be.

The theological basis and the ethical imperatives resounded strong and clear, internationally as well as nationally.[14] In Sweden, the Christian Council stood united in its persistent plea for the protection of the right of asylum and for humane migration policies. Hence, there was no lack of nutrition for the leadership backbone in these issues. Reassurance on the level of national and international leadership was strong. It became obvious, however, that the situation was much tougher for local leaders. Whereas practitioners find ample reassurance of the importance and meaningfulness of their daily work, local leaders and governance boards are much more prone to give in to fear of criticism. If they withdraw to

9. WCC et al., "Xenophobia, Racism and Populist Nationalism."

10. By "soul" I refer to shared values and their deep roots as well as our humanity (in the sense of humanhood) itself. See also Barker's chapter in this book, on "Crimes Against the Soul."

11. WCC et al., "Xenophobia, Racism and Populist Nationalism."

12. WCC et al., "Xenophobia, Racism and Populist Nationalism."

13. WCC, "Global Conference on Xenophobia."

14. Regarding the theological basis, see also Lillian's notes on a Jewish theology of migration in her chapter in this book, "Evolving Torah of Human Migration."

safe comfort zones, the practitioners at the front line are deprived of essential material and moral resources.

While, on the one hand, the call was very clear and the theological and ethical mandate did not change, everyday reality, on the other hand, has undergone significant shifts. Fears among host communities have not been dealt with constructively. Rather, they have become instruments in the process of "othering" migrants, especially Muslim migrants, and of changing policies. The past eight years or so have seen an increasing campaigning from the political (extreme) right wing, especially against the Church of Sweden. Even though the Roman Catholic Church and the Free Churches sometimes were even more outspoken on migration issues than the Church of Sweden, it was the latter that would be attacked. When a church leader in the public space would quote the Bible on the command to care for the stranger, typical accusations would be: "The church is political rather than Christian"; "the church promotes free immigration"; "the Church of Sweden betrays the Swedes"; and "the Archbishop is 'Islamicizing' the church."

At times, public debate became influenced by animosity towards Islam and Muslims. When media reported that Christian refugees were harassed by Muslim refugees in a refugee facility, debaters accused the Church of Sweden of not taking care of Christian brothers and sisters, and requested refugee facilities for Christians only. In fact, the local Church of Sweden congregation was already engaged in helping to address the problems in the refugee facility, which, however, did not make it into the headlines. When around the same time Roma migrants were subject to an arson attack, no voices were raised in public debate asking the Church to rush to the support of these Christians. It so happened that discussions were started to trigger and/or satisfy certain opinions in Sweden rather than to facilitate humanitarian aid to refugees in areas of conflict, on the move, and upon arrival in Sweden.[15]

Along similar lines, the Church was reproached for not paying enough attention to the persecution of Christians in the world. Rather than assisting people of other faiths, the Church should focus on helping Christians (only). The argument that Christians living with discrimination and oppression themselves caution against one-sided support, since that would inevitably worsen tensions, did not seem to convince the critics. These accusations tended to focus more on the alleged perpetrators

---

15. See, for example, Heberlein, "Svenska kyrkan"; Jackelén, "Ärkebiskopen svarar."

and their religion than on the needs of the oppressed themselves. Nevertheless, for Christian life, two things apply at the same time. Through baptism, there is a special bond between Christians. At the same time, the call of baptism to a life of faith and love means that commitment to vulnerable people cannot be made dependent on religious affiliation. In other words, we help people not because *they* are Christian but because *we* are Christian.

Over the years, comments on social media that were driven by Islamophobia and hate of Islam would get more frequent and brutal. The effect was obvious: interfaith engagement, rather than being driven by curiosity, joy, and love, became associated with fear, discomfort, and suspicion. Frequent accusations of having spoken with the wrong persons—for example a person who at some point in their life had been in touch with somebody associated with the Muslim Brotherhood—triggered anxiety, rather than a powerful response. The fact that dialogue comes with a dimension of inevitable risk-taking, so powerfully exemplified by Jesus, became hard to communicate. Instead, silence and self-censorship lured at the doorstep. Those engaged felt questioned. All too often, a retreat from the public sphere into the parochial was the result.[16]

The biased rhetoric in social media spilled over to traditional media. With low levels of religious literacy and ecclesial knowledge among journalists, social media would become a source of interview ideas. The strategy of consequently calling everything one does not like "political" and/or "leftist," and of creating suspicion around all contact between Christian and Muslim leaders paid off. If enough journalists ask, "you are being criticized for being political or being too Islam-friendly (!)—what's your comment?" a certain image of the Church is created: political, activist, embracing Islam rather than, as some would want to have it, fighting against it.

The development of hate speech against Islam and Muslims continues to be frightening. Even in this case, there is a spill-over from the most brutal excesses on social media to mainstream media. When the wordings "Islam(ism)" and "Islam(ists)" pass as normal, a border has been crossed.[17] One has given up on the distinction between a world religion

---

16. Regarding the effect of political campaigns on anti-refugee and anti-Muslim resentment, see Wilczynski's chapter in this book, "Social Media and Migration."

17. On February 4, 2024, Richard Jomshof, Chair of the Justice Committee in the Swedish Parliament, wrote on X: "Islam(ismen) är ett verkligt hot. Den är ett hot mot vår demokrati och allt som den står för. Det är dags att vakna upp ur törnrosasömnen.

and its extremist distortions, which is a step on the way to legitimizing persecution. Some alarm bells have been sounded[18]—amid deafening silence.

My concern over these developments has grown considerably over time. Even more so, my respect has increased for the practitioners who persevere, support each other, learn together and continue to work for change.[19]

CHANGE

This book brings a lot of treasures to the common table where everyone can be nourished and empowered to meet the challenges of our time. In the interest of further reflection and learning, I would like to conclude by highlighting seven issues.

First, in Europe, there is a continuing need to think seriously about decolonization. We must foster awareness of what Anya Topolski calls the "racialized reality of refugees in Europe."[20] Othering leads to dehumanization and eventually to violence. Topolski calls it an illusion that Europe after the Shoah has transcended its racist past. The difference in treatment of Ukrainian refugees and refugees from Africa and the Middle East, noticed by several contributors in this volume, is a case in point.[21] What do we say when someone confronts us with a reminder of "the nameless bodies on the oblivion of which our proud and loud *democracies* are built"?[22] There is an urgent call to rehumanize the dehumanized, as much as is still possible. Listening in a way that empowers others,

---

Det är dags att reagera, det är dags att agera [Islam(ism) is a real threat. It is a threat against our democracy and everything it stands for. It is time for the Sleeping Beauty to wake up. It is time to react, it is time to act]" (my translation). Similarly, in a chronicle in the magazine *Axess*, entitled "Dags att avsluta dialogen [Time to End the Dialogue]," Annika Borg wrote: "En ärkebiskop som tycker att dialog med islam(ister) är den nya väckelserörelsen [An archbishop who thinks that dialogue with Islam(ists) is the new revival movement]" (my translation). See Borg, "Dags att avsluta dialogen," 11.

18. See, for example, Aganović, "Islamofobin är varken dold eller skamlig att [sic] längre [Islamophobia is neither hidden nor shameful any longer]" (my translation).

19. See Esp's chapter in this book, "Sabina, You Must Promise Me."

20. See Topolski's chapter in this book, "Race, Religion, and Refugees in Europe."

21. Several chapters in this book address this discrepancy.

22. From Sathoud's chapter in this book, "The Vigil." Sathoud writes about the power of vigilant silence. See also Voorberg's chapter in this book, "Arriving with Empty Hands," which argues for a post-help praxis.

without forgetting the pros and cons of one's own power, recommends itself as a viable strategy.

However, decolonizing lived praxis alone is not enough. Majbritt Lyck-Bowen also requests the decolonizing of research ethics.[23] Yet this may prove more difficult and ambiguous than envisioned. "An initial aim is to blur the line between researchers and practitioners with the view to eventually eradicate the line," the author suggests. Yet, can blurring lines ever be desirable, if the goal—as it should be in research—is transparency?

Second, striving for clarity and transparency does not preclude caring about the complexity of contexts. It is good advice to hold on to the significance of contextualization and not shy away from trying to understand and communicate complexities.

When I was a young student of theology, the idea still prevailed that theology with a capital T was predominantly made in Germany, at the perceived centre, whereas contextual theologies, such as liberation theologies and feminist theologies, were phenomena at the perceived margins. Only gradually did it sink in that all theologies are contextual, and that acknowledging the contextuality of thinking is an achievement rather than a flaw. In these days, however, the pendulum seems to be on its way back from contextualization to a matter-of-factness that is fond of binaries. I have witnessed, for example, discussions about the situation in Israel and Palestine where speakers who referred to the complexities of history and context were accused of relativism. The same can occur when it comes to migration. And yet, migration can never be reduced to a contextless yes-or-no issue. Clearly, academia as a community of teaching and learning can benefit from AWoN as a community of practice and collaborative learning. The experiences of the in-between, of "life in the messy middle of things,"[24] which the work of AWoN brings, are an important asset for academic theology.

Third, another good piece of advice is to look for reliable information and statistics, so that myths regarding economic gains and burdens related to the receiving of refugees can be debunked. Even though the defence of human rights and humanitarian values cannot be reduced to economics, it is an advantage to find one's way around among the "hard" figures. It helps to counter reproaches that practitioners are naïve idealists

---

23. See Lyck-Bowen's chapter in this book, "Responsible Research Projects."
24. Brock, "Losing Your Innocence."

who neglect "the facts" that can be used to turn heroes into zeroes, as Maria Kjellsdotter Rydinger puts it.[25]

Fourth, at the same time, we should never stop believing in the power of meetings.[26] Likewise, we should never give up on the possibility and beauty of the ripple effect. Good things do happen—in ways that not even the most sophisticated statistics are able to predict. If nothing else, people can, as one practitioner puts it, create "those small cracks in the wall."[27] And, to say it with Leonard Cohen, that's how the light gets in.

Fifth, there are good reasons to insist on neighbourliness and neighbourhood as vital concepts. They are open enough to harbour a diversity of human relationships and yet distinct enough to focus on a common ground we share. We need to capitalize on the equalizing potential of neighbourliness. This will help to counteract polarization. In a best-case scenario, neighbourliness may even help to convert a racist—a mission enterprise worth its name! Inspired by the example of Mártha Bolba, how could anyone oppose building concrete and metaphoric table communities, where alongside bodily nourishment spiritual nourishment takes place?[28] Here dreams can be dreamt and imagination flow, without negating limitation and powerlessness. It is here that it is possible to "sit with the pain and stay there as long as necessary."[29] It is here that narratives take shape with the power to make a difference in the public space.

Sixth, persist in interfaith dialogue. It is a way of remaining faithful to one's own faith and tradition while at the same time being open to relate to others. Without dialogue, there is no way of building a socially cohesive society. Dialogue in a broad sense is both words and more than words. Sometimes common action (diapraxis) is what moves social cohesion forward. It is reassuring that defending the other's right to live and practice their faith in public, proves to be a sacred obligation in most religious traditions, as Jakob Wirén points out.[30] Dialogue is indispensable when it comes to resisting theologies of contempt, doing theology in

---

25. See Kjellsdotter Rydinger's chapter in this book, "Embroidering Theology."
26. See Sahlström's chapter in this book, "Collaboration Beyond Borders."
27. Anna Stamou interviewed in Sathoud's chapter in this book, "Fighting Now, Dreaming Ahead."
28. See the story in Bolba's chapter in this book, "At the Table of Jesus."
29. See Voorberg's chapter in this book, "Arriving with Empty Hands."
30. See Wirén's chapter in this book, "Making Space for the Other."

the presence of the other, minding the eschatological horizon and being rooted in one's own tradition in order to be open to the other.[31]

Interfaith dialogue needs to be sensitive to asymmetries when it comes to roots and space in society, organizational compatibility, resources, and the like. Atallah FitzGibbon's contribution on Muslim communities is helpful in this regard. Factors like fear of censure and retaliation, lack of capacity, differing understandings around support services and inner tensions can result in perceived invisibility or lack of interest.[32]

Seventh, Ulrich Schmiedel shows that AWoN's praxis promotes an ethics of care, that "revolves around the insight that life is sustained by relationships."[33] Not only sustained, I would add, but even constituted by relationships! A quick glance at Genesis 2 confirms this. God formed a human from the dust of the ground, from the *adamah* (Hebrew) or the *humus* (Latin). The human from humus becomes a living human being when God breathes the breath of life into those humus-nostrils. This is relationship number one: the relation between God and human. Second, God puts the human into the garden, to till and keep it. Thus, the relationship with the whole of creation is established. The message is: Humans are humans when they care for creation, when they are in relationship with that which grows and when they cultivate, create culture. Next, the human being encounters a being that is closer in likeness than any other being: the relationship to the fellow human being is established, the relationship to the neighbour. Fourth and finally, they eat the famous fruit from the tree in the middle of the garden. And they discover that they are naked—the relationship to their own selves is established. It is a fascinating order of relationships: God, creation, neighbour, self. Notwithstanding that in our day and age, we seem to have turned that order upside-down, life is relationality![34] To care for human life is to care for this fourfold web of relationality. And AWoN is right in having "relationality as its normative anchor"; an ethics that "revolves around the practice of encounters" is well justified.[35]

---

31. See Church of Sweden, *Sann mot sig själv*.

32. See FitzGibbon's chapter in this book, "Significance of Ethnic and Religious Identity."

33. See Schmiedel's chapter in this book, "Just Care."

34. See Jackelén, "Life."

35. Quotes taken from Schmiedel's chapter in this book, "Just Care."

Thus, AWoN is in a strong position to embody a theology of coexistence, resilience, and hope.[36] A theology of co-existence enables us to revisit some of the borders that are harmful to our working and living together as one human family. A theology of resilience[37] can make sense of the struggle of women and men for the health, wellbeing, and future of their children. It equips people again and again to draw God's mercy into this world with words and actions, whether words of prayer and words of advocacy for human rights, equality, peace, justice, and reconciliation, whether humanitarian help and support for development. A theology of resilience provides tools to confront the trends and powers that hamper constructive engagement with the greatest challenges of our time. With a theology of hope, finally, there is reason to expect change. Narratives of hate and fear can be overcome with narratives of love and hope. A credible hope has at least three elements. It can harbour the pain, frustration, grief, and anger about everything that is not right, such as hypocrisy and violence. It comes with a sense of humility and realism, because it relates wisely both to our strength, creativity, and power and to our vulnerability, weakness, imperfection, and mortality. And last not least, in most situations there are still choices. Hope choses the path that is more courageous than other alternatives.

All this considered, it must be concluded that churches are doing a good thing when they decide to be receptive to the theology that emerges from the work in and through A World of Neighbours.

BIBLIOGRAPHY

Aganović, Vildana. "Islamofobin är varken dold eller skamlig att längre." *Borås Tidning*, October 5, 2022. https://www.bt.se/boras/islamofobin-ar-varken-dold-eller-skamlig-att-langre-7e2c4d07.

Borg, Annika. "Dags att avsluta dialogen." *Axess* 5 (2022). https://www.axess.se/artiklar/dags-att-avsluta-dialogen.

Brock, Rita Nakashima. "Losing Your Innocence But Not Your Hope." In *Reconstructing the Christ Symbol*, edited by Maryanne Stevens, 30–53. Mahwah, NJ: Paulist, 1993.

Church of Sweden. *Sann mot sig själv—öppen mot andra*. Uppsala: Svenska kyrkan, 2011. https://www.svenskakyrkan.se/Sve/Bin%C3%A4rfiler/Filer/3368b0c8-9fb8-4a68-9c4d-2bd157e16b15.pdf.

Heberlein, Ann. "Svenska kyrkan måste värna om kristna flyktningar." *Dagens Nyheter*, February 9, 2016. https://www.dn.se/kultur-noje/kulturdebatt/ann-heberlein-svenska-kyrkan-maste-varna-om-kristna-flyktingar.

---

36. Jackelén, "Need for a Theology of Resilience."

37. On building a backbone of resilience by creating meaning and hope, see Kjellsdotter Rydinger's chapter in this book, "Embroidering Theology."

Hellqvist, Kristina, and Andreas Sandberg. *A Time of Encounters: The Work with Asylum Seekers and New Arrivals in the Parishes of the Church of Sweden 2015–2016.* Uppsala: Svenska Kyrkan, 2017. https://www.svenskakyrkan.se/forskning/a-time-of-encounters.

Jackelén, Antje. "Ärkebiskopen svarar. Diskussionen försvåras av det islamfientliga tankekomplexet." *Dagens Nyheter*, February 11, 2016. https://www.dn.se/arkiv/kultur/arkebiskopen-svarar-diskussionen-forsvaras-av-det-islamfientliga-tankekomplexet.

———. "Life: An Ill-Defined Relationship." In *What is Life?*, edited by Dirk Evers et al., 69–85. London: T&T Clark, 2015.

———. "The Need for a Theology of Resilience, Coexistence, and Hope." *Ecumenical Review* 71.1–2 (2019) 14–20. https://doi.org/10.1111/erev.12404.

Lutheran World Federation (LWF). "Refugees Lose Many Things but Never Their Human Rights." *Lutheran World Federation*, April 18, 2016. https://lutheranworld.org/news/refugees-lose-many-things-never-their-human-rights.

———. "Welcoming the Stranger, Shaping the Future." *Lutheran World Federation*, June 20, 2022. https://lutheranworld.org/news/welcoming-stranger-shaping-future.

World Council of Churches (WCC). "At Global Conference on Xenophobia, Refugees Speak Out on Role of the Church." *WCC*, September 18, 2018. https://www.oikoumene.org/news/at-global-conference-on-xenophobia-refugees-speak-out-on-role-of-the-church.

World Council of Churches (WCC), et al. "Xenophobia, Racism and Populist Nationalism in the Context of Global Migration." Conference held in Rome, September 18–20, 2018. https://familyofsites.bishopsconference.org.uk/wp-content/uploads/sites/8/2019/07/vatican-conference-xenophobia-migration-190918.pdf.

A World of Neighbours

What Guides Us

WHO WE ARE

We are neighbours!

We are a multi-faith grassroots network working with people on the move across Europe. We are driven by the conviction that everybody could and should be welcomed into our communities like a neighbour.

Neighbourliness is a core concern for both our religious and our non-religious ways of life. It is at the core of the commitments that characterize our network. We work with everybody in need, regardless of who they are.

WHAT WE DO

We work in acceptance, accompaniment, and advocacy. Everybody we encounter is treated equitably, with recognition and respect.

We encourage the visibility of religion in our work because all of us—religious and non-religious—are driven by a commitment that goes beyond ourselves. In our work, we cross intra- and inter-religious boundaries. We accept that crossing boundaries can come with conflicts. We aim to provide space for such conflicts. We acknowledge our own and other points of view. We aim to get to know each other better.

We are committed and courageous. Together with people on the move, we advocate for the causes of all people who have arrived or have attempted to arrive in Europe. We break down the barriers that keep us apart from each other. We aim to ensure that all people can participate in the decision-making processes on issues that concern them. We stand by each other. We stand up for each other. We speak out for each other.

WHAT WE DREAM OF

We pursue justice, envisioning a world where all people can live together peacefully.

We are guided by a vision for convivence that enables mutual transformation in dignity and diversity. Mutual transformation between people who are and people who are not on the move is the foundation for any authentic friendship.

We work together with religious and non-religious organizations for spiritual and social sustainability inside and outside Europe. Starting on a small scale, we want to change the world. The world needs it.

Index

accompaniment, 5, 21–22, 112, 117–18, 121, 167, 237, 262
advocacy, 5, 9, 125, 177, 260, 262
America, 36, 49, 59, 102, 113, 249, 252
antisemitism, 52, 58, 63–65, 106
Arendt, Hannah, 57, 61–69, 100, 150–51, 154, 231, 242
Armstrong, Andrea, 133–34, 137
asylum, 8, 33, 37–38, 40–42, 53, 61, 73–74, 80–81, 85, 87–89, 92–93, 95, 99, 110, 117, 140, 146–47, 150–51, 157, 167, 169, 198–99, 217, 220, 226, 234, 253

Bayoumi, Moustafa, 3–4, 16
belief, 9, 23, 57, 94, 103, 207, 212
belonging, 49, 65–66, 140, 148, 151, 190–91, 200, 247–48
Beaman, Lori, 9–10, 16
Benhabib, Seyla, 232–33, 238, 242
Berlin, 216, 218, 221
Bible, biblical, 26, 28, 181–82, 184–87, 193, 199, 208, 210, 232–33, 248, 252, 254
border, 3, 8, 21, 32–37, 39, 41–42, 59, 87–89, 102, 111, 140–42, 144, 157, 160, 166–67, 226, 230, 246
Brussels, 5, 99, 103, 110, 126, 160, 229, 235
bureaucracy, 33, 36, 217, 220–21
burnout, 119, 227

care, 15, 23, 27, 41, 46, 73, 85–86, 88–91, 118–19, 123, 142, 194–95, 197, 199, 208, 229, 235–41, 245, 252, 254, 259
Caputo, John, 112, 115
Cascant Sempere, Maria, 135–37
Christianity, Christian, 2, 4, 8, 58–60, 65–66, 109, 114, 131, 141, 157, 160, 168, 171, 175, 182, 199, 204, 207–8, 210–14, 240, 246, 248, 252–55
Church, 4–5, 11, 21–22, 25, 27, 40, 58–59, 65, 87, 90, 92, 95–97, 109, 113–16, 190–92, 194–96, 207, 210–11, 213, 249–52, 254–55
climate, 24, 268, 183, 186–87, 246
colonialism, Colonial, 3, 149, 232
conflict, xi, 15, 75, 96, 141, 200, 214, 220, 233, 235, 254
Cooke, Bill, 133, 137
crime, 11, 32 – 42, 170–71
criminalization, 33, 37–41
culture, 7, 11, 22, 26, 37, 58, 67, 90, 130, 171–72, 197, 202, 233, 259

decolonial, 57, 128–30, 132, 134–37, 256–57
dehumanization, 8, 23–24, 33, 35–36, 40, 42, 46, 56–60, (→ humanity), 62–64, 66–68, 89, 111–12, 148, 168, 236–37, 246, 268, 251, 256
democracy, democratic, 32–35, 37, 39, 62, 67–68, 100–101, 125, 226, 231, 237, 241, 256
dialogue, 22, 24–26, 29, 31, 119, 134, 142, 204–6, 209, 214, 248, 255–56, 258–59

dignity, 23, 30, 34, 36, 39, 45, 84, 90, 129, 134, 144, 192, 195, 198, 214, 220, 222, 251, 263
discrimination, 3–4, 11, 57, 67–68, 75, 151, 201, 224, 253–54
displacement, 2–3, 36, 38, 54, 61, 112, 147, 166, 169, 246, 252
Dublin Agreement, 88, 140

economics, economy, 12, 36, 72–82, 90, 130, 141, 149–51, 168, 170–71, 201, 249, 257
encounter, 4, 6–8, 11–15, 21–27, 30–31, 40, 95–96, 98–99, 113, 118–19, 124, 150, 204–5, 214, 220, 229–30, 232, 234–35, 238–41, 251, 259, 262
ethics, ethical, 11–15, 108, 128–37, 149, 181, 193, 202, 229–41, 253–54, 257, 259
exclusion, 34, 39, 57–58, 60–67, 132, 148, 215, 221, 232
empowerment, 53–54, 65, 103, 148, 190, 201, 215, 220, 256
European Union, 8, 32–34, 56, 74, 81, 140, 171, 191, 238, 246

faith-based, 5, 7, 23, 99, 101, 167
Ficca, Dirk, xii, xiv, 3, 5, 7, 16, 95–96, 103, 117, 126, 225, 248–51
Fiddian-Qasmiyeh, Elena, 233–34, 242

Gallant, Zachary, 182–83, 188
Germany, 3, 72, 96, 100, 139, 143, 163, 169–70, 216, 218, 221–22, 246, 250, 257
Gilligan, Carol, 235–37, 242
God, 8, 9, 22, 26, 28, 90–91, 104, 112–14, 183–86, 130, 192–93, 207–11, 213, 233, 259–60
Graeber, David, 6–8, 16
grassroots, 5, 31, 54, 110, 119, 525, 262

Hammad, Suheir, 102, 104
hate, 27, 45–46, 50–54, 67, 109, 114, 153, 199, 253, 255, 260

Hebrew Immigrant Aid Society 252
hope, 7–9, 12, 29, 35, 37, 46, 54, 86, 94, 101, 109, 113–14, 119, 121, 126, 142, 204, 213, 215, 224, 227, 245, 253, 260
hospitality, 3, 182–83, 187, 203–4, 248
humanity , 8, 23–24, 33, 35–36, 40, 42, 46, 56–60, (→ dehumanization) , 62–64, 66–68, 89, 111–12, 148, 168, 236–37, 246, 268, 251, 256
human rights, 23, 32, 34, 39, 63, 81–82, 107–8, 128, 144, 163, 225, 231–32, 252–53, 257, 260

ideology, 64, 148, 150
illegal (→ legal), 11, 23, 34, 36–38, 41–42, 66, 68, 75, 87–88, 114, 147, 153, 167, 172, 199, 218, 251
inclusion, 58, 62–63, 66–67, 125, 133, 232
influence, 5, 7, 22, 27, 97, 123, 125, 130, 132, 155, 177, 201–2, 253–54
integration, 63, 66, 76, 79–80, 82, 132, 147, 156, 166–67, 197, 215–16, 220, 226, 241, 245–47, 252
interreligious (→ multi-faith), 1, 6, 8, 10, 14, 22–23, 26, 29, 31, 95–96, 116, 136, 177, 204–9, 214, 229, 262
Islam, Islamic, Muslim, 2, 4, 6, 8, 14–15, 46, 49–50, 52–53, 57–561, 66–67, 72, 97, 100, 131, 156–59, 161–62, 175, 194, 197–202, 206, 208–9, 212–14, 223–25, 233–34, 240–41, 248, 250, 254–56, 259
Islamic Relief, 14, 197–98, 252
Islamophobia, Islamophobic, 4, 11, 50, 52, 56–57, 68, 109, 157, 159–61, 199, 201, 206, 225, 234, 240, 254

Jackelén, Antje, 4, 7, 9, 15–17, 26, 95, 244
Jesus, 14, 25, 113, 189–90, 192–94, 196, 211, 233, 238, 251–52, 255
Jesuit Refugee Serivice, 112

Judaism, Jewish, 2, 14, 53, 56–61, 63–67, 131, 151 181–88, 207–12, 233
justice, 8, 38–39, 43, 63, 111, 115, 144, 159, 161–62, 184, 196, 223–25, 236, 239, 241, 260, 263

language, 21, 24–25, 29, 31, 40, 45, 48, 99, 104, 143, 147–48, 151, 172, 190, 213, 222, 247
law, 37–38, 62, 88–89, 159, 162, 174
legal (→ illegal), 11, 23, 34, 36–38, 41–42, 66, 68, 75, 87–88, 114, 147, 153, 167, 172, 199, 218, 251
local, 21, 31, 38, 48–49, 51, 72, 79–80, 88, 96, 116, 118, 125–26, 164, 170, 182, 190, 192, 198–200, 205–7, 209, 244, 252–54
love, 7, 49, 54, 86–88, 102, 112, 134, 142, 145, 181, 184–85, 189, 208, 233, 248, 251–53, 255, 260
media (→ social media), 13, 29, 50–52, 54, 74, 80, 110, 115, 117, 155–57, 163, 167–69, 172, 177, 195, 206, 234, 254–55

Mediterranean, 32, 41, 144
Muhammad, Prophet, 46, 198, 212, 217
multi-faith (→ interreligious), 1, 6, 8, 10, 14, 22–23, 26, 29, 31, 95–96, 116, 136, 177, 204–9, 214, 229, 262

narrative, 2–3, 23–24, 53, 74, 101–2, 123, 125, 157, 163, 166–72, 185–87, 210, 253, 258, 260
nationalism, 39, 161, 252
needs, 13, 15, 21, 23, 25, 36, 68, 80, 90–91, 97, 111, 117, 122, 126, 132, 134, 136, 142, 149, 162, 199–200, 222, 227, 245–46, 253, 255, 259, 263
neighbour, neighbourliness, 1–2, 4, 6–7, 9, 12, 15, 21, 24, 27–29, 31, 33, 42, 46, 84, 86, 90, 95–97, 99, 100–103, 112, 114, 116, 128, 141, 157, 167, 177, 184, 191–92, 194–95, 204, 206, 215, 218, 221, 223, 229–35, 238–40, 244–46, 248, 250–51, 258–60, 262
network, 1, 4–8, 10, 13, 15, 21, 26, 33, 40, 52, 54, 96, 102, 116–17, 119–22, 124–26, 128, 131, 133–34, 177–78, 182, 204, 207, 229, 236–37, 250, 252, 262
Neusner, Jacob, 211–12, 214
normative, 237, 239, 259

pandemic, 5, 26, 73, 77–79, 117, 126, 146, 151, 248
passport, 32, 139, 144, 151, 168, 240, 246
peace, 27, 32–33, 46, 53, 60, 95, 113, 207–8, 216, 220, 222–23, 245–46, 252–53, 260, 263
philosophy, 9, 15, 29, 231
policy, 3, 5, 8, 30, 40, 51, 54, 67, 74, 77, 78, 80–81, 116–17, 125, 159, 161, 163–64, 166, 171, 225, 237–38
populism, 76, 156–57, 160, 162–64, 252–53
postmigrant, 15, 230, 238–39, 241
praxis, 11–12, 21–22, 25–26, 31, 107–8, 110, 112, 115–16, 119, 152, 204, 208, 212, 214, 257–59
public debate, 73, 76, 81, 156, 233, 254

Qur'an, qur'anic, 26, 46, 198, 208, 224

race, 11, 24, 31, 46, 53, 56–64, 67–68, 87, 133, 140, 190, 232
racism, 4, 11, 46, 49–52, 54, 56–59, 62–63, 66–68, 200–201, 234, 247, 252

secularism, secular, 25, 57–58, 62, 64–68, 91, 108–9
security, 13, 32, 35, 37–39, 87, 129, 139, 142–44, 157, 161–62, 165–66, 247, 249
Snyder, Suzanna, 232–33, 242
social cohesion, 21, 45–46, 51, 53–54, 117, 121, 181, 205, 249–51

social media (→ media), 13, 29, 50–52, 54, 74, 80, 110, 115, 117, 155–57, 163, 167–69, 172, 177, 195, 206, 234, 254–55
solidarity, 4, 33, 40, 89, 245, 251
soul, 11, 32–33, 35–37, 42, 58–60, 104, 181, 183, 211, 253
spirituality, spiritual, 90–91, 108, 110, 185–87, 195, 198, 200, 224, 248, 258, 263
statistics, 3, 23, 257–58

transformation, 12, 126, 237, 263
theology, theological, 9, 11–12, 14–15, 21–22, 24–27, 29, 31, 54, 58–60, 64, 95, 107–14, 181–82, 186–90, 195, 204–14, 230, 232–34, 238, 244, 247–48, 251, 253–54, 257–58, 260
Torah, 14, 181–85, 187–88

United Nations High Commissioner for Refugees (UNHCR) 2–3, 230

values, 23–24, 30, 3233, 35–37, 39, 53, 78–79, 90, 109, 113, 125, 133, 140, 147, 148, 150, 155, 157, 159, 161–62, 171, 196–97, 201, 228, 236, 250, 252–53, 257
Voorberg, Rikko, 5, 12, 102, 107, 256, 258
violence, 11, 32–33, 35–38, 40, 42, 46, 50–54, 60, 95, 150–51, 200, 206, 214, 253, 256, 260

xenophobia, xenophobic, 102, 159, 164, 181, 252

youth, 85–89, 94, 192

www.ingramcontent.com/pod-product-compliance
Lightning Source LLC
Chambersburg PA
CBHW070239230426
43664CB00014B/2358